TRADE POLICIES AND AGREEMENTS IN THE ERA OF GLOBALIZATION

TRADE POLICIES AND AGREEMENTS IN THE ERA OF GLOBALIZATION

PAUL B. LUCUS
EDITOR

Nova Science Publishers, Inc.
New York

For permission to use material from this book please contact us:
Telephone 631-231-7269; Fax 631-231-8175
Web Site: http://www.novapublishers.com

LIBRARY OF CONGRESS CATALOGING-IN-PUBLICATION DATA

Trade policies and agreements in the era of globalization / Paul B. Lucus (editor).
p. cm.
Includes bibliographical references and index.
ISBN-13: 978-1-60021-836-1 (hbk.)
ISBN-10: 1-60021-836-9 (hbk.)
1. Commercial policy. 2. Commercial treaties. 3. International trade. 4. International economic relations. I. Lucus, Paul B.
HF1411.T7116 2007
382'.3--dc22 2007030061

Published by Nova Science Publishers, Inc. ✦ New York

CONTENTS

PREFACE

Trade policies and agreements are a powerful weapon in the Era of Globalization. Most countries' strategy is to pursue muliple market-opening initiatives on a global, regional and bilateral basis, establishing models of success that can be used throughout all negotiations. This book presents some trade policies and agreements of the United States.

Chapter 1 - The 110th Congress has a full legislative and oversight agenda on international trade. The agenda may include considering legislation to implement a number of free trade agreements, possible renewal of trade promotion authority (TPA), as well as oversight of U.S. trade relations with China. This report provides information and context for many of these topics. It is intended to be read primarily by Members and staff who may be new to trade issues.

This report is divided into four sections in a question-and-answer format: trade concepts, U.S. trade performance, formulation of U.S. trade policy, and trade and investment issues. Additional suggested readings are provided in an appendix.

The first section, on trade concepts, deals with why countries trade, the consequences of trade expansion, and the relationship between globalization and trade. Key questions address the benefits of specialization in production and trade, efforts by governments to influence a country's comparative advantage, how trade expansion can be costly and disruptive to workers in particular industries and skill categories, and some unique characteristics of trade between developed countries.

The second section, on trade performance, focuses on the U.S. trade deficit and its impact on industries. Several questions address the causes of trade deficits, the role of foreign trade barriers, and how the trade deficit can be reduced. In terms of business impacts, the questions focus on which U.S. industries appear to be the most and least competitive, and on the relative size of the manufacturing sector.

The third section deals with the roles played by the Executive Branch, Congress, the private sector, and the Judiciary in the formulation of U.S. trade policy. Information on how trade policy functions are organized in Congress and the Executive Branch, as well as the respective roles of individual Members and the President, is provided. The formal and informal roles of the private sector and the involvement of the Judiciary are also covered.

The fourth section, on U.S. trade and investment policy, asks questions related to trade negotiations and agreements and to imports, exports, and investments. The justification, types, and consequences of trade liberalization agreements, along with the role of the World Trade Organization, are treated in this section. The costs and benefits of imports, exports, and investments are also discussed, including how the government deals with disruption and injury to workers and companies caused by imports and its efforts to both restrict and promote exports. The motivations and consequences of foreign direct investment flows are also discussed.

Chapter 2 - As imports from the People's Republic of China (PRC) have surged in recent years, posing a threat to some U.S. industries and manufacturing employment, Congress has begun to focus on not only access to the Chinese market and intellectual property rights (IPO) protection, but also the mounting U.S. trade deficit with China as well as allegations that China is selling its products on the international market at below cost (dumping), engaging in "currency manipulation," and exploiting its workers for economic gain. Members of the 109th Congress introduced several bills that would impose trade sanctions on China for intervening in the currency market or for engaging in other acts of unfair trade, while the Bush Administration has imposed anti-dumping duties and safeguards against some PRC products and pressured China to further revalue its currency and remove non-tariff trade barriers.

China runs a trade surplus with the world's three major economic centers — the United States, the European Union, and Japan. Since 2000, the United States has incurred its largest bilateral trade deficit with China ($201 billion in 2005, a 25% rise over 2004). In 2003, China replaced Mexico as the second largest source of imports for the United States. China's share of U.S. imports was 14.6% in 2005, although this proportion still falls short of Japan's 18% of the early 1990s. The United States is China's largest overseas market and second largest source of foreign direct investment on a cumulative basis. U.S. exports to China have been growing rapidly as well, although from a low base. In 2004, China replaced Germany and the United Kingdom to become the fourth largest market for U.S. goods and remains the fastest growing major U.S. export market. China is purchasing heavily from its Asian trading partners — particularly precision machinery, electronic components, and raw materials for manufacturing. China is running trade deficits with Taiwan and South Korea and has become a major buyer of goods from Japan and Southeast Asia.

In the past decade, the most dramatic increases in U.S. imports from China have been not in labor-intensive sectors but in some advanced technology sectors, such as office and data processing machines, telecommunications and sound equipment, and electrical machinery and appliances. China's exports to the United States are taking market share from other Pacific Rim countries, particularly the East Asian newly industrialized countries (NICS), which have moved most of their low-end production facilities to China.

This article provides a quantitative framework for policy considerations dealing with U.S. trade with China. It provides basic data and analysis of China's international trade with the United States and other countries. Since Chinese data differ considerably from those of its trading partners (because of how entrepot trade through Hong Kong is counted), data from both PRC sources and those of its trading partners are presented. Charts showing import trends by sector for the United States highlight China's growing market shares in many industries and also show import shares for Japan, Canada, Mexico, the European Union, and the Association for Southeast Asian Nations (ASEAN).

U.S. trade with the People's Republic of China (PRC) has raised several policy concerns. The trade is highly unbalanced in China's favor with a U.S. deficit of $201 billion in 2005. Year-to-date (January-October 2006), the U.S. deficit reached $190 billion. Many associate this deficit with the concomitant loss of American jobs in industries competing with rapidly rising imports from China. Some policymakers as well as leaders of industry and labor blame

China for unfair trade practices, including deliberately undervaluing its currency, which they claim create an uneven playing field for U.S. companies when competing against imports from the PRC. U.S.-China trade issues are often driven by larger policy objectives. U.S. trade with China is but one aspect of the overall U.S. policy of engagement with the PRC, a policy that serves broader U.S. interests. Trade also underpins Beijing's development strategy and contributes to domestic support for the PRC government.

This report presents data and analysis of China's trade that shed light on various policy issues, provides an overview of recent U.S. legislative initiatives, and examines the goals and constraints of U.S. trade policy toward the PRC. Some of the specific questions addressed are how the U.S. trade balance with China compares with those of the European Union and Japan, whether imports from China are merely replacing imports from other Pacific Rim nations, and how imports from China by industry compare with imports from other countries.

Chapter 3 - The United States is negotiating an unprecedented number of trade agreements. These agreements range from bilateral trade agreements with countries that account for meager shares of U.S. trade to multilateral negotiations that could affect large numbers of U.S. workers and businesses. During this process, Congress likely will be presented with an array of data estimating the impact of trade agreements on the economy, or on a particular segment of the economy.

An important policy tool that can assist Congress in assessing the value and the impact of trade agreements is represented by sophisticated models of the economy that are capable of simulating changes in economic conditions. These models are particularly helpful in estimating the effects of trade liberalization in such sectors as agriculture and manufacturing where the barriers to trade are identifiable and subject to some quantifiable estimation. Barriers to trade in services, however, are proving to be more difficult to identify and, therefore, to quantify in an economic model. In addition, the models are highly sensitive to the assumptions that are used to establish the parameters of the model and they are hampered by a serious lack of comprehensive data in the services sector. Nevertheless, the models do provide insight into the magnitude of the economic effects that may occur across economic sectors as a result of trade liberalization. These insights are especially helpful in identifying sectors expected to experience the greatest adjustment costs and, therefore, where opposition to trade agreements is likely to occur.

This report examines the major features of economic models being used to estimate the effects of trade agreements. It assesses the strengths and weaknesses of the models as an aid in helping Congress evaluate the economic impact of trade agreements on the U.S. economy. In addition, this report identifies and assesses some of the assumptions used in the economic models and how these assumptions affect the data generated by the models. Finally, this report evaluates the implications for Congress of various options it may consider as it assesses trade agreements.

Chapter 4 - For over 40 years, the United States has relied on unilateral trade preferences to promote export-led development in poor countries. Congressionally authorized trade preferences give market access to selected developing country goods, duty-free or at tariffs below normal rates, without requiring reciprocal trade concessions. The Caribbean Basin has benefitted from multiple preferential trade arrangements, the best known being those linked to the Caribbean Basin Initiative (CBI) begun in the mid-1980s. Since then, the growing number of reciprocal U.S. free trade agreements (FTAs) in the region have effectively replaced preferential trade arrangements, signaling a shift in U.S. trade policy and raising questions with respect to the future of those mostly smaller countries still relying on trade preferences. This report discusses the evolution of U.S. trade policy toward the Caribbean, focusing on the implications of moving from unilateral tariff preferences to reciprocal FTAs.

The U.S. Congress has approved multiple trade preference programs over the past three decades (production sharing, GSP, CBERA, CBI II, CBTPA, and HOPE Act of 2006). Each one amended trade rules and tariff preferences in ways designed to increase imports from CBI countries. Trade grew and many of the goals for development were supported. Evaluations of the benefits, however, suggested that they may not have been as robust as originally expected. Benefits tended to be concentrated in a few countries and products, often skirting industries with the greatest potential to stimulate exports. Also, the benefits of preferences are being eroded by multilateral trade liberalization and recently implemented FTAs.

A number of issues and circumstances are converging during the 110th Congress that will be a challenge for U.S. trade policy in the Caribbean region. Among these circumstances are the expiring trade preference programs, their limited use by remaining eligible countries, and the reluctance of these countries to make the transition to an FTA with the United States without some guarantee of a "development component" to the agreement. These concerns persist, despite the promise of permanent market access and increased investment that an FTA holds out. The Caribbean countries, long accustomed to dependent economic relationships, appear content to take a cautious and leisurely path toward any new arrangement with the United States.

For U.S. trade policy, which is still committed to achieving regional integration, these circumstances present a special challenge. Broader integration may be difficult to reconcile with the needs of very small developing countries, which are highly vulnerable to the vicissitudes of global economic trends and may require new and creative solutions, particularly if U.S. policy is still driven by the historical focus on development and regional security issues in addition to trade liberalization. In the context of continuing with trade preferences in similar or altered form, or opting for an FTA, the solution is not immediately obvious.

Chapter 5 - Trade promotion authority (TPA), formerly known as "fast-track" authority, is scheduled to expire July 1, 2007. With it will expire the authority: (a) that Congress grants the President to enter into certain trade agreements, and (b) for Congress to consider the agreements' implementing legislation under expedited procedures. Currently, the Administration is negotiating a number of trade agreements that may not be completed before the current TPA is set to expire. If these activities are to continue, TPA/fast-track renewal may be a central issue in the 110th Congress. Within the debate, a major issue is expected to be whether to include as a principal negotiating objective in trade agreements, "enforceable core labor standards."

Two TPA/fast-track authorities have incorporated labor provisions. The first, the *Omnibus Trade and Competitiveness Act of 1988* (OTCA), which expired in 1994, included the broad, general objective: "to promote worker rights." The *North American Free Trade Agreement*, with its labor side agreement, was negotiated under OTCA. The second and current TPA/fast-track authority with labor provisions, the *Trade Act of 2002,* includes protections for labor, modified by protections for country governments, businesses and investors. Seven free trade agreements (FTAs) — with Chile, Singapore, Australia, Morocco, Bahrain, Oman, and the Dominican Republic and Central America — were negotiated under this authority. All have only one enforceable labor requirement: that each country not fail to enforce its own labor laws in a manner affecting trade between the parties. (In contrast to this, the U.S.-Jordan FTA, negotiated in 2000 and approved in 2001 without TPA/fast track authority, includes enforceable labor provisions.)

Major options for labor provisions in renewed TPA focus on whether principal negotiating objectives should include "enforceable core labor standards." Supporters argue that including these could help: (1) slow the offshoring of certain U.S. jobs; (2) protect foreign workers against exploitative corporate behavior; (3) support the ability of workers to share in the gains from international trade; and (4) fend off an international "race to the bottom" based on labor costs. Opponents argue that: (1) core labor standards should be promoted by the International Labor Organization, not by trade agreements; (2) as countries develop, they adopt higher labor standards on their own; (3) stronger worker protections could discourage international investment; and (4) labor standards are disguised protectionism. History shows that with or without FTAs, trade will likely continue to grow.

This report examines issues relating to TPA/fast-track labor provisions in the larger context of global labor issues. It: (1) identifies the players and their positions; (2) tracks the enforceable labor provisions in TPA/fast-track laws and the FTAs negotiated under them; (3) presents some legislative options for new TPA/fast-track labor provisions; and (4) sets out arguments for and against enforceable core labor standards. Finally, it looks at possible outcomes and implications of the various legislative options

Chapter 6 - Mercosur is the Common Market of the South established by Brazil, Argentina, Uruguay, and Paraguay in 1991 to improve political and economic cooperation in the region following a lengthy period of military rule and mutual distrust. On July 2, 2006, Venezuela acceded to the pact as its first new full member, making Mercosur the undisputed economic counterweight to U.S. trade policy in the region, but raising questions about how it may shift regional political and trade dynamics. Collectively, the Mercosur countries have a diversified trade relationship with the world. The United States is the largest trade partner, the European Union (EU) a close second, with each claiming about 25% of total Mercosur trade. By contrast, the four Mercosur countries together account for only 2% of total U.S. trade. Including U.S. imports of Venezuelan oil, the "Mercosur 5" constitute 3.5% of total U.S. trade.

The Mercosur pact calls for an incremental path to a common market, but after 15 years only a limited customs union has been achieved. From the outset, Mercosur struggled to reconcile a basic inconsistency in its goals for partial economic union: how to achieve trade integration, while also ensuring that the benefits would be balanced among members and that each country would retain some control over its trade, production, and consumption structure. This delicate balance faced serious structural and policy asymmetries that became clear when Brazil and Argentina experienced financial crises and deep recessions. These economic setbacks disrupted trade flows among members, causing friction, the adoption of new bilateral safeguards, and a retreat from the commitment to deeper integration.

For now, Mercosur has turned to expanding rather than deepening the agreement. Many South American countries have been added as "associate members" and Mercosur has reached out for other South-South arrangements in Africa and Asia. These are limited agreements and unlikely paths to continental economic integration. Internal conflicts have highlighted Mercosur's institutional weaknesses and slowed the integration process. Uruguay has diversified its trade more toward the United States, and is showing signs of reconsidering the benefits of an "exclusive" Mercosur trade arrangement. Venezuela's accession to the pact adds a decidedly anti-American factor and may complicate both Mercosur's internal balance and regional trade relationships.

It appears Mercosur has opted for political cohesion over deeper economic integration. Mercosur, especially with Venezuela, will likely continue to resist movement toward a Free Trade Area of the Americas (FTAA), with Brazil in particular viewing the World Trade Organization (WTO) as the preferred alternative for achieving its trade policy goals. Given this impasse, it seems that the United States and Mercosur may continue to expand their influence through smaller trade agreements, presenting the possibility of two very different overlapping trading systems emerging in the Western Hemisphere centered around the U.S. and Brazilian economies. Few, if any, view this as an economically and administratively optimal alternative, presenting a formidable challenge to the future direction of U.S. trade policy in Latin America.

On March 26, 1991, Brazil, Argentina, Uruguay, and Paraguay signed the Treaty of Asunción, establishing the Common Market of the South (Mercado Común del Sur — Mercosur) with the intention of strengthening sub-regional economic and political cooperation. Since then, Mercosur has struggled to achieve deep economic integration, but has made strides toward political cohesion and emerged as an influential voice in regional trade negotiations. In particular, Mercosur has advocated its own expansion as an alternative to completing the proposed Free Trade Area of the Americas (FTAA).[1] On July 2, 2006, Venezuela acceded to the pact as its first new full member, making Mercosur the undisputed economic counterweight to U.S. trade policy in the region, and perhaps diminishing further expectations for a hemispheric-wide trade agreement. In December 2006, Bolivia also requested to become a full member. This report examines the evolution of Mercosur's policy decisions and performance as important elements for understanding the challenges to U.S. trade policy in Latin America.

Chapter 7 - On January 8, 2007, Canada initiated a World Trade Organization (WTO) dispute settlement case (DS357) against certain aspects of U.S. commodity programs in general, and the U.S. corn program in particular, by requesting consultations with the United States under the auspices of the WTO dispute settlement process. Canada's WTO case represents the present manifestation of long-simmering concerns that previously surfaced in 2005 in the form of an anti-dumping (AD) and countervailing (CV) duty case brought by Canadian corn producers who sought legal action for alleged unfair subsidization and dumping of U.S. corn in Canadian markets. Canada's International Trade Tribunal (CITT) ultimately ruled in favor of the United States on the 2005 AD/CV duty case. However, Canadian corn producers continued to press their concerns with the Canadian government about perceived unfair subsidization of U.S. corn. This pressure, and other supporting factors, likely contributed to the Canadian government's decision to request WTO consultations with the United States, thereby setting in motion the WTO dispute settlement process with its explicit rules and timetables for resolving a trade dispute.

In making its charges, Canada clearly seeks to build on Brazil's successful challenge of various provisions of the U.S. cotton program (WTO dispute settlement case DS267). Canada raises three explicit charges against U.S. farm programs. First, Canada contends that U.S. corn subsidies have caused serious prejudice to Canadian corn producers in the form of market price suppression in Canadian corn markets during the 1996 to 2006 period. Second, Canada argues that the U.S. export credit guarantee program operates as a WTO-illegal export subsidy. Third, Canada claims that U.S. fixed direct payments are not green-box compliant and should therefore be included with U.S. amber box payments, in which case the United States would be in violation of its $19.1 billion amber box spending limit for 1999, 2000, 2001, 2004, and 2005.

Since Canada's initial request for WTO consultations, several other WTO members — including Argentina, Australia, Brazil, the European Communities (EC), Guatemala, Nicaragua, Thailand, and Uruguay — have requested to join the consultations as interested third parties.

If successfully litigated, this case could affect all U.S. agricultural policy since the charges against the U.S. export credit guarantee and direct payment programs extend beyond corn to all major program crops. Should any eventual changes in U.S. farm policy be needed to comply with a WTO ruling in Canada's favor, such changes would likely involve action by Congress to produce new legislation. Congress will be revisiting U.S. farm legislation this year and could potentially address some of the issues raised by Canada's WTO challenge. U.S. Secretary of Agriculture, Mike Johanns, who has been advocating that a new Farm Act should be designed to make U.S. farm policy be "beyond challenge," has recently proposed changes to U.S. commodity programs that, if accepted in a new Farm Act, potentially could alleviate many of Canada's concerns while minimizing the likelihood of future WTO challenges.

Chapter 8 - This report is a brief overview of key issues addressed in CRS Report RL33864, *Trade Promotion Authority (TPA) Renewal: Core Labor Standards Issues*. Trade promotion authority (TPA), formerly known as "fast-track" authority, is scheduled to expire July 1, 2007. With it will expire the President's authority to negotiate trade agreements that Congress will then consider without amendment and with limited debate. For the 110th Congress, a likely issue in this debate is whether to include *enforceable core labor standards* as a principal negotiating objective in trade agreements. Accordingly, this report (1) identifies key labor provisions in the current TPA law and how they have translated into free trade agreements negotiated under it; (2) presents some legislative options, and summarizes arguments for and against listing enforceable core labor standards as a principal negotiating objective; and (3) looks at possible outcomes and implications of the legislative options.

Chapter 9 - U.S. merchandise trade is trade in goods only, not services. In 2006, U.S. exports, imports, and trade deficit reached their highest historical values: U.S. exports were $1.0 trillion, a 14.5% increase; U.S. imports were $1.9 trillion, a 10.9% increase; and the U.S. merchandise trade balance reached -$818 billion, a 6.6% increase.

Merchandise trade statistics are used to measure trade in commodities and with partner countries and groups. Latest official annual trade statistics of the U.S. Department of Commerce, used in this report, show that U.S. exports remain strong and growing and that U.S. imports remain even stronger, resulting in the largest annual merchandise trade deficit in U.S. history.

In: Trade Policies and Agreements in the Era of Globalization ISBN: 978-1-60021-836-1
Editor: Paul B. Lucus, pp. 1-31

Chapter 1

TRADE PRIMER: QS AND AS ON TRADE CONCEPTS, PERFORMANCE, AND POLICY*

Raymond J. Ahearn, Mary Jane Bolle, William H. Cooper, J. F. Hornbeck, James K. Jackson, Vivian C. Jones, Dick K. Nanto, Angeles Villarreal, Craig K. Elwell and Jeanne J. Grimmett

ABSTRACT

The 110th Congress has a full legislative and oversight agenda on international trade. The agenda may include considering legislation to implement a number of free trade agreements, possible renewal of trade promotion authority (TPA), as well as oversight of U.S. trade relations with China. This report provides information and context for many of these topics. It is intended to be read primarily by Members and staff who may be new to trade issues.

This report is divided into four sections in a question-and-answer format: trade concepts, U.S. trade performance, formulation of U.S. trade policy, and trade and investment issues. Additional suggested readings are provided in an appendix.

The first section, on trade concepts, deals with why countries trade, the consequences of trade expansion, and the relationship between globalization and trade. Key questions address the benefits of specialization in production and trade, efforts by governments to influence a country's comparative advantage, how trade expansion can be costly and disruptive to workers in particular industries and skill categories, and some unique characteristics of trade between developed countries.

The second section, on trade performance, focuses on the U.S. trade deficit and its impact on industries. Several questions address the causes of trade deficits, the role of foreign trade barriers, and how the trade deficit can be reduced. In terms of business impacts, the questions focus on which U.S. industries appear to be the most and least competitive, and on the relative size of the manufacturing sector.

The third section deals with the roles played by the Executive Branch, Congress, the private sector, and the Judiciary in the formulation of U.S. trade policy. Information on

* Excerpted from CRS Report L33944, dated March 27, 2007.

how trade policy functions are organized in Congress and the Executive Branch, as well as the respective roles of individual Members and the President, is provided. The formal and informal roles of the private sector and the involvement of the Judiciary are also covered.

The fourth section, on U.S. trade and investment policy, asks questions related to trade negotiations and agreements and to imports, exports, and investments. The justification, types, and consequences of trade liberalization agreements, along with the role of the World Trade Organization, are treated in this section. The costs and benefits of imports, exports, and investments are also discussed, including how the government deals with disruption and injury to workers and companies caused by imports and its efforts to both restrict and promote exports. The motivations and consequences of foreign direct investment flows are also discussed.

TRADE CONCEPTS[1]

Trade Expansion and Globalization

1. Why Do Countries Trade?

Economic theory indicates that trade occurs because it is *mutually enriching*. It has a positive economic effect like that caused by technological change, whereby economic efficiency is increased, allowing greater output from the same amount of scarce productive resources. By allowing each participant to specialize in producing what it is more efficient at and trading for what it is less efficient at, trade can increase economic well-being above what would be possible without trade. There is a broad consensus among economists that trade expansion has a favorable effect on overall economic well-being, but the gains will not necessarily be distributed equitably. Moreover, although most economists hold that the benefits to the overall economy exceed the costs incurred by workers who lose their jobs, some economists argue that the benefits are often overestimated and the costs are often underestimated.

2. What Is Comparative Advantage?

The idea of comparative advantage was developed by David Ricardo early in the 19th century and its insight remains relevant today. Ricardo argued that specialization and trade are mutually beneficial even if a country finds it is more efficient at producing everything than its trading partners. If one country produces a given good at a lower resource cost than another country, it has an *absolute advantage* in its production. (The other country, of course, has an *absolute disadvantage* in its production.) If all productive resources were highly mobile between countries, absolute advantage would be the criterion governing what a country produces and the pattern of any trade between countries. But Ricardo demonstrated that because resources, particularly labor and the skills and knowledge it embodies, are highly immobile, a comparison of a good's absolute cost of production in each country is not relevant for determining whether specialization and trade should occur. Rather, the critical comparison within each country is the *opportunity cost* of producing any good — *how much output of good Y must be forgone to produce one more unit of good X.* If the opportunity costs of producing

X and Y are different in each economy, then each country has a *comparative advantage* in the production of one of the goods. In this circumstance, Ricardo predicts that each country can realize gains from trade by specializing in producing what it does relatively well and in which it has a comparative advantage and trading for what it does relatively less well and in which it has a comparative disadvantage.

3. What Determines Comparative Advantage?

Most often, differences in comparative advantage between countries occur because of differences in the relative abundance of the factors of production: land, labor, physical capital (plant and equipment), human capital (skills and knowledge including entrepreneurial talent), and technology. Standard economic theory predicts that comparative advantage will be in activities that make *intensive* use of the country's relatively abundant factor(s) of production. For example, the United States has a relative abundance of high-skilled labor and a relative scarcity of low-skilled labor. Therefore, the United States' comparative advantage will be in goods produced using high-skilled labor intensively such as aircraft and comparative disadvantage will be in goods produced using low-skilled labor intensively such as apparel. In addition to differences in factor endowments, differences in productive technology among countries create differences in relative efficiency and may be a basis for comparative advantage. Nevertheless, some high skilled services jobs, such as computer programming and graphic design, can today be easily done in a country such as India because of the revolution in telecommunications.

4. Can Governments Shape or Distort Comparative Advantage?

Government actions to influence comparative advantage can be grouped in two broad categories: policies that *indirectly* nurture comparative advantage, most often by compensating for some form of market failure, but not targeted at any specific industry or activity; and policies that aim to *directly* create and nurture comparative advantage in particular industries. Indirect influence on comparative advantage can emanate from government policies that eliminate corruption, enforce property rights, remove unnecessary impediments to market transactions, assure macroeconomic stability, build transport and communication infrastructure, support mass education, and assist technological advance. Policies that try to exert a direct influence on comparative advantage may include infant industry policies, industrial policies, or strategic trade policies. They all have the essential goal of identifying and nurturing particular industries that are thought to have extra-ordinary economic potential. In this view, realizing that potential requires initial government support, including protection from foreign competition. The efficacy of direct government efforts to shape comparative advantage is likely to vary significantly according to stages of economic development. China and India, for example, have used industrial policies to restructure their economies and enable them better to take advantage of world markets.

5. What Is the Terms of Trade?

A nation's *terms of trade* — the ratio of an index of export prices to an index of import prices — is a measure of the export cost of acquiring desired imports. Increases and decreases in its terms of trade indicate whether a nation's *gains from trade* are rising or falling. A sustained improvement in the terms of trade expands what our income will buy on the world market and can make a significant contribution to the long-term growth of economic welfare.

Similarly, a falling terms of trade raises the export cost of acquiring imports, which reduces real income and the domestic living standard. Although trade is considered a process of mutual benefit, each trading partner's *share* of those benefits can change over time, and movement of the terms of trade is an indicator of that changing share.

6. What Are the Costs of Trade Expansion?

Like technological change and other market forces, international trade creates wealth by inducing a reallocation of the economy's scarce resources (capital and labor) into relatively more efficient exporting industries that have a comparative advantage and away from less efficient activities that have a comparative disadvantage. This reallocation of economic resources is often characterized as a process of "creative destruction," generating a net economic gain to the overall economy, but also being disruptive and costly to workers in adversely affected industries that compete with imports. Many of these displaced workers bear significant adjustment costs and many may find work only at a lower wage. Although economic analysis almost always indicates that the economy-wide gains from trade exceed the costs, the perennially tough policy issue is how or whether to secure those gains for the wider community while dealing equitably with those who are hurt by the process. Economists generally argue that facilitating the adjustment and compensating for the losses of those harmed by market forces, including trade, is economically less costly than policies to protect workers and industries from the negative impacts of trade. While it is debatable how well existing worker assistance policies have worked, funding is also a longstanding issue. The Peterson Institute for International Economics, for example, estimates the lifetime costs of worker displacement to be roughly $50 billion year, but calculates that the United States spends about $2 billion per year to address the costs connected to displacement.

7. Does Trade Destroy Jobs?

Trade creates and destroys jobs in the economy just as other market forces do. Economy-wide, trade creates jobs in industries that have a growing comparative advantage and destroys jobs in industries that have a growing comparative disadvantage. In the process, the economy's composition of employment changes, but there may not be a *net* loss of jobs due to trade. Consider that over the course of the last economic expansion, from 1992 to 2000, U.S. imports increased nearly 240%, but total employment grew by 22 million jobs and the unemployment rate fell from 7.5% to 4.0% (the lowest unemployment rate in more than 30 years.).

8. Does Trade Reduce the Wages of U.S. Workers?

International trade can have strong effects, good and bad, on the wages of American workers. Concurrent with the large expansion of trade over the past 25 years, real wages (i.e., inflation adjusted wages) of American workers grew more slowly than in the earlier post-war period, and inequality of wages between the skilled and less skilled worker rose sharply. Trade based on comparative advantage tends to increase the return to the abundant factors of production — capital and high-skilled workers in the United States — and decrease the return to the less-abundant factor — low-skilled labor in the United States.[2] Therefore, it is reasonable to expect that, other factors constant, the large increase in trade over this period, particularly increased trade with economies with vast supplies of low-skilled labor, could harm the wages of low-skilled U.S. workers. However, other economic factors such as technological change and the shifting structure of production among emerging economies may have mitigated the potential adverse effect of trade on wages. While there may be no strong evidence that expanding trade has depressed the *average* wages of U.S. workers, some evidence suggests that increased trade may have caused 10% to 20% of the increase in wage inequality.[3] Many observers believe the larger share of increased inequality of U.S. wages was likely caused by advancing technology's tendency to pull up the wages of high-skilled workers and increased immigration's tendency to push down the wages of low-skilled workers.

9. What Is Intra-Industry Trade?

A sizable portion of world trade sees countries exporting and importing to each other goods from the same industry. This phenomenon is called *intra-industry trade.* This type of trade is particularly characteristic of the large flows of products between advanced economies, which have very similar resource endowments. This suggests that there is another basis for trade than comparative advantage behind intra-industry trade: the exploitation of *economies of scale.* Economies of scale exist when a production process is more efficient (i.e. has lower unit cost) the larger the scale at which it takes place. This scale economy becomes a basis for trade because while the United States and Germany, for example, could be equally proficient at producing any of a wide array of goods such as automobiles and pharmaceuticals that consumers want, neither has the productive capacity to produce the full range of goods at the optimal scale. Therefore, a pattern of specialization tends to occur with countries producing and trading some sub-set of these goods at the optimal scale.

10. Why Is Intra-Industry Trade Important?

A significant attribute of intra-industry trade is that it tends not to generate the strong effects on the distribution of income that can occur with trade based on comparative advantage. This attribute may explain why the large trade expansion that took place in the 1950-1980 period was less politically contentious than has been true for trade expansion since 1980. The earlier period was dominated by rising trade between advanced economies with similar endowments of productive resources and similar levels of technology. Therefore, trade at that time was largely an expansion of intra-industry trade that had no relatively abundant factor of production to exploit. As a consequence, it had little adverse affect on the return to the factors of production, including the wages of U.S. workers. In contrast, a much larger portion of the trade expansion since 1980 has been with less-developed economies with their relative abundance of low-skilled and priced labor — a likely source of downward pressure on wages in the developed economies.

11. What Is Globalization?

Globalization has come to represent many things, but economic globalization refers specifically to the increasing integration of national economies into a world wide trading system. Globalization involves trade in goods and services, and trade in assets (i.e. currency, stocks, bonds, and real property), as well as the transfer of technology, and the international flows (migration) of labor. Since 1950, world trade in merchandise has consistently grown faster then world production. In the recent period of 1990-2005 world trade in merchandise grew at about 6.0% per year as compared to about 2.0% for world output.[4] As a result, world exports as a percent of world GDP rose from about 12% to about 32%. In the United

States global integration has advanced quickly, with imports as a share of GDP rising from about 10% in the 1950s to about 17% today. More recent but far more dramatic has been the growth of international trade in assets. In the 1990s gross capital flows leaped by 300% as compared to a 63% advance of trade in goods. The rising economic integration of the world economy has been facilitated by two types of events: the myriad of technical advances in transport and communication that have reduced the natural barriers of time and space that separate national economies; and national and multi-national policy actions that have steadily lowered various man-made barriers (i.e. tariffs, quotas, subsidies, and capital controls) to international exchange.

12. What Is the Global Supply Chain and How Does It Relate to Globalization?

A supply chain is the interrelated organizations, resources, and processes that create and deliver a product to the final consumer. A global supply chain organized mostly by multinational corporations (MNCs) means that products that were once produced in one country may now be produced by assembling components fabricated in several countries. This supply chain has meant that as much as 30% of the recent growth of world trade has been through trade in intermediate products. Not only does such geographically fragmented production raise the level of trade associated with a particular final product, it also tends to raise the level of trade with both developing countries and developed countries. This growth of the global supply chain has been facilitated by technological advances that have increased the speed and lowered the cost of international transport and, perhaps most importantly, accelerated the international flow of information that allows MNCs to coordinate geographically fragmented production with relative ease. In addition, government action has achieved a substantial reduction of various man-made trade barriers and promoted movement toward a market based economy.

13. How Does Globalization Affect Job Security?

A greater degree of international economic integration can add to disruptive forces in the marketplace, including concerns that an estimated 30 to 40 million high-wage and high-skilled U.S. service sector jobs may now be vulnerable to "outsourcing" over time. Although this increased integration is unlikely to have a negative effect on overall employment rate or the average worker wage, greater volatility of worker incomes and employment is a possible effect. While the precise causes remain unclear, some evidence for the United States indicates a steady rise in wage and employment volatility since the 1980s.[5] In response to this rise, some argue that because increased volatility raises the economic risk attached to employment and earnings, the "social safety net" that protects workers from periodic market disruptions should be expanded commensurately.

U.S. TRADE PERFORMANCE[6]

U.S. Trade Deficit

14. What Is Meant by the Trade Deficit?

The U.S. trade deficit is the difference between the value of U.S. exports and U.S. imports. The deficit on trade in goods (merchandise) that reached a record $836 billion in

2006 is what the media generally calls the trade deficit. The United States, however, usually runs a surplus in trade in services with the world. By adding net exports of services to the calculation, the trade deficit on goods and services was $764 billion in 2006. Adding in net transfers of investment income and remittances by individuals to foreign countries gives the broader measure of the trade deficit that is called the current account. In 2006, the current account deficit was $857 billion.

15. Why Are Different Numbers Reported for the Trade Deficit?

The data on imports and exports are reported in two ways that give similar but different numbers. When goods or services pass through U.S. borders, the Customs Service compiles the figures from shipping manifests and other documents and reports it to the U.S. Census Bureau. The Bureau then produces data on imports and exports and calculates the trade deficit on a Census basis. The detail in these data allows the import and export flows to be broken out into trade by countries, sectors, and major ports. The Census data are then adjusted to a balance-of-payments basis by accounting for military sales, adding private gift parcels, including foreign official gold sales from U.S. private dealers, and making other refinements. The following table shows U.S. trade data on both a Census and balance-of-payments basis.

Table 1. U.S. Exports, Imports, and Merchandise Trade Balances 2002-2006 (billions of U.S. dollars)

	Census Basis			Balance-of-payments Basis		
Year	Exports	Imports	Balance	Exports	Imports	Balance
2002	693.5	1,163.6	-470.1	681.8	1,164.7	-482.9
2003	724.8	1,257.1	-532.3	713.1	1,260.7	-547.6
2004	818.8	1,469.7	-650.9	807.5	1,472.9	-665.4
2005	906.0	1,673.5	-767.5	894.6	1,677.4	-782.8
2006	1,037.3	1,855.4	-818.1	1,023.7	1,859.8	-836.1

Source: U.S. Department of Commerce, Bureau of Economic Analysis, U.S. International Transactions Accounts Data.

16. What Are the Causes of the Record Trade Deficits?

The fundamental cause of the U.S. trade deficit is excess spending by U.S. consumers, business, and government. In essence, Americans consume more than they produce. This allows other countries to sell more to the United States than they buy from the United States. Economists characterize this as a lack of savings by U.S. consumers, business, and government. Households buy much on credit; businesses invest much with borrowed funds; and the government runs budget deficits. As long as foreigners (both governments and private entities) are willing to loan the United States the funds to finance the lack of savings in the U.S. economy, the trade deficit can continue. The United States, however, accumulates more and more debt.

17. What Role Do Foreign Trade Barriers Play in Causing Trade Deficits?

Trade barriers tend to affect bilateral trade in specific products and with particular countries, but they do not necessarily affect the size of the overall U.S. trade deficit. For example, trade with Burma or North Korea is non-existent or small because of U.S.-imposed export barriers. Foreign countries also impose barriers to imports and limit foreign access to their markets by a variety of measures. Some barriers are overt, such as high tariffs or import quotas. Others are less visible, such as income tax audits by tax authorities of persons buying foreign automobiles or controls over foreign exchange that prevent citizens wishing to purchase imports from obtaining the foreign currency necessary. If, for example, a government requires exporters to sell their dollars to the government at a fixed exchange rate, and that government invests the dollars in U.S. securities rather than allowing businesses and consumers to use the dollars to buy American exports, then this combination of government intervention in currency markets plus exchange controls can increase the size of the U.S. trade deficit.

Foreign trade barriers also can affect the profitability of U.S. exporters and thereby influence the size of the overall U.S. trade deficit. If U.S. exporters are able to sell more to a country that has lowered its trade barriers, the exporting companies can increase their profits, hire more American workers, and possibly increase the overall U.S. saving rate. This can occur only if the economy is operating at less than full employment.

18. How Does the Trade Deficit Affect the Exchange Value of the Dollar?

Without sufficient inflows of capital, a trade deficit causes other parts of the economy to adjust, particularly the country's exchange rate — for the United States, this is the value of the dollar relative to that of the Chinese yuan, Japanese yen, Canadian dollar, British pound, or European euro. The way the adjustment mechanism works is that the excess of U.S. imports causes a surplus of U.S. dollars to flow abroad. If these dollars are then converted to other national currencies, their excess supply tends to lower their price (exchange rate) relative to other currencies, and the value of the dollar depreciates. This causes imports to be more expensive for American consumers and U.S. exports to be cheaper for foreign buyers. This process gradually causes U.S. imports to decrease and exports to increase and for the trade deficit to be diminished.

The dollar, however, may not be exchanged for foreign currencies because of its special status in global financial markets and because the U.S. economy is viewed both as a safe haven for storing wealth and as an attractive destination for investments. In some countries, the dollar is used as a medium of exchange, and in most countries it is used as a reserve currency by central banks. Foreign governments can intervene to keep the value of their currency from appreciating relative to the dollar by buying excess dollars and sending them back to the United States by buying Treasury securities or other U.S. assets. This is what China has been doing. In Japan's case, the government has not intervened since the spring of 2004 to keep the value of the yen low, but private Japanese investors are causing the same result by investing their savings overseas where interest rates are higher (financiers also are borrowing in Japan and lending the funds abroad).[7] The surplus of dollars, therefore, may not cause the dollar to depreciate and for the trade deficit to decrease.

19. How Is the Trade Deficit Financed?

The U.S. trade deficit is financed by borrowing from abroad. This takes the form of net financial inflows into the United States. In 2006, U.S. net financial inflows amounted to $719 billion. Foreigners acquired $1,765 billion in assets in the United States, while Americans acquired $1,046 in assets abroad. Foreigners purchased an additional $29 billion in Treasury securities and $621 billion in other securities, while increasing their deposits at U.S. banks by

$441 billion and acquiring $13 billion in U.S. currency. Foreigners also invested $184 billion in their companies located in the United States.

20. Is the Trade Deficit a Problem for the U.S. Economy?

The U.S. trade deficit is a dual problem for the economy. In the long term, it generates debt that must be repaid by future generations. Meanwhile, the current generation must pay interest on that debt. Whether the current borrowing to finance imports is worthwhile for Americans depends on whether those funds are used for investment that raises future standards of living or whether they are used for current consumption. If American consumers, business, and government are borrowing to finance new technology, equipment, or other productivity enhancing products, the deficit can pay off in the long term. If the borrowing is to finance consumer purchases of clothes, household electronics, or luxury items, it pushes the repayment of funds for current consumption on to future generations without investments to raise their ability to finance those repayments.

In the short term, the trade deficit could lead to a large and sudden fall in the value of the dollar and financial turmoil both in the United States and abroad. The current account deficit now exceeds 6% of GDP and is placing downward pressure on the dollar. If foreign investors stop offsetting the deficit by buying dollar-denominated assets, U.S. interest rates would have to rise to attract more foreign investment. Rising interest rates can cause havoc in financial markets and also may raise inflationary pressures. Global financial markets are now so closely intertwined that turmoil in one market can quickly spread to other markets in the world.

21. How Long Can the United States Keep Running Trade Deficits?

U.S. deficits in trade can continue for as long as foreign investors are willing to buy and hold U.S. assets, particularly government securities and other financial assets.[8] Their willingness depends on a complicated array of factors including the perception of the United States as a safe haven for capital, relative rates of return on investments, interest rates on U.S. financial assets, actions by foreign central banks, and the savings and investment decisions of businesses, governments, and households. The policy levers that influence these factors that affect the trade deficit are held by the Federal Reserve (interest rates) as well as both Congress and the Administration (government budget deficits and trade policy), and their counterpart institutions abroad.

22. How Can the Trade Deficit Be Reduced?

In reducing the U.S. trade deficit, the policy tool kit includes direct measures (trade policy) that are aimed at imports, exports, and the exchange rate, and indirect measures (monetary and fiscal policies) aimed at U.S. interest rates, saving rates, budget deficits, and capital flows. Monetary and fiscal policy, however, usually address conditions in the U.S. macroeconomy and generally consider the trade deficit only as a secondary target. It is ironic that the most effective method of reducing the trade deficit is through monetary and fiscal policy, yet monetary and fiscal policy is rarely determined by the trade deficit.

23. What Is the Role for Trade Policy in Reducing the Trade Deficit?

Trade policy consists of the strategies, goals, and initiatives by governments to change the laws, regulations, and agreements that provide the framework for international trade and to take action to remedy distortions in the movement of goods, services, and capital flows across national borders. U.S. trade policy operates along three paths: (1) in opening markets abroad for U.S. exporters, (2) in protecting U.S. industries from imports that are unfairly traded (sold at prices lower than those in the exporting country) or from import surges that cause, or threaten to cause, substantial harm, and (3) trying to ensure that exchange rates are not manipulated by other nations to hinder the process by which trade is brought into balance or to gain competitive advantage.

Currently, U.S. trade policy to open markets abroad is conducted at three levels: through bilateral negotiations and trade/investment agreements, through establishing free-trade agreements, and through multilateral negotiations under the WTO. Trade policy plays a proactive role in leveling the playing ground for U.S. business, a remedial role in correcting distortions in trade caused by foreign government intervention, and a reactive role in addressing specific problems raised by U.S. businesses. The specifics of U.S. trade policy are discussed in the section on U.S. Trade and Investment Policy below.

Trade policy aims at reducing the U.S. trade deficit by increasing U.S. exports or decreasing U.S. imports. U.S. trade policy, however, operates under multiple constraints. Trade policy, for example, can affect specific trade flows but the overall trade deficit tends to be determined by macroeconomic conditions (savings and investment flows). The U.S. government, moreover, faces legal obligations, political resistance, and other constraints on policy aimed at decreasing imports or increasing exports. Free market principles and U.S. law, for example, preclude the government from moving against big box retailers that sell low-cost imports from China. U.S. obligations under the World Trade Organization preclude arbitrary increases in import tariffs or large direct subsidies for U.S. exporters, and only under special circumstances, usually related to national security or severe offenses to international humanitarian values (e.g., genocide) does the United States block trade with a specific country (e.g., Cuba or Burma).

24. Who Are the Leading U.S. Trade Partners?

As shown in the following table, in 2006, Canada was America's largest merchandise trading partner, but China passed Mexico to take second place in the ranking. Fourth was Japan, then Germany, and the United Kingdom.

Sectoral Issues

25. Which Industries Appear to Be the Most Competitive as Measured by the Size of Their Trade Surpluses? Which Are the Least Competitive as Measured by Their Trade Deficits?

The international competitive advantage of specific industries can be measured in a number of ways — one of which is their trade balances. Other measures include profitability, value added, productivity, employment, and technological change. The table below shows the balance of trade for U.S. industries (as defined by 2-digit Harmonized System tariff classifications). By this measure, the industries with the largest surpluses, in 2006, include aircraft and spacecraft, cereals, optical and medical instruments; plastic, chemical products, grains/seed/fruit, cotton/yarn/fabric, animal feed, and wood pulp. These U.S. industries can be considered the most competitive in international trade. The table also shows those industrial sectors with the largest deficits in trade. These include mineral fuel and oil, motor vehicles, electrical machinery, machinery, woven and knit apparel, furniture and bedding, toys and sports equipment and footwear.

Table 2. Top U.S. Trading Partners Ranked by Total Merchandise Trade in 2006 (Millions of U.S. Dollars)

Rank	Country	Total Trade	Balance	Exports	Imports
1	Canada	533,997	-72,835	230,581	303,416
2	China	342,997	-232,549	55,224	287,773
3	Mexico	332,426	-64,092	134,167	198,259
4	Japan	207,740	-88,442	59,649	148,091
5	Germany	130,392	-47,753	41,319	89,073
6	UK	98,830	-8,044	45,393	53,437
7	South Korea	78,285	-13,374	32,455	45,830
8	France	61,366	-12,931	24,217	37,149
9	Taiwan	61,238	-15,191	23,023	38,215
10	Malaysia	49,082	-23,982	12,550	36,532
11	Venezuela	46,177	-28,153	9,012	37,165
12	Brazil	45,617	-7,161	19,228	26,389
13	Italy	45,219	-20,086	12,567	32,652
14	Saudi Arabia	39,497	-23,881	7,808	31,689
15	Ireland	37,155	-20,125	8,515	28,640
16	India	31,917	-11,735	10,091	21,826
17	Thailand	30,624	-14,319	8,152	22,472
18	Nigeria	30,147	-25,686	2,231	27,916
19	Russia	24,500	-15,066	4,717	19,783
20	Sweden	17,967	-9,714	4,126	13,841
21	Algeria	16,594	-14,391	1,102	15,492
22	Indonesia	16,482	-10,326	3,078	13,404
23	Chile	16,350	-2,770	6,790	9,560
24	Colombia	15,973	-2,557	6,708	9,265

Source: Data from U.S. Department of Commerce.

Note: Total trade = imports + exports. Data are on a Census basis. Imports are on a Customs basis.

Despite the large trade deficit by the mineral fuel and oil sector, the major oil companies remain quite competitive. They are multinational firms who, themselves, do much of the importing of crude oil for their refineries often from their own sources of oil. The deficit in trade in electrical machinery, moreover, may reflect more the global supply chain of multinational producers who may be located in the United States and have competitive products but manufacture their machinery abroad.

Table 3. U.S. Industries with the Largest Trade Surpluses and Deficits in 2006 (Million U.S. Dollars)

	Largest Trade Surpluses		Largest Trade Deficits	
	Description	2006	Description	2006
1	Aircraft, Spacecraft	49,161.4	Mineral Fuel, Oil, etc	-298,638.1
2	Cereals	12,392.6	Vehicles, Not Railway	-122,675.9
3	Optics, Medical Instruments	11,376.8	Electrical Machinery	-83,322.0
4	Plastic	8,351.1	Machinery	-61,912.8
5	Misc. Chemical Products	8,058.8	Woven Apparel	-36,130.1
6	Misc Grain, Seed, Fruit	7,976.0	Knit Apparel	-33,018.8
7	Cotton+yarn, Fabric	4,944.3	Furniture and Bedding	-32,229.6
8	Food Waste; Animal Feed	3,276.2	Toys and Sports Equipment	-20,362.7
9	Woodpulp, Etc.	2,679.6	Other Special Import Provisions	-20,194.1
10	Tanning, Dye, Paint, Putty	2,462.3	Footwear	-18,332.2
11	Ores, Slag, Ash	2,107.6	Pharmaceutical Products	-17,112.9
12	Meat	2,098.7	Wood	-16,384.8
13	Hides and Skins	2,018.5	Iron and Steel	-16,255.9
14	Soap, wax, etc; Dental Prep	1,888.9	Iron/steel Products	-14,936.6
15	Miscellaneous Food	1,592.2	Beverages	-13,491.0
16	Tobacco	1,194.7	Precious Stones, Metals	-12,497.8
17	Ships and Boats	1,144.9	Organic Chemicals	-10,036.6
18	Arms and Ammunition	1,122.2	Special Other	-9,062.1
19	Railway; Traffic Sign eq	969.7	Aluminum	-8,878.2
20	Photographic/Cinematography	866.7	Misc Textile Articles	-8,694.2
21	Knit, Crocheted Fabrics	671.6	Leather Art Saddlery; Bags	-8,339.2
22	Book, Newspaper; Manuscript	636.4	Rubber	-7,929.3
23	Other Base Metals, etc.	526.0	Copper and Articles Thereof	-7,641.6
24	Edible Fruit and Nuts	516.3	Fish and Seafood	-6,354.4
25	Wadding, Felt, Twine, Rope	484.7	Paper, Paperboard	-5,572.2

Source: CRS. Underlying data from U.S. Department of Commerce. Data are on a Census Basis.

26. Is the U.S. Manufacturing Sector Shrinking?

Imports are often blamed for what is perceived as the shrinking of the U.S. manufacturing sector. Media reports of factories being closed, workers laid off, and the plethora of labels on merchandise that indicate the product was made in China, Italy, or any of a number of foreign countries reinforce that perception. Employment in U.S. manufacturing has declined moderately over the past 46 years. In 1960, 15.4 million persons were employed in manufacturing. That number peaked at 19.4 million in 1979 and has declined to 14.2 million in 2006.[9] (See figure 1 below.) Since total U.S. employment has risen, however, manufacturing employment as a share of total nonfarm employment has dropped from 29% in 1960 to 10% in 2006.

Most of the new jobs are being created by the service sector. In 1960, 35.1 million persons worked in service-producing industries. By 2006, employment in services had more than tripled to 113 million persons.

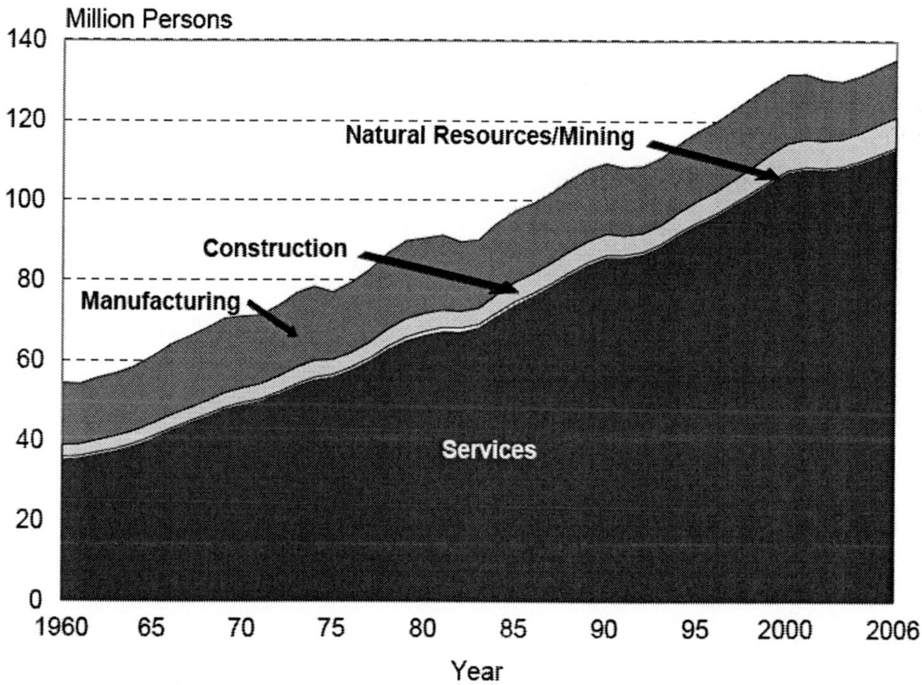

Source: U.S. Department of Labor. Based on reports from employing establishments.

Figure 1. Employees on Nonagricultural Payrolls by Major Industry, 1960-2006.

Even with reduced employment, production by the manufacturing sector as a whole continues to rise, although production in some sectors has been stagnant or declining. What appears to be happening depends on the industry, but studies of de-industrialization generally conclude that it is being caused primarily by developments internal to the economy and not by trade. These include technological change, the shift in consumer demand from manufactured products toward services as incomes rise, and the declining relative price of manufactured items. Import competition has played a role in certain industries. One study concludes that import competition has contributed less than one-fifth to the relative decline of manufacturing in the advanced economies and has had little effect on the overall volume of manufacturing output in those countries.[10]

27. Which Industries Are Losing the Most Jobs?

The industries that are incurring large deficits in their balance of trade are under heavy competition from imports and have been reducing employment. Table 3 shows certain of those industries with the recent peaks in their employment and their employment in 2007. The peak dates range from 1991 to 2004, while the declines since then range from 299.8% for the apparel industry to 165.0% for textile mills, and to 7.5% for furniture and related products.

Table 4. Recent Peaks and Current Employment for Industries with Heavy Import Competition (Thousand Persons)

Industry	Recent Peak	Peak Employment	2007 Employment	Change
Motor Vehicles and Parts	Feb. 2000	1,330.3	1,015.7	-23.6%
Electrical Equipment and Appliances	Jul. 2000	595.8	436.6	-26.7%
Computer and Electronic Products	Jan. 2001	1,872.2	1,394.0	-25.5%
Machinery	Mar. 1998	1,522.9	1,212.8	-20.4%
Textile Mills	Feb. 1995	480.9	181.5	-62.3%
Textile Product Mills	May 2004	179.9	157.1	-12.7%
Apparel	Dec. 1991	917.6	229.5	-75.0%
Furniture and Related Products	Apr. 2004	575.3	535.3	-7.0%
Plastics and Rubber Products	Feb. 2000	959.9	794.0	-17.3%

Source: U.S. Bureau of Labor Statistics. Most Recent Industry-specific Peak and Through Employment and Change. Accessed March 6, 2007.

Formulation of U.S. Trade Policy

Role of Congress[11]

28. What Role Does Congress Play in the Making of Trade Policy?

The role of Congress in formulating international economic policy and regulating international trade is based on express powers set out in Article 1, section 8 of the U.S. Constitution, "to lay and collect taxes, duties, imposts and excises" and "to regulate commerce with foreign nations, and among the several states," as well as the general provision to "make all laws which shall be necessary and proper" to carry out these specific authorities. Congress exercises this power in many ways, among the most important being the enactment of tariff schedules and trade remedy laws, and the approval and implementation of reciprocal trade agreements.

29. What Committees Take the Lead in Exercising Congressional Authority over Trade?

Because of the revenue implications inherent in most trade agreements and policy changes, the House Ways and Means Committee and Senate Finance Committee have responsibility for trade matters. Each Committee has a subcommittee dedicated exclusively to trade issues. Other committees may have a role should trade agreements, policies, and other trade issues include matters under their jurisdiction.

30. What Explicit Ways Does Congress Make Trade Policy?

U.S. trade policy is founded on statutory authorities, as passed by Congress. These include laws authorizing trade programs and governing trade policy generally in areas such as: tariffs, non-tariff barriers, trade remedies, import and export policies, political and economic security, and trade policy functions of the Federal Government. Congress also sets trade negotiating objectives in law, requires formal consultation from and opportunity to advise on trade negotiations with the Executive Branch (in part through the Congressional

Oversight Committee — COG), and conducts oversight hearings on trade programs and agreements to assess their conformity to U.S. law and congressional intent.

31. How Can Individual Members Affect Trade Policy Decisions?

Individual Members affect trade policy first as voting representatives who determine collectively the statutes governing trade matters. They may also exercise influence as sitting Members on relevant committees, in testimony before those committees, whether as a Member of it or not, and in exercising informal influence over other Members through the exercise of the political authority and power invested in them by the electorate.

32. What Is Meant by Fast Track or Trade Promotion Authority (TPA)?

TPA (formerly fast track) refers to a statutory mechanism under which Congress authorizes the President to enter into reciprocal trade agreements governing tariff and non-tariff barriers, and allows their implementing bills to be considered under expedited (fast track) legislative procedures, provided the President observes certain statutory obligations in negotiating trade agreements, including notifying and consulting Congress. The purpose of TPA is to preserve the constitutional role of Congress with respect to consideration of implementing legislation for trade agreements that require changes in domestic law, while also bolstering the negotiating credibility of the Executive Branch by assuring the trade implementing bill will receive expedited and unamended consideration.

Role of the Executive Branch[12]

33. Who Is in Charge?

The President directs overall trade policy in the Executive Branch and performs specific trade functions granted him in statute. The principal adviser to the President on trade matters is the United States Trade Representative (USTR). A cabinet-level appointment, the USTR has primary responsibility for developing and coordinating the implementation of U.S. trade policy (19 U.S. C. 2171).

34. Why Was the USTR Created?

Congress created the USTR in 1962 (originally as the Office of the Special Representative for Trade Negotiations) to heighten the profile of trade and provide better balance between competing domestic and international interests in the formulation and implementation of U.S. trade policy and negotiations, which were previously managed by the U.S. Department of State.

35. How Are Trade Decisions Made?

The USTR has primary responsibility for trade policy decisions within the executive branch; however, they often involve areas of responsibility that fall under other cabinet-level departments, at times requiring a multi-department process. To implement this process, Congress established the Trade Policy Committee, chaired by the USTR and consisting of the Secretaries of Commerce, State, Treasury, Agriculture, Labor, and other department heads as the USTR deems appropriate. The USTR subsequently established two sub-cabinet groups — the Trade Policy Review Group (TPRG) and the Trade Policy Staff Committee (TPSC). The

Executive Branch also solicits advice from a three-tiered congressionally-established trade advisory committee system that consists of private sector and non-Federal government representatives.

36. What Are the Functions of the Executive Branch in U.S. Trade?

The Executive Branch executes trade policy in a variety of ways. It negotiates, implements, and monitors trade agreements, and has responsibility for customs enforcement, collection of duties, implementation of trading remedy laws, budget proposals for trade programs and agencies, export and import policies, and agricultural trade, among others.

37. When Does the President Get Involved in Trade Decisions?

The President is responsible for influencing the direction of trade legislation, signing trade legislation into law, and making other specific decisions on U.S. trade policies and programs where he deems the national interest or political environment requires his direct participation. This can take place in many areas of trade policy, such as requesting TPA/fast track authority, initiating critical trade remedy cases, meeting or communicating with foreign Heads of State or Government, and other areas subject to or requiring high political visibility.

Role of the Private Sector[13]

38. What Is the Formal Role of the Private Sector?

The formal role of the private sector in the formulation of U.S. trade policy is embodied in a three-tiered committee system that the Congress has provided in section 135 of the Trade Act of 1974, as amended. These committees advise the President on negotiations, agreements and other matters of trade policy. At the top of the system is the 45-member Advisory Committee for Trade Policy and Negotiations (ACTPN) consisting of presidentially-appointed representatives from local and state governments and representatives from the broad range of U.S. industries and labor. The USTR administers the ACTPN in cooperation with the Departments of Agriculture, Commerce, Labor, and other relevant departments. At the second tier are industry-specific policy advisory committees, each one consisting of representatives of a specific U.S. industry who provide advice on their specific industry. The third tier consists of sector-specific representatives who provide technical advice. The USTR and the relevant department Secretary appoint members of the sector-specific committees in the latter two tiers.

39. What Is the Informal Role that the Private Sector Plays in the Formulation of U.S. Trade Policy?

The private sector helps shape U.S. trade policy in a number of informal ways. For example, representatives from industry and non-government organizations may be invited to testify or ask to testify before congressional committees on trade matters. Private sector representatives are also invited or request to testify before the United States International Trade Commission (USITC), the U.S. Department of Commerce, or other government bodies to provide assessments of the potential impact of pending trade actions, such as an antidumping or countervailing duty orders, on their industries and sectors. Private sector organizations also lobby Congress and the Executive Branch to forward their interests in U.S. trade policy actions and agreements.

40. Why Are Trade Decisions So Heavily Lobbied?

Trade is becoming a larger and increasingly integral part of the U.S. economy. Virtually all kinds of agricultural and manufactured goods are tradeable — they can be exported and imported. In addition, a growing number of services — once considered non-tradeable because of their intangibility — can be bought and sold across borders because of technology advancements, such as the internet. As a result, how U.S. trade policy is shaped and implemented can affect a broad spectrum of people in the United States. For some industries, firms, and workers, congressional decisions to support a particular free trade agreement or Department of Commerce rulings on antidumping cases, subsidies, and other cases could affect both employment and growth. Those decisions could also influence product choices of U.S. consumers. Consequently, groups representing the multinational national corporations, small businesses, farmers, workers, consumers, and other segments of the economy strive to make sure that their clients' views on trade policy decisions are represented.

Role of the Judiciary[14]

41. How Do Federal Courts Get Involved in Trade?

Legal challenges may be brought in federal court by importers, exporters, domestic manufacturers and producers, and other parties affected by governmental actions and decisions concerning trade. Cases may involve, for example, customs classification decisions, agency determinations in antidumping and countervailing duty (CVD) proceedings, presidential decisions to (or not to) restrict imports under trade remedy statutes, or the constitutionality of state economic sanctions. The federal government may also initiate legal proceedings against individuals and firms to enforce customs laws or statutory restrictions on particular imports and exports. Some trade statutes may preclude judicial review. For example, most preliminary determinations in antidumping and CVD proceedings and governmental actions involving the implementation of WTO and free trade area agreements may not be challenged in federal court.[15] While most federal cases involving trade laws are heard in the U.S. Court of International Trade (see below), cases may also be filed in other federal courts depending on the cause of action or proceeding involved. Court decisions may significantly affect U.S. trade policy when they examine whether an agency has properly interpreted its statutory mandate, determine whether an agency has acted outside the scope of its statutory authority, decide how much deference should be granted the Executive Branch under a particular statute, or rule on whether a trade statute violates the U.S. constitution.

42. What Is the U.S. Court of International Trade?

The U.S. Court of International Trade (USCIT) is an Article III federal court located in New York City with exclusive jurisdiction over a number of trade-related matters, including customs decisions, antidumping and countervailing duty determinations, import embargoes imposed for reasons other than health and safety, and the recovery of customs duties and penalties. Formerly known as the Customs Court, the USCIT was renamed in the Customs Court Act of 1980, which also significantly enlarged its jurisdiction. The court consists of nine judges, no more than five of whom may be from the same political party. Judges are appointed by the President with the consent of the Senate. USCIT decisions are appealable to the U.S. Court of Appeals for the Federal Circuit and to the U.S. Supreme Court. Statutory provisions related to the USCIT may be found at 28 U.S.C. §§ 251-258 (establishment) and 28 U.S.C. §§ 1581-1585 (jurisdiction).

U.S. Trade and Investment Policy Issues

Trade Negotiations and Agreements[16]

43. Why Does the United States Negotiate Trade Liberalizing Agreements?

The United States negotiates trade liberalizing agreements for economic and commercial reasons, including:

- to encourage foreign trade partners to reduce or eliminate tariffs and non-tariff barriers and, in so doing, increase market access for U.S. exporters;
- to gain an advantage for U.S. exporters over foreign competitors in a third-country market;
- to increase access to lower cost imports that help to control inflation and offer domestic consumers a wider choice of products; and
- to encourage trading partners, especially developing countries, to rationalize their trade regimes, and thereby improve the efficiency of their economies.

The United States has also negotiates trade liberalizing agreements for political/national security reasons, including:

- to strengthen established alliances;
- to forge new strategic relationships; and
- to establish a presence in a geographic region.

44. What Are the Various Types of Trade Liberalizing Agreements?

In general, reciprocal trade agreements can be categorized by the number of countries involved: bilateral agreements, such as free trade agreements (FTAs), are between two countries; regional agreements, such as, the North American Free Trade Agreement (NAFTA), involve three or more countries in a geographic region; and multilateral agreements, such as those negotiated in the World Trade Organization (WTO), involve many countries from virtually all regions.

45. Who Benefits from Trade Liberalizing Agreements? Who Loses?

Economic theory suggests and empirical studies have generally concluded that economies as a whole benefit when trade barriers are removed because economic resources (land, labor, and capital) are employed more efficiently. However, economic theory and studies also point out that the benefits of trade liberalization are not distributed evenly within an economy and not even among economies. Some industries, firms, and workers "lose" if they cannot adjust to the increased foreign competition resulting from the trade agreement or if particular provisions of the trade agreement disadvantages their interests. Other industries, firms, and workers "win" if they can take advantage of new market opening opportunities presented by the trade agreement or if particular provisions of the trade agreement favors or promotes their interests.

46. What Is the WTO?

The World Trade Organization (WTO) is a 150-member body that establishes through negotiations and implements the multilateral system of rules on trade in goods and services and on other trade-related matters and adjudicates disputes under the rules. A fundamental principle of the WTO is non-discrimination in trade among the members. The WTO was established in January 1995 as a part of the agreements reached by the signatories to the General Agreement on Tariffs and Trade (GATT) at the end of the Uruguay Round negotiations. The WTO's primary purpose is to administer the roughly 60 agreements and separate commitments made by its members as part of the GATT (for trade in goods), the General Agreement on Trade in Services (GATS — for trade in services), and the agreement on trade-related aspects of intellectual property rights (TRIPS).

47. How Are Disputes Resolved under WTO Agreements?

If a WTO Member believes that another Member has adopted a law, regulation, or practice that violates a WTO agreement, the Member may initiate dispute settlement proceedings under the WTO Dispute Settlement Understanding. The process begins with consultations and, if these fail to resolve the dispute, the Member may request that the WTO establish a dispute panel. A panel report may be appealed to the WTO Appellate Body by either disputing party. If the defending Member is found to have violated a WTO obligation, the Member will be expected to remove the challenged measure. If this is not done by the end of the established compliance period, the prevailing Member may request authorization from the WTO to take temporary retaliatory action. In most cases, retaliation consists of tariff increases on selected products from the defending Member. To date, over 350 complaints have been filed since the WTO agreements entered into force, with the majority of disputes resolved through consultations and negotiations rather than the panel process.

WTO decisions do not have direct effect in U.S. law. Thus, in the event a U.S. statute is found to violate a WTO obligation, the dispute findings may not be implemented except through legislative action. Where an administrative action is successfully challenged, the United States Trade Representative (USTR) decides what, if any, compliance action will be taken. If sufficient statutory authority exists to amend or modify a regulation or practice or to issue a new determination in a challenged administrative proceeding, the USTR may direct the agency involved to make the change, provided that certain statutory procedures for such actions are followed.[17]

48. What Is the Doha Round?

Since the GATT was signed in 1947, its signatories (member countries) have revised and expanded the trade rules in various rounds of negotiations. The Doha Development Agenda (DDA)is the ninth round and the first under the WTO. It is named after the city where it was launched in November 2001 — Doha, Qatar. The WTO members included "development" in the title to reflect their intention to emphasize issues of importance to developing countries. The negotiations have primarily focused on three areas — agriculture, non-agricultural goods, and services, although members have conducted negotiations in other areas as well, such as rules. As of this writing, negotiators have not been able to reach agreements and conclude the round.

49. What Are Free Trade Agreements (FTAs)?

At a minimum, FTAs are agreements between/among two or more countries under which they agree to eliminate tariffs and non-tariff barriers on trade in goods and services among them, but each country maintains its own trade policies and regulations, including tariffs, on trade outside the FTA. FTA partner countries may also agree to reduce barriers or otherwise establish rules of behavior in other economic activities — investment, intellectual property rights (IPR), labor rights and environmental protection.

50. How do FTAs that the United States Has Negotiated Generally Differ from Those Negotiated among other Countries?

The FTAs that the United States negotiates are often more comprehensive than those that are negotiated among other countries, particularly developing countries. The standard U.S. FTA model includes not only the elimination of tariffs on trade in goods among the FTA partners, but also reduction of barriers on trade in services, rules on foreign investment, requirements for intellectual property rights protection, and provisions on labor rights and environment protection. These rules may not necessarily guarantee "free trade," but may condition or influence the terms of competition in specific markets.

51. What are Trade and Investment Framework Agreements (TIFAs)?

A TIFA is an agreement between the United States and another country (for example Afghanistan) or group of countries (for example, ASEAN) to consult on issues of mutual interest in order to promote trade and investment among the participants. Most U.S. TIFAs are with developing countries. The United States and its TIFA partner(s) agree to establish a joint ministerial-level council as the overall mechanism for consultation with the possibility of establishing issue-oriented working groups. A TIFA is a non-binding agreement and does not involve changes in U.S. law; therefore, TIFAs do not require congressional approval. In some cases, TIFAs have led to FTA negotiations.

Import Issues[18]

52. Why Do Countries Import Goods and Services from other Countries?

Some goods that are imported into the United States, such as bananas or crude oil, cannot be produced at home or produced in sufficient quantities to satisfy domestic demand. Many other goods and services are imported because they can be produced less expensively or more efficiently by other countries.

53. What Are other Benefits of Imports?

Consumers can benefit through access to a wider variety of goods at lower costs. Producers can benefit through access to lower priced components or inputs that can be utilized in the production process. Longer term, imports can also provide pressures for companies to reduce costs through innovation and research and development, thereby serving as a spur to economic growth.

54. What Are the Costs of Imports?

By providing increased competition to companies producing similar or competing products, imports can contribute to job losses and business failures. If these job losses and company failures are concentrated in a region, imports can also be a cause of considerable economic distress in a community.

55. How Does the Government Deal with Disruption and Injury to Producers and Workers?

The government tries to help producers and workers who are adversely affected by trade though application of various trade remedy laws. These laws include responses to unfair trade practices and to increased levels of injurious imports, as well as the Trade Adjustment Assistance program.

56. What Are the Main Trade Remedy Laws?

Two primary trade remedy laws aimed at unfair trade practices are the antidumping (AD) and countervailing duty (CVD) laws. Other trade remedy laws include Section 201 (see below), Section 301 (focuses on violations of trade agreements or other foreign practices that are unjustifiable and restrict U.S. commerce), and Section 337 (focuses on unfair practices in import trade such as patent and copyright infringement).

57. What Is the Purpose of the Countervailing Duty Law?

The purpose of the CVD law is to offset any unfair competitive advantage that foreign manufacturers or exporters might enjoy over U.S. producers as a result of receiving a subsidy. As defined by the WTO, a subsidy is a financial contribution, such as a loan, grant, or tax credit, provided by a government or other public entity that confers a benefit on manufacturers or exporters of a product. Countervailing duties, if imposed, are designed to equal the net amount of the foreign subsidy and are levied upon importation of the subsidized goods into the United States.

58. What Is the Purpose of the Antidumping Law?

Dumping generally refers to a situation where goods are sold in one export market at prices lower than the prices at which comparable goods are sold in the home market of the exporter, or in its other export markets. It is thought that companies dump products to gain market share or to deter competition. U.S. law provides for the assessment and collection of antidumping duties when an administrative determination is made that foreign goods are being dumped or sold at less than fair value in the United States and that such imports are materially injuring a U.S. industry.

59. What Is the Import Relief (Safeguards) Law?

U.S. trade law (chapters 1 and 2 of the Trade Act of 1974, as amended) provides the President with the authority to provide domestic industry with temporary import relief, which could include tariffs and quotas, if it is found to be seriously injured from surges of imports that do not necessarily involve unfairly traded products. This provision is based on the recognition that liberalization of trade barriers could cause individual sectors of the U.S. economy economic adjustment problems, and that domestic industries should provide a period of relief to allow them to adjust to changed competitive conditions. The U.S. International Trade Commission investigates and recommends on import relief cases, and the President takes final action.

60. What Is the Trade Adjustment Assistance Program?

The first trade adjustment assistance program was adopted as part of the Trade Expansion Act of 1962. In proposing the program, the Kennedy Administration argued that "those injured by trade competition should not be required to bear the full brunt of the impact. Rather, the burden of economic adjustment should be borne in part by the federal government ... [because] there is an obligation to render assistance to those who suffer as a result of national trade policy."[19]

The current trade adjustment assistance program has three parts: Part A for workers, Part B for firms, and Part C for farmers. Under Part A, certified workers may be eligible for remedial education, wage reimbursement, job search and relocation allowances, and tax credits for health insurance costs. Under Part B, firms may be eligible for technical assistance to help them develop strategies to remain competitive in the changing international economy. Under Part C, farmers impacted by competing imports may be eligible for cash benefits.[20]

61. What Are the Arguments for and Against Extending Trade Adjustment Assistance (TAA) to All Dislocated Workers?

Some observers have suggested extending TAA to all dislocated workers —roughly defined as workers who lose their job involuntarily, for reasons not related to job performance.[21] Supporters point to an inequity in eligibility among trade-related job losers: Many who lose their jobs directly or indirectly to trade are not eligible for benefits under the current TAA program. These include (1) virtually all service sector job losers; (2) certain manufacturing sector job losers, depending on the country to which the job is outsourced, whether the United States has a trade agreement with it, and whether or not imports of "like"or "directly competitive" articles are expected to increase; (3) some job losers in "upstream" supply operations and "downstream" user operations; (4) those who lose their jobs to a decline in U.S. *exports*; and (5) those who lose their jobs to automation designed to increase exports or improve competitiveness against imports. Supporters also argue for an expanded and simplified program of eligibility in order to eliminate the difficulties of administering a program with such a complex set of eligibility criteria.

Opponents question why trade-related job losses should be treated any differently than non-trade related job losses; some oppose any adjustment programs "because they imply that there is something wrong with the operation of the free market." The National Association of Manufacturers reportedly has warned, "Business enterprises and their employees are continuously affected for better or for worse by all sorts of events beyond their control.... All experience warns that programs of this type inevitably expand and proliferate."[22] Others my be concerned with definitions, administering such a complex program, and its fiscal impact.

Export Issues[23]

62. What Are the Benefits of Exports?

From the perspective of individual companies, export markets provide opportunities to expand production runs and reduce costs. Companies may also be able to sell goods and services at higher prices than they can obtain at home. From the perspective of individual workers, jobs in export-oriented industries often provide higher than average wages.

63. What Are Some Costs of Exporting?

From an economic perspective that views higher levels of consumption as being the goal of economic activity, countries export goods and services in order to earn the foreign currency with which they can buy imports. Exports, according to this view, are foregone production that could have been consumed domestically.

64. What Factors Most Determine U.S. Export Levels?

Economists maintain that the overall level of U.S. exports is determined primarily by the same macroeconomic conditions that generate the U.S. trade deficit. These include the level of savings and investment, the foreign exchange rate, and willingness of foreigners to invest in U.S. assets. U.S. exports also depend on economic growth rates in major markets. The higher the rate of economic growth in Asia (particularly Japan and China), Europe (particularly Germany, the U.K., and France), Canada, and Latin America, the more people in those markets are likely to buy U.S. exports, other things being equal.

65. What Factors Determine the Exporting Success of Specific Sectors?

The level of American exports in specific sectors depends both on the overall level of exports and on an interplay of factors such as the relative competitiveness of the American industry, trade barriers abroad, and sometimes the degree of U.S. export promotion. The higher the overall level of exports, the more individual sectors are likely to sell abroad, but given the impact of macroeconomic factors, export surges by a particular sector often are offset by a decline in exports by other sectors. In a world of floating exchange rates, a large export surge will cause foreigners to buy more dollars to pay for those exports. This raises the demand for dollars and increases its price relative to other currencies. Since the United States does not intervene in currency markets to fix its exchange rate, the higher value of the dollar makes U.S. exports more expensive and may reduce their sales.

66. How Does the U.S. Government Promote Exports?

For many years, the U.S. government has promoted exports by providing credit, finance, and insurance programs that are administered by the Export-Import Bank, the Department of Agriculture, and the Overseas Private Investment Corporation. In addition, the Department of Commerce through the Foreign Commercial Service in the International Trade Administration of the Department of Commerce acts to promote U.S. exports of goods and services, particularly by small and medium-sized companies. Nearly every country promotes its exports as well.

67. What Does the U.S. Government Do to Restrict Exports?

Congress has authorized the President to control the export of various items for national security, foreign policy, and economic reasons. Separate programs and statutes for controlling different types of exports exist for nuclear materials and technology, defense articles and services, and dual-use goods and technology. Under each program, licenses of various types are required before an export can be undertaken. The Departments of Commerce, State, and Defense administer these programs.

Investment Issues[24]

68. What Are the Main Kinds of Capital Flows?

Generally, the two main kinds of capital flows are foreign direct investments and foreign portfolio investments. Foreign direct investments involve the acquisition of real assets such as real estate, a manufacturing plant, or controlling interest in an ongoing enterprise by a person or entity from another country. Foreign portfolio investments involve purchase of foreign equities or bonds, loans to foreign residents, or the opening of foreign bank accounts. Direct investments involve a long-term commitment and usually have direct employment stimulation advantages for the host country while portfolio investments are extremely liquid and can be withdrawn often times at the click of a computer mouse. In addition, there are official capital flows generated by governments for various purposes such as humanitarian assistance and other foreign aid.

69. Which Is Larger — Trade or Capital Flows?

It depends. Recent data indicate that from 1985 to 2005, global trade in goods and services, as measured by exports, doubled from $6 trillion a year to $12 trillion a year. During the same twenty-year period, capital flows, as measured in the balance of payments accounts (direct, portfolio, and other official investments), more than quadrupled from $1.1 trillion a year to $5.2 trillion a year. But during this time period, there also has been an explosion in growth in other types of capital flows, known as foreign exchange and over-the-counter derivatives markets. These markets facilitate trade in foreign exchange and other types of assets. While the capital flows associated with these markets do not directly relate to transactions in the balance of payments, they do affect the international exchange value of the dollar, which in turn affects the prices of goods and services and the cost of securities. A survey in 2004 by the world's leading central banks indicated that the daily trading of foreign currencies totals more than $1.9 trillion.

70. Why Do Companies Invest Abroad?

For the most part, firms invest abroad to increase their profits. Economists and other experts generally conclude, however, that a broad range of factors influence a firm's decision to invest abroad. The major determinants of foreign direct investment are the presence of ownership-specific competitive advantages in a transnational corporation, the presence of locational advantages such as resource endowments or low-cost labor in a host country, and the presence of superior commercial benefits in an intra-firm relationship as opposed to an arm's-length relationship between investor and host country. Multinational firms apparently are motivated by more than a single factor, and likely invest abroad not only to gain access to a low-cost resource but to improve their efficiency or to improve their market share.

71. Why Has Foreign Investment Increased So Dramatically in Recent Decades?

From 1990 to 2005, the stock, or the cumulative amount, of foreign direct investment in the world grew from $1.8 trillion to $10.7 trillion, or by nearly 600 percent. This rapid growth arises from a number of factors. One of the most important factors has been a change in public policies toward foreign direct investment among most countries. Foreign direct investment has come to be viewed favorably not only by the economically advanced countries, but also by developing economies, which now often compete to bring in much-needed capital, technology, and technical expertise. Currently, about three-fourths of all direct investment is placed among the highly developed economies where consumer tastes and workers wages are comparable.

72. What Are Some of the Benefits of Direct Foreign Investment?

Generally, economists argue in favor of unimpeded international flows of capital, such as direct investment, because they estimate that such flows positively affect both the domestic (home) and foreign (host) economies. For the home country, direct investment benefits the individual firms that invest abroad, because they are better able to exploit their existing competitive advantages and to acquire additional skills and advantages. Direct investment also seems to be associated with a strengthened competitive position, a higher level of skills of the employees, and higher incomes of firms that invest abroad. Host countries benefit from inward direct investment because the investment adds permanently to the capital stock and often to the skill set of the nation. Direct investment also brings technological advances, since firms that invest abroad generally possess advanced technology, processes, and other advantages. Such investment also boosts capital formation and contributes to a growth in a competitive business environment and productivity. In addition, direct investment contributes to international trade and integration into the global trading community, since most firms that invest abroad are established multinational firms.

73. What Are Some of the Costs of Direct Foreign Investment?

Concerned observers argue that U.S. direct investment abroad supplants U.S. exports, thereby reducing employment and wages in the U.S. economy. While it appears unlikely that the overall U.S. employment level is affected by direct investment flows, jobs in particular companies and sectors can be eliminated when a company decides to produce similar products abroad. For example, if a U.S. auto company closed an assembly line in the United States and opened one in Mexico assembling the same product line, U.S. auto assembly jobs are lost. Similarly, while inward flows of foreign direct investment tend to create new jobs, there sometimes is concern that the new foreign owners may not serve as stable and dependable community partners as the previous nationally-based ownership.

74. What are BITs?

Bilateral investment treaties (BITs) are agreements between two countries for the reciprocal encouragement, promotion and protection of investments in each other's territories. Most treaties contain basic provisions that cover the following areas: scope and definition of investment, admission and establishment, national treatment, most-favored-nation treatment, fair and equitable treatment, compensation in the event of expropriation or damage to the investment, guarantees of free transfers of funds, and dispute settlement mechanisms, both state-state and investor-state. U.S. BITs have to be ratified by the Senate.

75. What is CFIUS?

The Committee on Foreign Investment in the United States (CFIUS) is an interagency committee that serves the President in overseeing the national security implications of foreign investment in the economy. CFIUS was established by an Executive Order of President Ford in 1975 with broad responsibilities and few specific powers. Legislation currently pending in Congress could affect the role and membership of CFIUS.

Additional Readings

CRS Reports

CRS Report RS20088, Dispute Settlement in the World Trade Organization: An Overview, by Jeanne J. Grimmett.

CRS Report RS21554, Free Trade Agreements and the WTO Exceptions, by Jeanne J. Grimmett and Todd B. Tatelman.

CRS Report RS21763, WTO Dispute Settlement: Stages and Pending U.S. Activity Before the Dispute Settlement Body, by Todd B. Tatelman and Cynthia M. Brougher.

CRS Report RS22154, WTO Decisions and Their Effect in U.S. Law, by Jeanne J. Grimmett.

CRS Report 97-896, Why Certain Trade Agreements Are Approved as Congressional-Executive Agreements Rather Than as Treaties, by Jeanne J. Grimmett.

CRS Report RL31032, The U.S. Trade Deficit: Causes, Consequences, and Cures, by Craig K. Elwell.

CRS Report RL31356, Free Trade Agreements: Impact on U.S. Trade and Implications for U.S. Trade Policy, by William H. Cooper.

CRS Report RL32371, Trade Remedies: A Primer, by Vivian C. Jones.

CRS Report RL32461, Outsourcing and Insourcing Jobs in the U.S. Economy: Evidence Based on Foreign Investment Data, by James K. Jackson.

CRS Report RL32964, The United States as a Net Debtor Nation: Overview of the International Investment Position, by James K. Jackson.

CRS Report RL33144, WTO Doha Round: The Agriculture Negotiations, by Charles E. Hanrahan and Randy Schnepf.

CRS Report RL33274, Financing the U.S. Trade Deficit, by James K. Jackson.

CRS Report RL33743, Trade Promotion Authority: Issues, Options, and Prospects for Renewal, by J. F. Hornbeck and William H. Cooper.

CRS Report RL33388, The Committee on Foreign Investment in the United States (CFIUS), by James K. Jackson.

CRS Report RL33463, Trade Negotiations During the 110th Congress, by Ian F. Fergusson.

CRS Report RL33553, Agricultural Export and Food Aid Programs, by Charles E. Hanrahan.

CRS Report RL33577, U.S. International Trade: Trends and Forecasts, by Dick K. Nanto.

CRS Report 98-928, The World Trade Organization: Background and Issues, by Ian F. Fergusson.

Other Readings

Burtless, Gary, Robert Z. Lawrence, and Robert Litan, *Globaphobia,* (Washington, DC: The Brookings Institution, 1998).

Destler, I. M., *American Trade Politics,* Institute for International Economics, Washington, DC, 2005.

The Economist, "Globalization and Its Critics," September 27, 2001.

Friedman, Thomas, *The Lexus and the Olive Tree* (London: Harper Collins, 2000).

Mankiw, N. Gregory, *Principles of Economics* (New York: Dryden Press, 1997).

Mann, Catherine L., *Is the U.S. Trade Deficit Sustainable?* Institute for International Economics, Washington, DC, 1999.

Office of the United States Trade Representative, *2007 Trade Policy Agenda and 2006 Annual Report* (March 2007), at [http://www.ustr.gov/Document_Library/Reports_Publications/2007/2007_Trade_Policy_Agenda/Section_Index.html].

Office of the United States Trade Representative, *2006 National Trade Estimate Report on Foreign Trade Barriers* (March 2006), at [http://www.ustr.gov/Document_Library/Reports_Publications/2006/2006_NTE_Report/Section_Index.html].

Stiglitz, Joseph, *Globalization and Its Discontents,* Yale University Press, 2003.

U.S. Congress. House Ways and Means Committee. Overview and Compilation of U.S. Trade Statutes, Parts I and II, June 2005

U.S. International Trade Commission, *The Year in Trade 2005; Operation of the Trade Agreements Program* (Pub. 3875, Aug. 2006), at [http://hotdocs.usitc.gov/ docs/pubs/year_in_trade/pub3875.pdf].

Wolf, Martin, *Why Globalization Works,* (New Haven: Yale University Press, 2004). World Trade Organization, *Dictionary of Trade Policy Terms* (Cambridge, UK: Cambridge University Press, 2003).

List of Questions

Trade Concepts

1. Why do countries trade?
2. What is comparative advantage?
3. What determines comparative advantage?
4. Can governments shape or distort comparative advantage?
5. What is the terms of trade?
6. What are the costs of trade expansion?
7. Does trade destroy jobs?
8. Does trade reduce the wages of U.S. workers?
9. What is intra-industry trade?

10. Why is intra-industry trade important?
11. What is globalization?
12. What is the global supply chain and how does it relate to globalization?
13. How does globalization affect job security?

U.S. Trade Performance

14. What is meant by the trade deficit?
15. Why are different numbers reported for the trade deficit?
16. What are the causes of the record trade deficits?
17. What role do foreign trade barriers play in causing trade deficits?
18. How does the trade deficit affect the exchange value of the dollar?
19. How is the trade deficit financed?
20. Is the trade deficit a problem for the U.S. economy?
21. How long can the United States keep running trade deficits?
22. How can the trade deficit be reduced?
23. What is the role for trade policy in reducing the trade deficit?
24. Who are the leading U.S. trade partners?
25. Which industries appear to be the most competitive as measured by the size of their trade surpluses? Which are the least competitive as measured by their trade deficits?
26. Is the U.S. manufacturing sector shrinking?
27. Which industries are losing the most jobs?

Formulation of U.S. Trade Policy

28. What role does Congress play in the making of trade policy?
29. What committees take the lead in exercising congressional authority over trade?
30. What explicit ways does Congress make trade policy?
31. How can individual Members affect trade policy decisions?
32. What is meant by fast track or Trade Promotion Authority (TPA)?
33. Who is in charge?
34. Why was the USTR created?
35. How are trade decisions made?
36. What are the functions of the Executive Branch in U.S. trade?
37. When does the President get involved in trade decisions?
38. What is the formal role of the private sector?
39. What is the informal role that the private sector plays in the formulation of U.S. trade policy?
40. Why are trade decisions so heavily lobbied?
41. How do federal courts get involved in trade?
42. What is the U.S. Court of International Trade?

U.S. Trade and Investment Policy Issues

43. Why does the United States negotiate trade liberalizing agreements?
44. What are the various types of trade liberalizing agreements?
45. Who benefits from trade liberalizing agreements? Who loses?
46. What is the WTO?
47. How are disputes resolved under WTO agreements?
48. What is the Doha Round?
49. What are free trade agreements (FTAs)?
50. How do FTAs that the United States has negotiated generally differ from those negotiated among other countries?
51. What are Trade and Investment Framework Agreements (TIFAs)?
52. Why do countries import goods and services from other countries?
53. What are other benefits of imports?
54. What are the costs of imports?
55. How does the government deal with disruption and injury to producers and workers?
56. What are the main trade remedy laws?
57. What is the purpose of the countervailing duty law?
58. What is the purpose of the antidumping law?
59. What is the import relief (safeguards) law?
60. What is the Trade Adjustment Assistance Program?
61. What are the arguments for and against extending Trade Adjustment Assistance (TAA) to all dislocated workers?
62. What are the benefits of exports?
63. What are some costs of exporting?
64. What factors most determine U.S. export levels?
65. What factors determine the exporting success of specific sectors?
66. How does the U.S. government promote exports?
67. What does the U.S. government do to restrict exports?
68. What are the main kinds of capital flows?
69. Which is larger — trade or capital flows?
70. Why do companies invest abroad?
71. Why has foreign investment increased so dramatically in recent decades?
72. What are some of the benefits of direct foreign investment?
73. What are some of the costs of direct foreign investment?
74. What are BITs?
75. What is CFIUS?

REFERENCES

[1] This section was prepared by Craig K. Elwell, Specialist in Macroeconomics, Government and Finance Division, CRS.

[2] Only 10% of the U.S. labor force has less than a secondary level of education as compared to over 60% below this level in China's labor force. See U.S. Department of

Labor, Bureau of Labor Statistics, *Current Population Survey,* 2006 and Barro, Robert and Jong-Wha Lee, "International Data on Educational Attainment," *NBER Working Papers 7911,* September 2000.

[3] For a survey of this evidence see Douglas Irwin, F*ree Trade Under Fire*, Princeton University Press, 2002, pp. 90-97.

[4] See International Monetary Fund, *World Economic Outlook,* June 2006.

[5] See Dani Roderik, *Has Globalization Gone too Far?* Institute for International Economics, 1997.

[6] This section was prepared by Dick K. Nanto, Specialist in Industry and Trade, Foreign Affairs. Defense, and Trade Division.

[7] See Nakamae, Tadashi. Weak Yen Conundrum. *The International Economy*, Winter 2007, pp. 42-45.

[8] See Mann, Catherine L. *Is the U.S. Trade Deficit Sustainable?* Washington, Institute for International Economics, 1999. 224 p. See also: CRS Report RL33274, *Financing the U.S. Trade Deficit*, by James K. Jackson. CRS Report RL31032, *The U.S. Trade Deficit: Causes, Consequences, and Cures*, by Craig K. Elwell.

[9] These data are based on reports from employing establishments and do not include proprietors, self-employed persons, unpaid family workers, private household workers, and those employed in agriculture.

[10] Brady, David and Ryan Denniston, "Economic Globalization, Industrialization and Deindustrialization in Affluent Democracies," *Social Forces,* 85 no. 1 (Sep 2006): pp. 297-310, 312, 315-316, 318, 320-327.

[11] Prepared by J. F. Hornbeck, Specialist in International Trade and Finance, Foreign Affairs, Defense, and Trade Division; and Jeanne J. Grimmett, Legislative Attorney, American Law Division.

[12] Prepared by J. F. Hornbeck, Specialist in International Trade and Finance, Foreign Affairs, Defense, and Trade Division, and Jeanne J. Grimmett, Legislative Attorney, American Law Division.

[13] Prepared by William H. Cooper, Specialist in International Trade and Finance, Foreign Affairs, Defense, and Trade Division.

[14] Prepared by Jeanne J. Grimmett, Legislative Attorney, American Law Division.

[15] For further information, see CRS Report RS22154, *WTO Decisions and Their Effect in U.S. Law*, by Jeanne J. Grimmett.

[16] This section was prepared by William H. Cooper, Specialist in International Trade and Finance, Foreign Affairs, Defense, and Trade Division.

[17] Uruguay Round Agreements Act, P.L. 103-465, §§ 123(g), 129, 19 U.S.C. §§ 3535(g), 3538.

[18] This section was prepared by Vivian C. Jones and Mary Jane Bolle, Specialists in International Trade and Finance, Foreign Affairs, Defense, and Trade Division.

[19] Trade Adjustment Assistance: The More We Change the More It Stays the Same, by Howard Rosen, in *C. Fred Bergsten and the World Economy,* edited by Michael Mussa, Peterson Institute for International Economics, December 2006, pp. 79-113.

[20] See *Trade Act of 2002*, P.L. 107-210, August 6, 2002, Division A: Trade Adjustment Assistance.

[21] Rosen, op. cit., p. 101, footnote 32.

[22] Rosen, op. cit., p. 80-81.

[23] Prepared by Angeles Villarreal, Analyst in International Trade and Finance and Dick K. Nanto, Specialist in Industry and Trade, Foreign Affairs, Defense, and Trade Division.

[24] Prepared by James K. Jackson, Specialist in International Trade and Finance, Foreign Affairs, Defense, and Trade Division.

In: Trade Policies and Agreements in the Era of Globalization ISBN: 978-1-60021-836-1
Editor: Paul B. Lucus, pp. 33-72

Chapter 2

CHINA'S TRADE WITH THE UNITED STATES AND THE WORLD*

Thomas Lum and Dick K. Nanto

ABSTRACT

As imports from the People's Republic of China (PRC) have surged in recent years, posing a threat to some U.S. industries and manufacturing employment, Congress has begun to focus on not only access to the Chinese market and intellectual property rights (IPO) protection, but also the mounting U.S. trade deficit with China as well as allegations that China is selling its products on the international market at below cost (dumping), engaging in "currency manipulation," and exploiting its workers for economic gain. Members of the 109th Congress introduced several bills that would impose trade sanctions on China for intervening in the currency market or for engaging in other acts of unfair trade, while the Bush Administration has imposed anti-dumping duties and safeguards against some PRC products and pressured China to further revalue its currency and remove non-tariff trade barriers.

China runs a trade surplus with the world's three major economic centers — the United States, the European Union, and Japan. Since 2000, the United States has incurred its largest bilateral trade deficit with China ($201 billion in 2005, a 25% rise over 2004). In 2003, China replaced Mexico as the second largest source of imports for the United States. China's share of U.S. imports was 14.6% in 2005, although this proportion still falls short of Japan's 18% of the early 1990s. The United States is China's largest overseas market and second largest source of foreign direct investment on a cumulative basis. U.S. exports to China have been growing rapidly as well, although from a low base. In 2004, China replaced Germany and the United Kingdom to become the fourth largest market for U.S. goods and remains the fastest growing major U.S. export market. China is purchasing heavily from its Asian trading partners — particularly precision machinery, electronic components, and raw materials for manufacturing. China is running trade deficits with Taiwan and South Korea and has become a major buyer of goods from Japan and Southeast Asia.

In the past decade, the most dramatic increases in U.S. imports from China have been not in labor-intensive sectors but in some advanced technology sectors, such as

---

* Excerpted from CRS Report RL31403, dated January 4, 2007.

office and data processing machines, telecommunications and sound equipment, and electrical machinery and appliances. China's exports to the United States are taking market share from other Pacific Rim countries, particularly the East Asian newly industrialized countries (NICS), which have moved most of their low-end production facilities to China.

This report provides a quantitative framework for policy considerations dealing with U.S. trade with China. It provides basic data and analysis of China's international trade with the United States and other countries. Since Chinese data differ considerably from those of its trading partners (because of how entrepot trade through Hong Kong is counted), data from both PRC sources and those of its trading partners are presented. Charts showing import trends by sector for the United States highlight China's growing market shares in many industries and also show import shares for Japan, Canada, Mexico, the European Union, and the Association for Southeast Asian Nations (ASEAN).

U.S. trade with the People's Republic of China (PRC) has raised several policy concerns. The trade is highly unbalanced in China's favor with a U.S. deficit of $201 billion in 2005. Year-to-date (January-October 2006), the U.S. deficit reached $190 billion. Many associate this deficit with the concomitant loss of American jobs in industries competing with rapidly rising imports from China. Some policymakers as well as leaders of industry and labor blame China for unfair trade practices, including deliberately undervaluing its currency, which they claim create an uneven playing field for U.S. companies when competing against imports from the PRC. U.S.-China trade issues are often driven by larger policy objectives. U.S. trade with China is but one aspect of the overall U.S. policy of engagement with the PRC, a policy that serves broader U.S. interests. Trade also underpins Beijing's development strategy and contributes to domestic support for the PRC government.

This article presents data and analysis of China's trade that shed light on various policy issues, provides an overview of recent U.S. legislative initiatives, and examines the goals and constraints of U.S. trade policy toward the PRC. Some of the specific questions addressed are how the U.S. trade balance with China compares with those of the European Union and Japan, whether imports from China are merely replacing imports from other Pacific Rim nations, and how imports from China by industry compare with imports from other countries.

THE RATIONALE FOR U.S. POLICY AND INITIATIVES

Allowing trade with China to develop is part of the overall U.S. strategy of engagement with the PRC. The rationale behind engagement is that working with China through economic, diplomatic, informational, and military interchanges helps the United States to achieve important national security goals such as preventing nuclear proliferation, defeating global terrorism, defusing regional conflicts, fostering global economic growth, and championing aspirations for human dignity.[1] These goals are aimed at achieving U.S. national interests of security and prosperity for all Americans and projecting U.S. values abroad.

U.S. trade policy toward China is based upon the assumption that trade between the two countries has both economic and political benefits: (1) in general, trade with China benefits both sides and allows for a more efficient allocation of available resources; (2) the rapidly developing Chinese economy affords a rare opportunity for U.S. businesses to become part of a huge and rapidly expanding market; (3) China's membership in the World Trade Organization (WTO) compels the PRC to comply with international trading rules and spurs the development of market forces in the country; and (4) foreign trade and investment create a dependency on exports, imports, and foreign investment and other interaction with the outside world in China, which in turn strengthen its relations with the Western world, create centers of power outside the Chinese Communist Party, and foster economic and social pressures for democracy; (5) a country as significant as China — accounting for a quarter of the world's population, armed with nuclear weapons, and a member of the U.N. Security Council — cannot be ignored or isolated. According to some experts, globalization and economic interests may be exerting a moderating influence on Beijing's policies toward protecting China's national security interests. However, the Chinese Communist Party's determination to maintain political legitimacy through economic growth also creates tensions with other countries and with emerging non-Party political actors.

The possible problems or challenges raised by the U.S. strategy of economic engagement with China include adjusting to economic competition in sectors where China has a comparative advantage, responding to PRC unfair trade practices, and the rise of an economically powerful China that is becoming more assertive in global affairs: (1) Imports from China may be entering in such increased quantities that they are a substantial cause of serious injury, or threat thereof, to competing U.S. industries;[2] (2) Imports from China may be dumped, subsidized, or unfairly aided by government entities in China, which still wield considerable influence in the economy;[3] (3) According to some economists and many policymakers, the U.S. trade deficit with the PRC stems in large part from Beijing's policy of maintaining an undervalued currency; (4) China has a poor record of adopting or enforcing internationally recognized standards for working conditions and environmental regulation which, in addition to violating human rights and harming the environment, may provide PRC businesses with unfair competitive advantages; and (5) U.S. economic engagement with China arguably contributes to the legitimacy of the socialist government and the strengthening of China's military by facilitating general economic development.

U.S. trade law and WTO regulations can deal with injury from imports and unfair trade practices. Trade disputes with China would normally be first discussed bilaterally before taking the case to the WTO for dispute resolution. China's alleged violations of international labor and environmental standards, as well as its own laws and government regulations, have fewer institutional remedies for the United States. Policy options include working to improve China's compliance through bilateral consultations and technical assistance, international organizations (such as the International Labor Organization), non-governmental organizations, and multilateral treaties (such as the U.N. Framework Convention on Climate Change and Kyoto Protocol),[4] and the threat of trade sanctions.

Trade Policy Developments

In the past few years, the United States has taken numerous actions in response to PRC trade practices that is has deemed unfair while China taken some incremental steps to heed U.S. demands.[5]

- In December 2006, China hosted the first China-U.S. Strategic Economic Dialogue led by U.S. Treasury Secretary Henry Paulson and PRC Vice-Premier Wu Yi. Talks focused on the following issues: China's exchange rate flexibility, the bilateral trade imbalance, PRC intellectual property rights violations, energy, and the environment. The U.S. Treasury Department released a report on December 19, 2006, that did not refer to China as engaging in currency manipulation for the purpose of gaining a trade advantage.

- On January 13, 2006, the Bush Administration announced that it would apply the so-called military catch-all rule to items on the Commodity Control List which could require licenses for the export of items to China that could be used to strengthen China's military power.
- On November 8, 2005, the United States Trade Representative (USTR) announced that the United States and China had, after three months of intense negotiations, reached a broad agreement on textile trade. The Agreement lasts through the life of the China WTO Textile Safeguard (through 2008), covers more than 30 individual products, and contains quotas that begin at low levels.[6]
- On July 21, 2005, the PRC government announced that its currency, the yuan, would be revalued upward (from 8.3 yuan to 8.11 yuan to the U.S. dollar) and that its future value would be "referenced" to a basket of currencies. However, according to most experts, China's central bank continues to intervene in the currency market in order to maintain a stable exchange rate.[7]
- In May 2005, the Bush Administration imposed "safeguard" quotas on 16 categories of Chinese apparel in response to a surge in such imports following the lifting of textiles and apparel quotas worldwide in January 2005.
- In December 2004, the U.S. government imposed anti-dumping duties on imported Chinese bedroom furniture. This case, the largest anti-dumping action against China, reportedly has both supporters and opponents in the U.S. furniture industry.[8]
- In September 2004, the U.S. government rejected a Section 301 (Trade Act of 1974) complaint filed by the China Currency Coalition alleging that China's fixed exchange rate constituted currency manipulation. In November 2004, the Administration rejected a similar petition filed by Members of Congress, while continuing to press and advise China on revaluing or floating its currency.
- In April 2004, the Bush Administration rejected a Section 301 petition filed by the AFL-CIO alleging unfair trade practices based upon exploitation of labor in the PRC and calling for a tariff of up to 77% on goods imported from China. In July 2006, the USTR rejected another, similar Section 301 petition filed by the AFL-CIO.
- In March 2004, the Bush Administration filed the United States' first complaint against China under the WTO's dispute settlement mechanism, charging that the PRC unfairly taxed imported semiconductors.[9] In July 2004, China eliminated the tax breaks for domestically-produced semi-conductors.

Congressional Actions

On December 15, 2006, Representative Sander Levin, who is to chair the House Ways and Means Trade Subcommittee in the 110th Congress, declared that he would support policies that would address what many regard as China's unfair trade advantage, gained largely through the PRC government's manipulation of the value of its currency. These measures include legislation that would impose countervailing duties against non-market economies such as China's and the filing of a Section 301 petition requesting the Administration to file a WTO case against China. Senator Max Baucus, incoming Chairman of the Senate Finance Committee, stated that "greater flexibility for China's currency is long overdue."[10]

In the 109th Congress, several bills aimed at reducing the U.S. trade imbalance with the PRC were introduced. These bills addressed issues such as China's currency practices, other alleged unfair trade practices (including dumping and export subsidies), violation of intellectual property rights, and non-compliance with WTO regulations. The following are selected bills from the 109th Congress related to U.S.-China trade:

- H.R. 4808 (Jones: Introduced February 28, 2006) To prohibit the importation of motor vehicles of the PRC until the tariff rates that China imposes on motor vehicles of the United States are equal to the rates of duty applicable to motor vehicles of the PRC.
- S. 2267 (Dorgan/Graham: Introduced February 9, 2006) To withdraw normal trade relations treatment from, and apply certain provisions of Title IV of the Trade Act of 1974 to, the products of the People's Republic of China. Related bill: H.R. 728 (Sanders).
- H.R. 3283 (English: Introduced July 14, 2005) Amends the Tariff Act of 1930 to impose countervailing duties on certain merchandise from nonmarket economy countries. Passed in the House on July 27, 2005. Related bill: S. 1421 (Collins).
- H.R. 1498 (Ryan: Introduced April 6, 2006) To clarify that exchange-rate manipulation by the People's Republic of China is actionable under the countervailing duty provisions and the product-specific safeguard mechanisms of the trade laws of the United States.
- S. 377 (Lieberman: Introduced February 15, 2005) To require negotiation and appropriate action with respect to certain countries that engage in currency manipulation.
- S. 295 (Schumer/Graham: Introduced February 3, 2005) To authorize the imposition of a 27.5% tariff on goods imported from China unless the President certifies that China has made a good faith effort to revalue its currency to reflect its fair market value. Related bills: S. 14 (Stabenow), H.R. 1575 (Myrick), S.Amdt. 309 (Schumer) to S. 600.
- H.Con.Res. 33 (Ryan: Introduced January 26, 2005) Urging the President to take immediate steps to establish a plan to adopt the recommendations of the United States-China Economic and Security Review Commission in its 2004 Report to the Congress in order to correct the current imbalance in the bilateral trade and economic relationship between the United States and China.

Summary of Trade Data

What light do the trade data shed on the controversy over economic relations with China? First, China has burst onto the U.S. trading scene in recent years. In 2003, the PRC surpassed Japan to become America's third largest trading partner, after Canada and Mexico,[11] while the United States is the PRC's second largest trading partner, after the expanded European Union (25 nations).[12] In 2005, according to PRC data, EU-China trade was valued at

$217.3 billion compared to U.S.-China trade of $211.6 billion.[13] China's largest export market is the United States followed by the EU-25 and Japan. Although China is a new player in international trade, it is taking major shares of markets once dominated either by other countries and U.S. domestic industries.

China is the second largest source of U.S. imports of merchandise ($243 billion in 2005) after Canada ($287 billion). PRC imports surpassed those of Mexico in 2003 and of Japan in 2002. China now accounts for over 14% of U.S. imports (2005), up from 12% in 2003, 8% in 1999, and 3% in 1990, although this share still falls short of Japan's 18% in the early 1990s.

Second, the data show that while U.S. trade with China is unbalanced, the same is also true for Europe and Japan, although to a lesser extent. China runs a trade surplus with the world's three major economic centers. The U.S. bilateral deficit in 2005 ($201 billion), however, was 1.6 times larger than that of the EU-15 ($121.8 billion; the EU-25 deficit was $133 billion) and seven times that of Japan ($28.5 billion). (As reported by the United States, EU, and Japan.)

Third, the data show that the U.S. trade deficit with China is rising with the overall U.S. trade deficit or growing at a slightly faster rate. Between 1996 and 1998, China's share of the overall U.S. merchandise trade deficit averaged 24%; between 1999 and 2001, China's share was 18%, and between 2002 and 2004, 22%. In 2005, the United States trade deficit with China constituted 26% of its global trade deficit. Over the same period, the shares of the U.S. deficit in goods trade accounted for by Japan, the Association of Southeast Asian Nations (ASEAN), and the East Asian newly industrialized countries (NICs) have decreased while the European Union's share has increased.

Fourth, the data show that U.S. exports to China are growing faster than U.S. exports to other nations. U.S. exports to China (up 157% between 2000 and 2005) have grown faster than U.S. exports to Canada (up 19.8% over the same period), Mexico (7.5%), and Japan (-15%), although exports to China have grown from a low base.[14] In 2004, China replaced Germany and the United Kingdom to become the 4th largest market for U.S. goods, moving up from 11th place in 1999. The United States exported somewhat more to China ($41.8 billion) than it did to the United Kingdom ($38.6 billion) in 2005. According to Japanese, European, and Korean data, in 2005, Japan was the largest overseas supplier of products to China with $79.9 billion in exports. South Korea and the EU-15 and were the second and third largest exporters to China in 2005 with $69.8 billion and $61.9 billion in exports, respectively.[15]

Fifth, the U.S. industrial sectors most at risk from import competition from China are generally labor intensive, but China is moving quickly up the technology ladder. The sectors in which the United States runs the largest trade deficits are generally those that depend on abundant and low-cost labor, while the United States accrues surpluses with China in some advanced technology items, such as aircraft, as well as in some agricultural products. In China's trade with the developed countries, over two-thirds of its exports are "low-end manufactures" — appliances, toys, furniture, footwear, apparel, and plastic goods — while 85% of its imports are capital-intensive machinery and equipment, electronic goods, and natural resource-related products.[16]

The United States has incurred large trade deficits with China in some high value-added sectors as well. These sectors include office and data processing machines, telecommunications and sound equipment, and electrical machinery and appliances. In 2003, China became the third largest car market and the fourth largest maker of automobiles with an output of 4.4 million vehicles. Production of cars reached an estimated 5.5 million units in 2005, putting the PRC on par with Germany in automobile production. However, China is not a major global importer or exporter of cars and it remains heavily reliant upon foreign technology in this sector.[17]

Sixth, PRC data show much smaller bilateral trade deficits than those claimed by its trading partners. PRC trade data differ from U.S. data primarily because of the treatment of products from or to China (mainland) that pass through the Hong Kong Special Administrative Region (SAR). Other reasons include different accounting systems and a lack of transparency in China's data reporting. China counts Hong Kong as the destination of its exports sent there, even goods that are then transshipped to other markets. By contrast, the United States and many of China's other trading partners count Chinese exports that are transshipped through Hong Kong as products from China,[18] not Hong Kong, including goods that contain Hong Kong components or involve final assembly or processing in Hong Kong. Furthermore, the United States counts Hong Kong as the destination of U.S. products sent there, even those that are then re-exported to China. However, the PRC counts many of such re-exported goods as U.S. exports to China. Some analysts argue that the U.S. Department of Commerce overstates the U.S. trade deficit with China by as much as 21% because of the way that it calculates entrepot trade through Hong Kong.[19]

According to PRC data, China's trade surplus with the United States in 2005 was $114 billion — not $201 billion as reported by the United States government. In Japan's case, both countries claim to be running trade deficits with each other. According to PRC data, in 2005, China ran deficits with many of its major trading partners, including Taiwan ($57.9 billion), South Korea ($41.7 billion), Japan ($16.3 billion), Malaysia ($9.5 billion), Saudi Arabia ($8.4 billion), Philippines ($8 billion), Thailand ($6 billion), Australia ($5 billion), Brazil ($5 billion) Iran ($3.5 billion).[20]

Seventh, some trade specialists suggest that the surge of U.S. imports from China do not pose an additional threat to U.S. industries and workers because it merely represents a shift of investment and production from other Pacific Rim countries. China's share of U.S. imports has been rising while those of other Pacific Rim nations have been falling or holding steady. In terms of absolute values, until recently, U.S. imports from all major Pacific Rim countries continued to rise, although at slower rates than imports from China. In 2005, U.S. imports from the East Asian NICS — South Korea, Taiwan, Hong Kong, and Singapore — fell or barely rose from the previous year.

Eighth, the rapid growth of the Chinese economy is adding to world demand for basic commodities that is causing upward pressure on world prices. Particularly significant are Chinese net imports of crude oil, copper, and soybeans.

China's Trade Balance and Imports

As shown in figure 1 and Appendix table A1, according to PRC data, with the exception of 1993, China has run a global trade surplus in goods each year since 1990. That surplus emerged at the beginning of the 1990s, entered into a deficit of $11 billion in 1993 (when the government temporarily loosened controls on imports), and reached a peak of $43.3 billion in

1998 before declining to $22.6 billion in 2001. In 2005, China's global trade surplus leapt to $102 billion (PRC data).

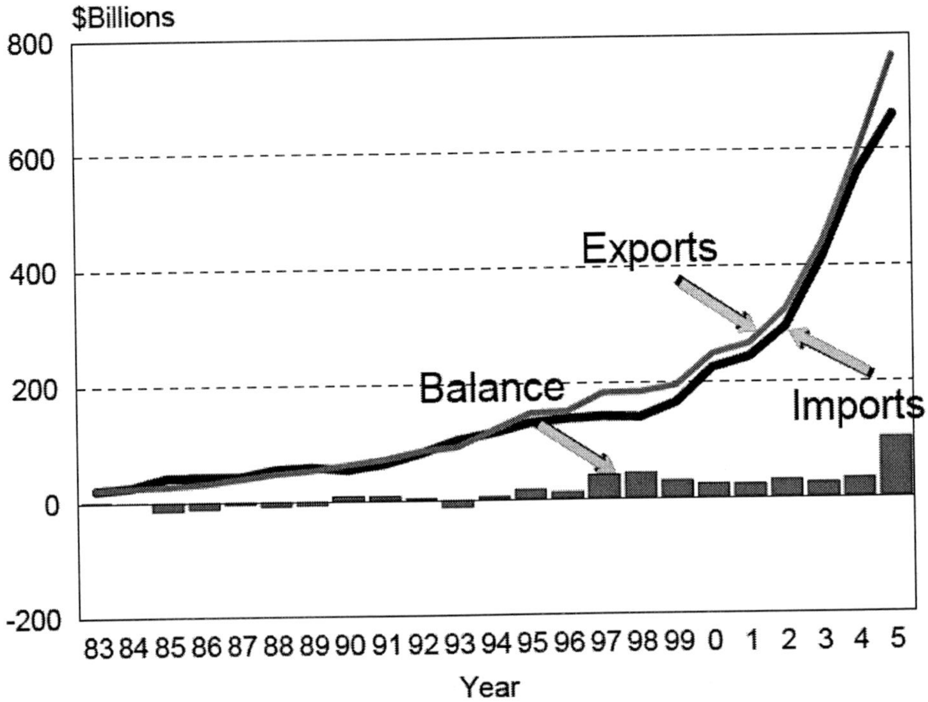

Sources: PRC General Administration of Customs; Global Trade Atlas (PRC data).

Figure 1. China's Exports, Imports, and Balance of Merchandise Trade, 1983-2005 (PRC data).

Between 1995 and 2001, China's current account surplus (includes trade in goods, services, and unilateral transfers such as remittances and government to government payments) was smaller than its surplus in merchandise trade because of a deficit in its services trade. Since 2002, the current account surplus has exceeded the merchandise trade surplus due to large increases in services exports and remittances. In 2005, the current account surplus was $160.8 billion compared to the merchandise trade surplus of $102 billion. According to one projection, China's global current account balance will remain in surplus "for some years to come," due to continued high rates of foreign investment, strong exports, and excessive savings in the non-state sector.[21]

As mentioned in the previous section, PRC data show much smaller bilateral trade deficits than those claimed by its trading partners. In 2005, the United States claimed it had incurred a $201 billion trade deficit with China, while China reported a trade surplus of only $114 billion with the United States. Japan reported a $28.5 billion merchandise trade deficit with China, while China likewise claimed a $16.3 billion trade deficit with Japan. In 2005, the European Union's trade deficit with China ($121.8 billion) was only $63 billion according to Chinese data. In 2005, the 156 countries categorized as the "world" by the International Monetary Fund reported an aggregate trade deficit with China of $342 billion. This is approximately 3.3 times the $102 billion global merchandise trade deficit reported by China for that year.[22] (See Appendix tables A1-A5.)

Not only have the surge in imports from China affected U.S. markets, but China has become a major importer of world commodities or primary goods. Table 1 shows China's imports by major commodity. Imports of machinery (including electrical) have soared from a total of $63.1 billion in 1999 to $271.3 billion in 2005. Such an increase in demand for machinery, however, has only a moderate effect on overall prices. China's imports of mineral fuel, organic chemicals, iron and steel, ores, copper, cotton, and wood, however, can affect world prices, particularly when combined with rising world demand or tightening supplies. In 2004-2005, Chinese demand for mineral fuel, in particular, including crude petroleum added to upward world price pressures.

Table 1. China's Imports by Major Commodity, 1999-2005 (billions of dollars)

	1999	2000	2001	2002	2003	2004	2005
Electrical Machinery	35.3	50.7	55.9	73.3	104.0	142.1	174.9
Machinery	27.8	34.4	40.6	52.2	71.6	91.5	96.4
Mineral Fuel, Oil, etc.	8.9	20.7	17.5	19.3	29.3	48.0	64.2
Optics, Medical. Instr.	5.0	7.3	9.8	13.5	25.1	40.1	49.9
Plastic	11.6	14.5	15.3	17.4	21.0	28.0	33.3
Organic Chemicals	5.5	8.3	9.0	11.2	16.0	23.8	28.0
Iron and Steel	7.2	9.6	10.9	13.2	22.2	23.6	26.2
Ores, Slag, Ash	2.2	3.1	4.2	4.3	7.2	17.3	25.9
Copper and Articles Thereof	3.1	4.7	4.9	5.7	7.2	10.5	12.9
Vehicles, Not Railway	2.4	3.6	4.5	6.5	11.8	12.9	12.2
Misc. Grain, Seeds, Fruit	1.6	3.1	3.3	2.8	5.7	7.3	8.1
Cotton and Yarn, Fabric	2.4	2.8	2.9	3.3	4.7	6.9	7.0
Aircraft, Spacecraft	3.2	2.2	4.4	4.1	4.5	4.9	6.6
Paper, Paperboard	1.6	2.6	2.7	2.9	3.9	5.2	6.3
Misc. Chemical Products	2.2	2.5	2.6	3.8	4.9	5.1	6.0
Wood, Articles of Wood	2.9	3.7	3.5	4.1	4.6	5.2	5.7
Source: Global Trade Atlas using Chinese data.							

CHINA AND THE ASIA PACIFIC REGION

While China is gaining manufacturing prowess and its trade surplus with the United States is spiraling, the country is purchasing heavily from neighboring trading partners. In 2004, China's imports rose by 35%, including machinery, raw materials, and components for manufacturing, although this growth in imports slowed to 17% in 2005.[23] In addition, the bulk of China's exports are manufactured under foreign brand names, and over half of China's exports are produced by foreign-owned companies. According to PRC official estimates, 70% of PRC exports to the United States contain foreign components, particularly from Taiwan, South Korea, and Singapore.[24]

China (not including Hong Kong) has become the largest trading partner of Taiwan and the second largest trading partner of Japan. The PRC has become South Korea's largest foreign investment destination and largest export market. According to Taiwanese and Korean data, in 2005, Taiwan's estimated trade surplus with China was $31.9 billion, while South Korea's surplus was $31.2 billion.[25]

China has become a huge buyer of raw materials, agricultural commodities, industrial machinery, and electronic components from Southeast Asia, as well as an important source of foreign investment and second largest source of foreign tourists in the region.[26] China's top exports to Southeast Asia include machinery, electronic goods, iron and steel, mineral fuels, textiles and apparel, and optical, photographic, and medical equipment. Despite worries about economic competition, in 2004, ASEAN, which ran a trade surplus of $20 billion with China that year (PRC data),[27] agreed to establish a free trade zone with China which would be implemented gradually over five years.[28] In the view of many of its major trading partners in Asia, China's economic growth and open trade policies have presented both competitive challenges and economic opportunities. However, according to some analysts, China's appetite for imports is slowing, while its export production shows little sign of abating.[29] Although ASEAN accumulated a trade surplus with China again in 2005 ($19.5 billion, according to PRC data), China's exports to ASEAN grew 50% faster than its imports from Southeast Asia.

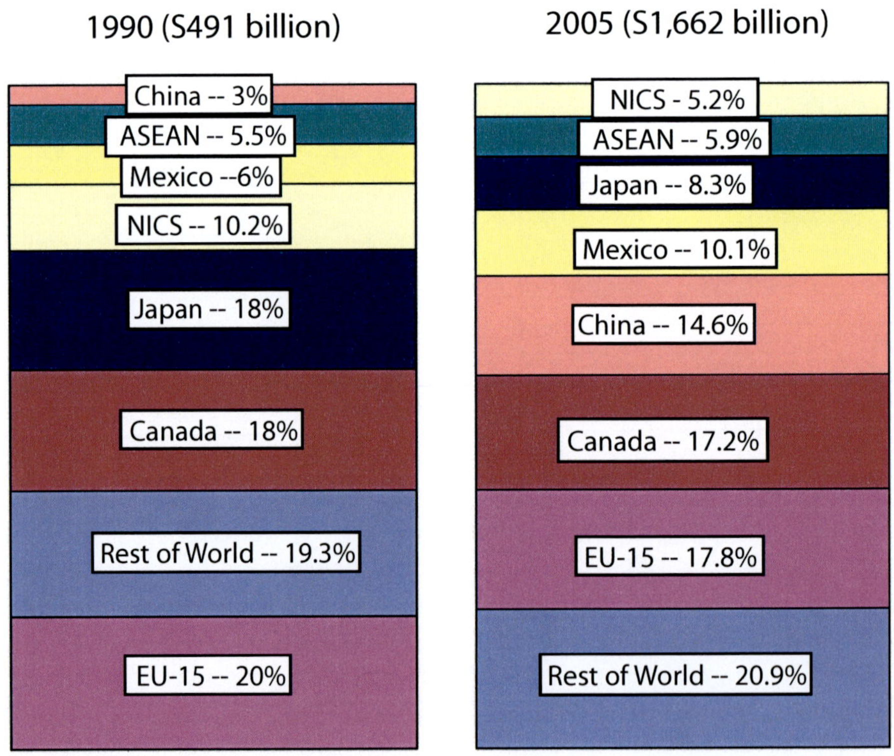

Figure 2. Shares of Total U.S. Imports by Country and Country Group, 1990 and 2005.

Some trade specialists suggest that the surge of U.S. imports from China do not pose an additional threat to U.S. industries and workers because it merely represents a shift of investment and production from other Pacific Rim countries. In other words, expanding imports from China have been offset by declining imports from other East Asian or Pacific Rim countries.[30] These countries include those at a similar level of development which are competing directly with China, such as Malaysia and Thailand, and more industrialized countries or special administrative regions that have moved their lower-end production to the

PRC, such as Macao, Hong Kong, South Korea, and Taiwan. In sectors such as footwear, handbags, apparel, furniture, and building and lighting fixtures, U.S. imports from China have been displacing those from Hong Kong, South Korea, Taiwan, and Mexico and reducing imports those from other developing Asian nations.

As shown in figure 2, China's share of U.S. imports grew from 3% in 1990 to 14% in 2005 (out of total U.S. imports of $491 billion and $1.66 trillion, respectively),[31] while the rest of East Asia's share (Japan, NICS,[32] and ASEAN) fell from 36% to 19%. Mexico's share of U.S. imports grew from 6% in 1990 to 11.6% in 2002. It fell to 10.6% in 2004 and further to 10.1% in 2005.

CHINA'S TRADE WITH THE UNITED STATES, EUROPE, AND JAPAN

As shown in figure 3 and Appendix table A2, by either Chinese or U.S. data, China runs a trade surplus with the United States. Although Chinese figures show it at only $114 billion in 2005, the United States reports it to be $201 billion. According to PRC data, China has run a trade surplus with the United States since 1993. According to U.S. data, the United States has incurred trade deficits with China since 1983.

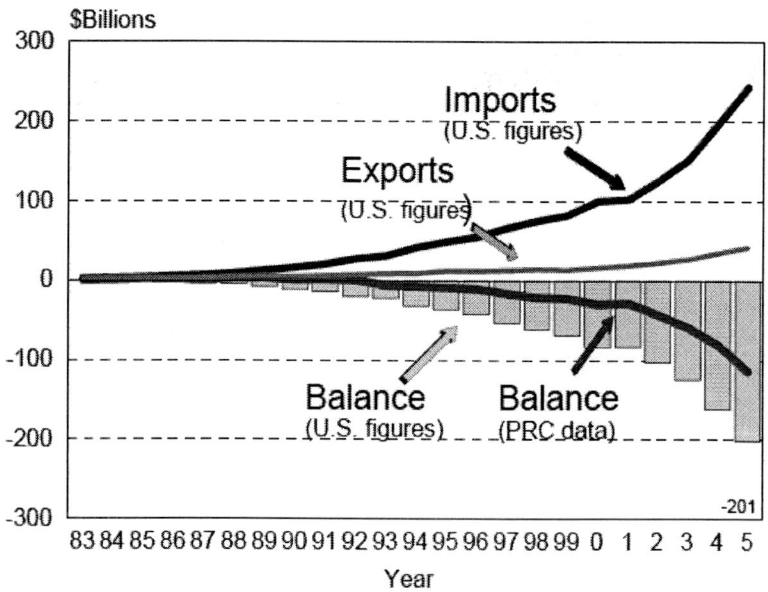

Sources: U.S. Department of Commerce IMF. *Direction of Trade Statistics Yearbook* Global Trade Atlas.

Figure 3. U.S. Exports, Imports, and Balance of Trade with China, 1983-2005.

As is the case with the United States, Japan has run a trade deficit with China since the 1980s (according to Japanese data). As shown in figure 4 and in Appendix table A3, Japan's balance of trade with China dropped from a surplus of $6 billion in 1985 to a deficit of nearly $6 billion in 1990. Japan's trade deficit with China reached a peak of $26.5 billion in 2001, which was surpassed in 2005 ($28.5 billion). Japan's exports to China have grown dramatically in the past few years, its largest exports to the PRC being electronics, general machinery, iron and steel, optical, photographic, and medical equipment, and organic chemicals.[33]

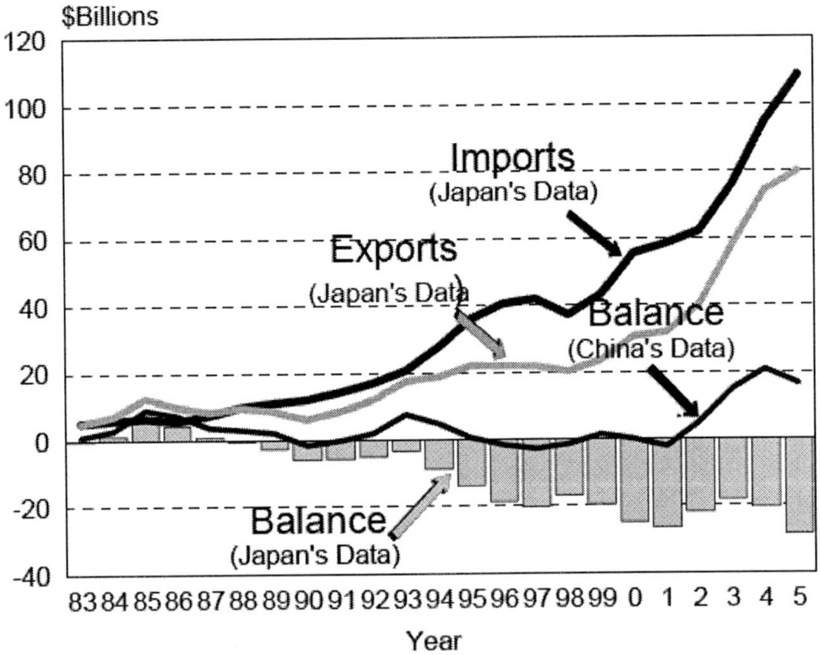

Sources: IMF.Direction of Trade Statistics Quarterly Global Trade Atlas.

Figure 4. Japan's Merchandise Imports, Exports, and Balance of Trade with China, 1983-2005.

As shown in figure 5 and Appendix table A4, according to EU data, the European Union incurred a trade deficit with China of $947 million in 1988, which grew to $121.8 billion in 2005. According to Chinese figures, however, the EU trade deficit with China began in the late 1990s and grew to $63 billion in 2005.

Compared to the world's two other major economic centers, the U.S. trade deficit with China at $201 billion in 2005 was the largest, followed by the EU-15 deficit with China at $121.8 billion and Japan at $28.5 billion. Within the EU, according to trading partner 2005 data, Germany's trade deficit with China was $23 billion, the U.K.'s was $18.8 billion, and France's was $9.9 billion. As shown in Appendix table A5, however, China's trade statistics indicate smaller European trade deficits or even surpluses.

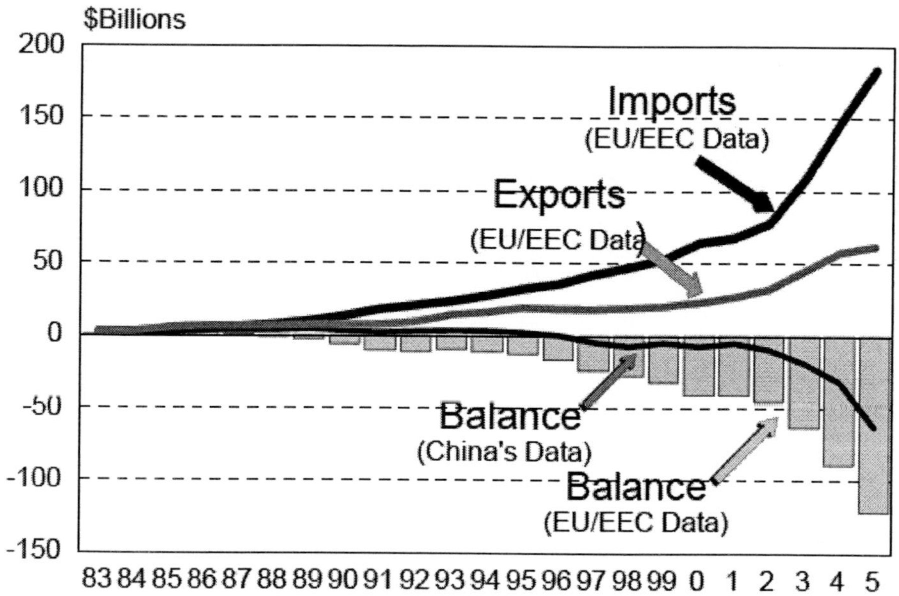

Note: For 1980-88, data are for the EEC12 nations. After 1988, data are for the EU 15.
Sources: IMF.*Direction of Trade Statistics Quarterly* Global Trade Atlas.

Figure 5. European Union Merchandise Imports, Exports, and Balance of Trade with China, 1983-2005.

U.S. Merchandise Trade Balances with Major Trading Partners

The U.S. trade deficit with China is notable for not only its size but also the large imbalance between imports from and exports to China. In 2005, Japan exported 2.5 times more to the United States than it imported, while Canada and Mexico exported 1.3 times and 1.4 times more, respectively, than they imported. China, by comparison, exported 5.8 times more to the U.S. market in 2005 than it imported from the United States. This indicates that the Chinese market has been vastly underdeveloped as a destination for U.S. exports.

U.S. Trade with China by Sector

U.S. Exports to China

As shown in table 2, among the top twenty U.S. exports to China in 2005, the top five by dollar value were electrical machinery, transport equipment, metalliferous ores, oil seeds and fruits, and general industrial machinery. Exports of metalliferous ores and oil seeds and fruits have grown by over 12 times and 6 times, respectively, since 1999, suggesting that China's appetite for raw materials and agricultural commodities has grown relative to that for general industrial machinery and office machines. Among the top 20 U.S. export items to China, textile fibers have experienced the largest growth in the past five years (969%). China's top ten imports from the world in 2005 were: electrical machinery, machinery, mineral fuels, optical and medical instruments, plastics, organic chemicals, iron and steel, iron ores, copper articles, and vehicles.

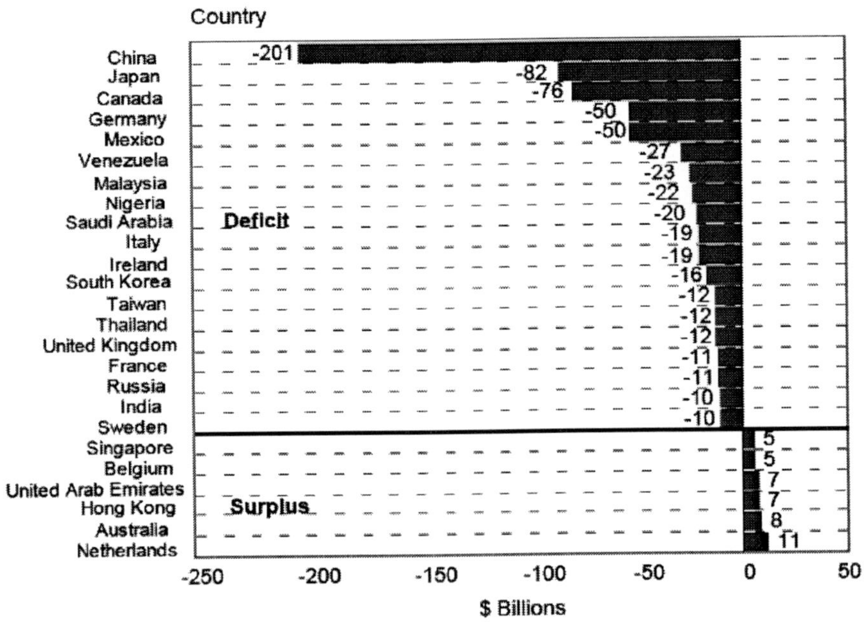

Source: U.S.Department of Commerce.

Figure 6. U.S. Merchandise Trade Balances with Selected Countries in 2005.

Table 2. Top Twenty U.S. Exports to China, 1997-2005 (millions of dollars)

Category	1997	1998	1999	2000	2001	2002	2003	2004	2005
Electrical Mach.	741	1,013	1,380	1,747	2,109	2,657	3,722	4,631	5,170
Transport Equip.	2,127	3,604	2,325	1,695	2,471	3,443	2,495	2,025	4,479
Metalliferous Ores	180	195	285	618	919	956	1,525	2,198	3,482
Oil Seeds and Fruits	419	288	354	1,020	1,014	890	2,832	2,332	2,256
Gen. Ind. Mach./Equip.	766	674	685	838	1,080	1,145	1,404	1,912	2,067
Office Machines	343	878	842	1,498	1,602	1,193	1,274	1,396	1,835
Plastics in Prim. Forms	340	320	394	545	628	740	931	1,342	1,793
Prof. and Scientific Instr.	429	527	538	583	886	931	1,167	1,568	1,710
Textile Fibers	682	199	98	154	160	278	909	1,638	1,657
Organic Chemicals	208	212	302	473	373	554	1,054	1,542	1,457
Specialized Industrial Machinery	770	538	481	758	819	1,124	1,218	1,744	1,325
Telecom, Sound Recording Equip.	644	655	573	817	1,204	1,110	978	1,104	1,299
Power Gen. Equip.	603	542	505	312	507	462	640	965	1,042
Pulp and Waste Paper	148	156	193	276	330	414	600	753	992
Road Vehicles	348	140	192	185	223	272	506	624	903
Nonferrous Metals	172	120	140	289	144	161	315	333	872
Misc. Manufactures	297	247	242	384	440	509	515	647	750
Hides, Furskins	112	126	96	237	402	397	457	521	629
Chemical Materials	124	143	177	247	285	312	403	582	604
Metalworking Mach.	173	190	162	211	265	367	304	618	547

Note: Ranked by data for 2005.

Source: U.S. Department of Commerce, International Trade Commission.

U.S. Imports from China

As shown in figure 7 and table 3, among the top twenty U.S. imports from China in 2005 by dollar amount, the top six were office machines and automatic data processing machines, telecommunications and sound equipment, miscellaneous manufactured articles, apparel and accessories, electrical machinery, and furniture and bedding. The value of U.S.-imports of PRC office and data processing machines alone ($42.2 billion) exceeded total U.S. exports to China in 2005 ($41.8 billion). While U.S. imports in all these categories have increased, the most dramatic percentage changes have been not in traditional labor-intensive industries but in sectors that encompass advanced technology, such as office and data processing machines (up 284% between 2000 and 2005), telecommunications and sound equipment (245%), and general industrial machinery (234%).

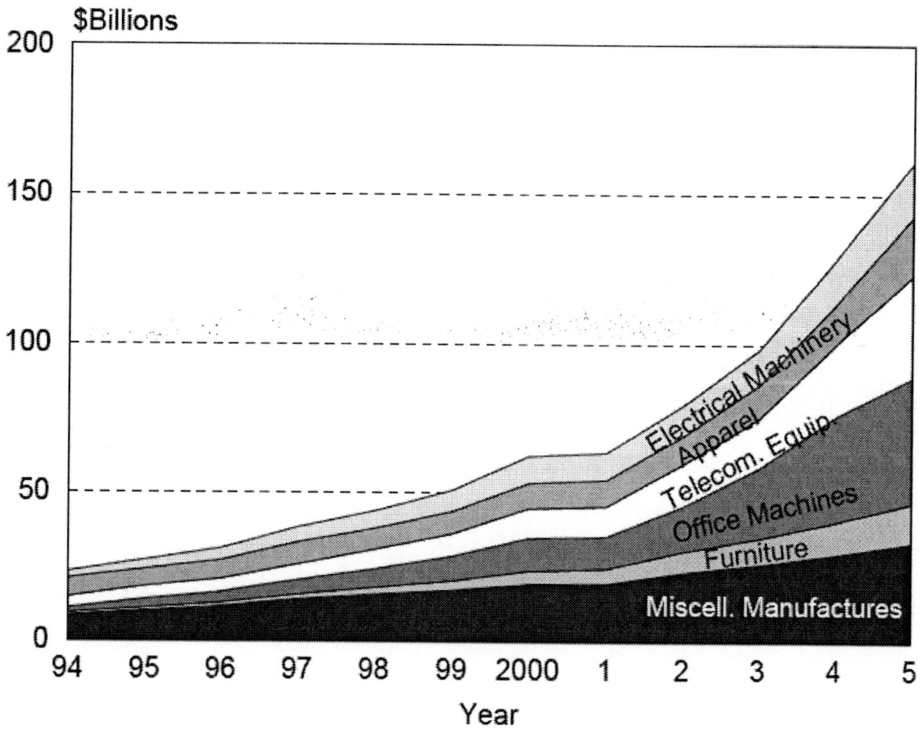

Source: U.S. Department of Commerce.

Figure 7. Top Six Imports from China by Industry, 1994-2005.

Table 3. Top Twenty U.S. Imports from China, 1997-2005
(millions of dollars)

Category	1997	1998	1999	2000	2001	2002	2003	2004	2005
Office Machines, Data Processing	5,019	6,329	8,239	10,980	10,763	15,230	23,646	35,620	42,242
Telecom and Sound Equip.	5,126	6,405	7,382	9,812	10,118	14,144	16,937	24,388	34,249
Misc. Manufactured Articles	14,155	15,872	17,291	19,445	19,763	23,494	26,287	29,505	33,573
Apparel and Accessories	7,406	7,133	7,351	8,473	8,866	9,538	11,381	13,607	19,931
Electrical Machinery, Parts, and Appliances	4,877	5,707	7,022	9,037	9,110	10,217	11,875	15,270	18,102
Furniture and Bedding	1,545	2,183	3,261	4,476	5,018	6,954	8,749	10,910	13,187
Footwear	7,354	8,016	8,438	9,206	9,758	10,241	10,546	11,350	12,721
Manufactures of Metals	1,816	2,238	2,878	3,651	4,119	5,219	6,302	8,257	10,110
General Industrial Machinery	1,180	1,449	1,833	2,087	2,414	3,259	41,213	5,528	7,007
Textile Yarn, Fabrics	1,369	1,432	1,583	1,816	1,854	2,501	3,365	4,253	5,605
Travel Goods, Handbags	1,917	1,942	1,974	2,214	2,171	2,741	3,319	4,044	4,658
Road Vehicles	574	731	923	1,800	1,406	1,796	2,373	3,265	4,170
Building Fixtures/Fittings	1,194	1,444	2,073	2,555	2,377	2,962	3,202	3,700	4,143
Nonmetallic Mineral Manufactures	1,216	1,441	1,681	2,059	2,165	2,431	2,624	2,953	3,510
Professional & Scientific Instruments	634	715	837	1,025	1,177	1,301	1,666	2,180	2,490
Iron and Steel	314	398	349	623	439	441	483	1,609	2,354
Photographic Optical Equip, Watches, Clocks	1,211	1,400	1,600	2,016	1,935	1,842	2,030	2,248	2,176
Misc. Low-Valued Items	282	425	586	759	784	957	1,229	1,652	2,068
Cork and Wood (Non-Furniture)	335	445	568	710	792	990	1,162	1,612	2,006
Organic Chemicals	335	337	392	467	488	564	772	1,071	1,600
Power Generating Machinery	314	354	408	505	553	694	842	1,112	1,573
Paper Products	310	401	471	611	627	792	1,022	1,263	1,535

Note: Ranked by data for 2005.
Source: U.S. Department of Commerce, International Trade Commission.

Balance of Trade By Sector

In modern economies, trade by sector generally follows two patterns. The first is based on traditional comparative advantage in which one country trades with another in those products in which it has an abundance of resources or in which it is comparatively productive. The United States economy is characterized by high technology, extensive farmland with high agricultural yields, expensive labor, and deep capital. As such, the United States would be expected to be strong in exports of high-technology goods, food and grains, and capital intensive products. The Chinese economy, on the other hand, is characterized by abundant and cheap labor, low capital intensity, and a mix of low, medium and high technology both in manufacturing and agriculture. As such, China would be expected to be strong in exports of not only labor-intensive manufactures, such as textiles and apparel, shoes, toys, and light manufactures, but also items produced under the tutelage of foreign companies that have invested in Chinese factories. These could include household appliances, electronics, tools, or automobile parts. One would expect trade that is conducted on the basis of comparative advantage to be unbalanced on a sector-by-sector basis. The United States, for example, would run a surplus with China in aircraft but a deficit in apparel.

The second trade pattern occurs among industrialized countries and is called intra-industry or trade within industrial sectors. This is typical of trade among North America, the European Union, and industrialized nations of Asia (e.g., Japan, South Korea, and Taiwan). The products traded usually carry brand names, are differentiated, and may be protected by intellectual property rights. For example, the United States both imports and exports items such as automobiles, machinery, electronic devices, prepared food, and pharmaceuticals. A considerable share of U.S. intra-industry trade is carried out within a multinational corporation (e.g., between Ford Motors and one of its related companies, such as Mazda in Japan, Jaguar in the United Kingdom, or with other subsidiaries abroad). A large deficit in an intra-industry trading sector in which the United States is competitive may indicate that the trading partner country is using import barriers to tip the trade balance in its favor.

Table 4 shows the U.S. balance of trade with China by major sector. Most of the sectors in which the United States runs the largest trade deficits with China are, as expected, those that depend on mostly abundant and low-cost labor. These include toys and sports equipment, furniture and bedding, footwear, textiles and apparel, and leather goods. Among the large deficit sectors, however, are machinery and mechanical appliances and electrical machinery, which reflect China's foreign investment and growing technological sophistication. In plastic articles, optical and medical instruments, books and magazines (indicated by shading in the table), the United States runs a surplus in its balance of trade with the world but a deficit with China.

Table 4. U.S. Balance of Trade with China by Sector, 2003-2005 (millions of dollars)

	2003	2004	2005
Total China	-123,960	161,977	201,625
Major U.S. Deficit Sectors (HTS Categories)			
Machinery/Mechanical Appliances	-25,262	-37,628	-46,375
Electrical Machinery	-24,007	-34,113	-46,249
Toys and Sports Equipment	-16,070	-17,163	-19,074
Furniture and Bedding	-11,739	-14,339	-16,942
Footwear	-10,528	-11,318	-12,679
Woven Apparel	-5,484	-6,606	-10,220
Knit Apparel	-3,192	-4,092	-6,553
Leather Art; Saddlery; Bags	-5,040	-5,708	-6,247
Articles of Iron and Steel	-3,086	-4,376	-5,886
Plastic Articles	-3,032	-3,402	-4,380
Misc. Textile Articles	-2,353	-3,052	-3,953
Vehicles, Not Railway	-1,947	-2,729	-3,268
Misc. Art of Base Metal	-1,414	-1,809	-2,243
Precious Stones and Metals, Pearls	-1,391	-1,714	-2,065
Wood and Articles of Wood	-1,019	-1,454	-1,847
Tools, Cutlery, of Base Metals	-1,373	-1,554	-1,774
Optical, Medical Instruments	-1,650	-1,704	-1,729
Rubber and Rubber Articles	-698	-1,036	-1,551
Miscellaneous Manufactures	-1,023	-1,203	-1,404
Ceramic Products	-1,112	-1,203	-1,316
Artificial Flowers, Feathers	-1,091	-1,109	-1,145
Books, Newspapers, Manuscripts	-653	-892	-1,130
Major U.S. Surplus Sectors (HTS Categories)			
Aircraft, Spacecraft	2,388	1,870	4,296
Misc. Grain, Seed, Fruit	2,787	2,260	2,165
Cotton and Cotton Fabrics	587	1,260	1,215
Wood pulp, Etc.	599	752	990
Hides and Skins	477	527	624
Copper and Articles Thereof	436	344	545
Ores	34	105	373
Iron and Steel	879	45	336

Note: Categories in italics are those in which the United States runs a trade surplus with the world but a trade deficit with China. Classification is by Harmonized System tariff codes at the 2-digit level.
Source: U.S. Department of Commerce, International Trade Commission.

The sectors in which the United States runs a trade surplus with China mirror U.S. competitive advantages and include aircraft, agricultural products, and cotton fabrics. In 2005, U.S. trade surpluses with China in aircraft, copper, iron ores, and iron and steel rose dramatically.

U.S. Imports from China — Sector Charts and Data

This section presents charts and data on U.S. imports from China by selected industrial sectors. The charts show imports from China as compared with imports from other major exporting countries or groups of countries. These include the European Union (fifteen original countries), the Association of Southeast Asian Nations (ASEAN, which includes,

Indonesia, Malaysia, Singapore, Thailand, the Philippines, Brunei, Vietnam, Laos, and Myanmar [Burma]), Taiwan, Mexico, South Korea, Japan, Hong Kong, and Canada.

The data in this section are presented according to two-digit standard international trade classification (SITC) codes as reported by the U.S. Department of Commerce. The industries selected are those in which the share of imports from China has risen to a significant level or trade policy has played a significant role (e.g. iron and steel and automobiles) even though U.S. imports from China in those industries might be relatively small.

Iron and Steel

In iron and steel products, China is becoming a major exporter to the United States. In 2005, China was the fourth largest foreign supplier of iron and steel products to the United States (surpassing Russia, South Korea, Germany, and Japan), up from seventh place in 2003. In 2005, China also bought $445 million worth of iron and steel products from the United States, making it the third largest market for U.S. exports of iron and steel. In 2005, the United States incurred a trade deficit with China in the SITC 67 category (iron and steel), which includes semi-finished products, tubes and pipes, iron and steel rods, and ferroalloys. However, the United States attained a trade surplus with China in the HTS 72 category (iron and steel), which includes more items in "primary form."

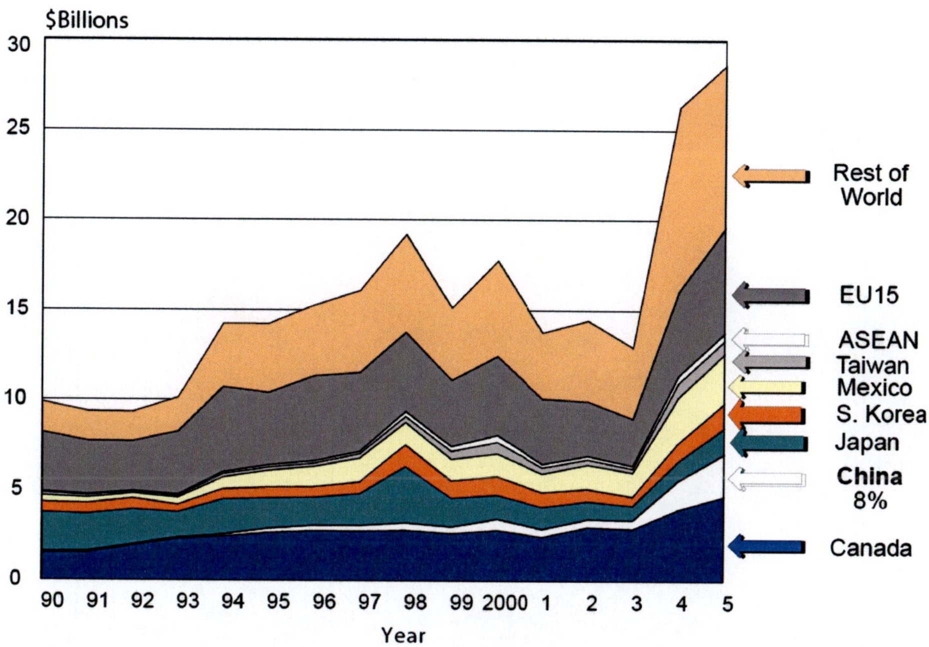

Figure 8. U.S. Imports of Iron and Steel Products (SITC 67) by Country and Group, 1990-2005.

Table 5. U.S. Imports of Iron and Steel Products (SITC 67) from Selected Countries and Country Groups, 1991, 2000-2005 (millions of dollars)

	1990	2001	2002	2003	2004	2005
EU15	3,303	3,637	3,041	2,621	4,697	5,828
Canada	1,504	2,437	2,981	2,885	3,979	4,699
Mexico	357	1,021	1,340	1,334	2,530	2,738
China	71	439	441	490	1,610	2,340
Japan	2,097	1,213	991	799	1,072	1,468
Korea	574	815	687	505	1,031	1,374
Taiwan	154	346	290	219	803	735
ASEAN	65	191	193	161	395	406
Hong Kong	2	2	3	2	3	10
Rest of World	1,691	3,657	4,469	3,929	10,204	9,034
World	9,818	13,758	14,436	12,945	26,324	28,632

Source: U.S. Department of Commerce.

Specialized Industrial Machinery

China is becoming an important supplier of specialized industrial machinery, which includes machine tools and sewing machines, but lags behind the European Union, Japan, and Canada and competes with other newly industrialized countries such as Mexico, South Korea, and Taiwan. China accounted for only 4.5% of U.S. imports in this category in 2005.

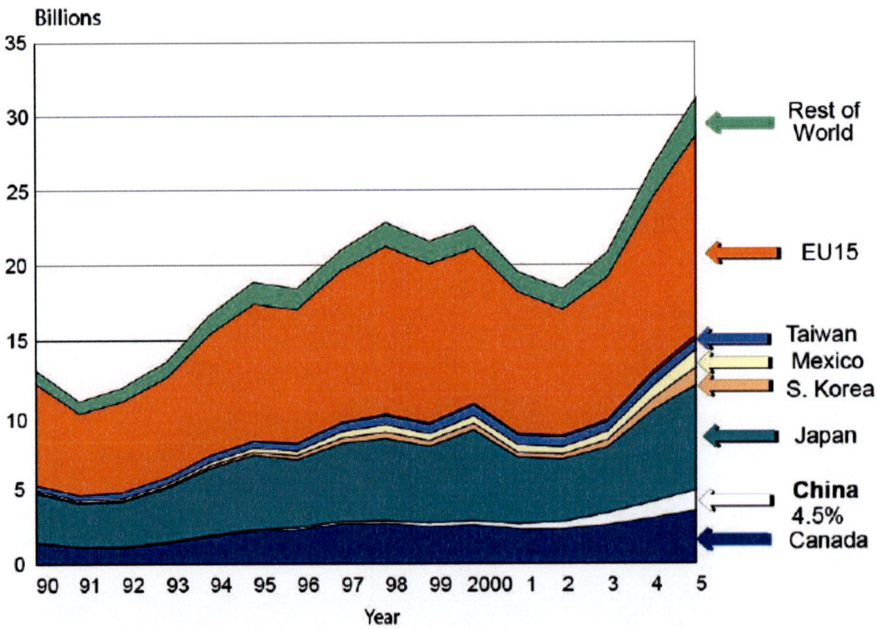

Source: U.S. Department of Commerce.

Figure 9. U.S. Imports of Specialized Industrial Machinery (SITC 72) by Country and Group, 1990-2005.

Table 6. U.S. Imports of Specialized Industrial Machinery (SITC 72) from Selected Countries and Country Groups, 1990, 2001-2005 (millions of dollars)

	1990	2001	2002	2003	2004	2005
EU15	6,786	9,511	8,463	9,586	11,656	13,419
Japan	3,340	4,479	4,217	4,445	6,105	7,019
Canada	1,384	2,297	2,294	2,556	3,010	3,482
China	23	331	485	791	1,069	1,415
Mexico	139	537	490	578	862	1,241
Korea	69	305	325	467	746	1,159
Taiwan	313	626	638	623	730	684
ASEAN	13	101	113	145	250	287
Hong Kong	18	12	17	15	18	17
Rest of World	868	1,314	1,373	1,614	2,049	2,464
World	12,953	19,513	18,415	20,820	26,495	31,187

Source: U.S. Department of Commerce.

Office Machines and Computers

In U.S. imports of office machines and automatic data processing machines (including television sets, computers and computer hardware), China has quickly become the largest supplier, surpassing ASEAN. Imports of such products from China rose by over 75% between 2003 and 2005 and now account for 42% of U.S. imports in this category. Office machines and computers from other East Asian countries — Japan, Taiwan, and South Korea — have been leveling off or decreasing, although many of their high tech manufacturers have built plants in China and export from there. The top exporters of office machines and data processing machines to the United States in 2005 were China, Malaysia, Japan, Mexico, and Singapore.

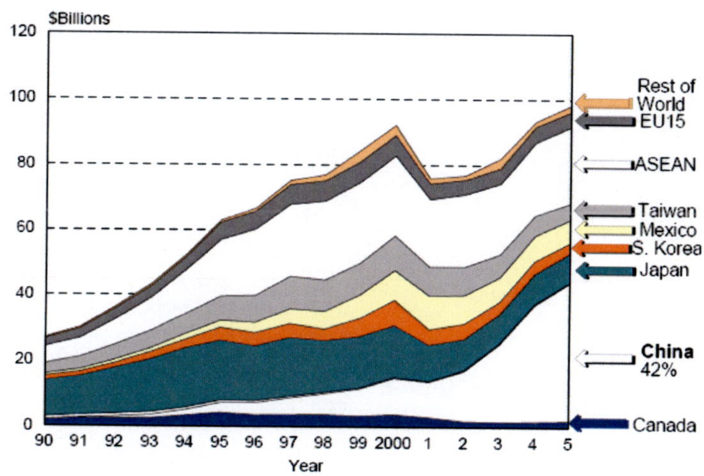

Source: U.S. Department of Commerce.

Figure 10. U.S. Imports of Office Machines and Automatic Data Processing Machines (SITC 75) by Country and Group, 1990-2005.

Table 7. U.S. Imports of Office Machines and Automatic Data Processing Machines (SITC 75) from Selected Countries and Country Groups, 1990, 2001-2005 (millions of dollars)

	1990	2001	2002	2003	2004	2005
China	117	10,761	15,230	23,612	35,579	42,169
ASEAN	5,150	20,676	22,043	21,571	22,460	23,473
Japan	11,007	11,055	9,464	8,978	9,282	8,936
Mexico	706	10,377	8,828	7,516	7,726	7,075
Taiwan	3,084	8,751	8,659	6,996	6,132	4,879
EU15	2,461	4,676	4,505	4,815	4,810	4,516
Korea	1,347	4,657	4,632	3,779	3,885	3,104
Canada	1,893	2,942	1,825	1,644	1,865	1,966
Hong Kong	809	276	392	328	304	210
Rest of World	297	1,729	1,342	2,947	1,492	2,015
World	26,871	75,900	76,920	80,542	93,535	98,343

Source: U.S. Department of Commerce.

Telecommunications and Sound Equipment

China's share of U.S. imports of telecommunications and sound equipment has risen to 33%. Such imports from China rose from $1.1 billion in 1990 to $34 billion in 2005. Imports of these products from elsewhere in Asia, particularly from ASEAN countries, have also been rising rapidly. The largest suppliers of telecommunications and sound equipment to the United States in 2005 were China, Mexico, Malaysia, Japan, and South Korea.

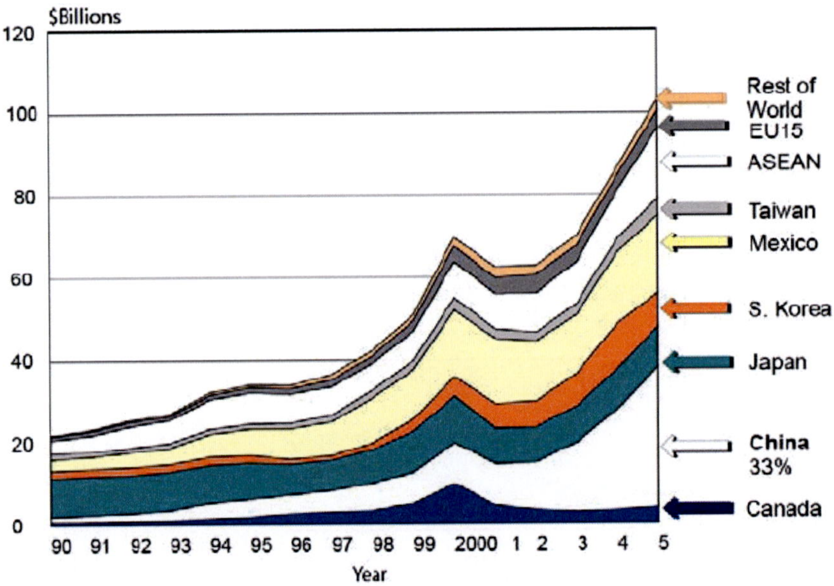

Source: U.S. Department of Commerce.

Figure 11. Imports of Telecommunications and Sound Equipment (SITC 76) by Country and Group, 1990-2005.

Table 8. U.S. Imports of Telecommunications and Sound Equipment (SITC 76) from Selected Countries and Country Groups, 1990, 2001-2005 (millions of dollars)

	1990	2001	2002	2003	2004	2005
China	1,142	10,062	14,144	16,723	24,311	34,140
Mexico	2,302	15,765	14,483	14,239	17,475	18,840
ASEAN	3,122	8,548	9,514	10,218	11,779	17,114
Korea	1,632	6,001	6,353	7,955	10,942	8,214
Japan	9,061	8,577	8,473	8,889	9,967	9,707
EU15	890	3,883	4,559	4,051	3,707	4,382
Canada	972	4,533	3,543	3,053	3,435	4,103
Taiwan	1,426	2,361	2,137	2,655	3,261	4,125
Hong Kong	478	224	357	522	647	672
Rest of World	322	2,446	2,264	2,363	1,941	2,637
World	21,347	62,400	65,827	70,668	87,465	103,934

Source: U.S. Department of Commerce.

Electrical Machinery and Parts

U.S. imports of electrical machinery and parts (including semi-conductors) have been growing dramatically from nearly all major suppliers. At 18% of such imports in 2005, China has become a significant supplier — surpassing the EU, Japan, and ASEAN. Mexico remains the leading foreign supplier.

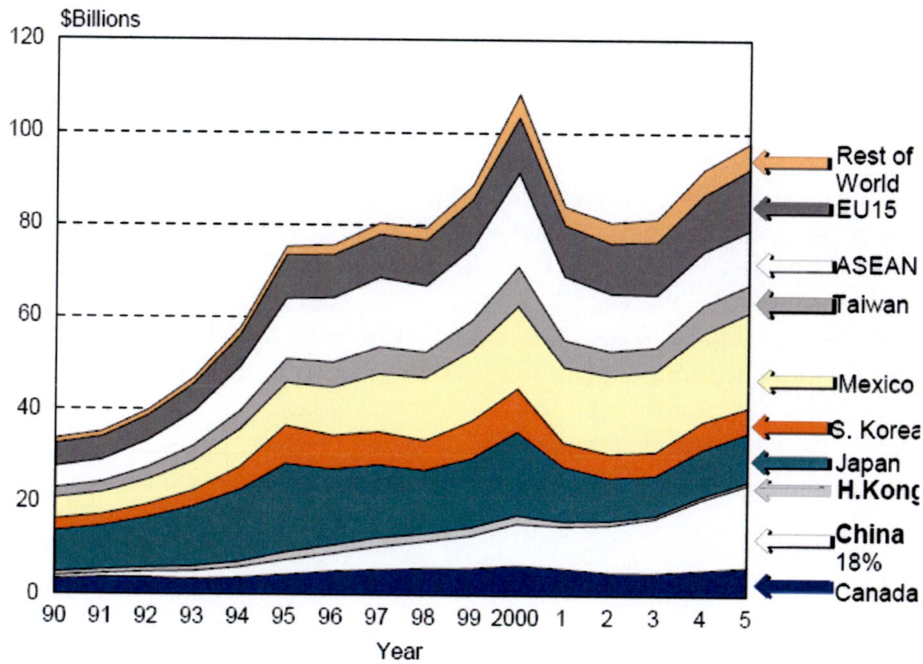

Source: U.S. Department of Commerce.

Figure 12. U.S. Imports of Electrical Machinery and Parts (SITC 77) by Country and Group, 1990-2005.

Table 9. U.S. Imports of Electrical Machinery and Parts (SITC 77) from Selected Countries and Country Groups, 1990, 2001-2005 (millions of dollars)

	1990	2001	2002	2003	2004	2005
Mexico	4,406	16,290	16,930	17,547	19,120	20,671
China	652	9,047	10,217	11,808	15,197	17,980
EU15	4,898	11,009	10,881	11,462	12,314	13,360
ASEAN	4,644	13,748	12,427	11,308	11,557	11,736
Japan	8,658	11,941	9,406	8,713	10,251	10,665
Canada	3,323	5,871	5,025	4,920	5,619	6,210
Taiwan	2,180	5,878	5,296	5,160	6,170	6,077
Korea	2,504	5,194	5,150	5,105	5,992	5,437
Hong Kong	792	1,050	881	585	637	593
Rest of World	1,080	4,112	4,359	4,916	5,414	5,560
World	33,137	84,140	80,572	81,524	92,271	98,289

Source: U.S. Department of Commerce.

Road Motor Vehicles

China is the world's third largest auto market and fourth largest auto producer. China's automobile sector has absorbed heavy foreign investment — roughly 70% of the country's car market is held by Chinese-foreign joint ventures such as Shanghai General Motors (GM), Shanghai Volkswagen, and First Auto Works-Toyota — and is aimed primarily at Chinese buyers.[34] China became a net exporter of vehicles for the first time in 2005, with exports of 172,800 vehicles and imports of 161,900 units. Most of China's vehicle exports are sold in Middle Eastern, North African, and South American countries. In addition, China has become a major supplier of motorcycles to Southeast Asia. Chinese auto makers Geely and Chery reportedly have plans to begin exporting passenger cars to the United States in 2007 or 2008.[35]

Currently, China is not a significant player in the U.S. car market. U.S. road vehicle and related imports from China mainly consist of auto parts, bicycles and motorcycles, and specialty vehicles such as golf carts and beach go-carts. China has become an important supplier of auto parts to the United States, with $2 billion in selected auto parts in 2005, but trails Canada ($11.8 billion), Japan ($8.8 billion), Mexico ($7.7 billion), and Germany ($2.3 billion). China exported $290 million worth of motorcycles to the United States in 2005, accounting for 8% of U.S. motorcycle imports compared to Japan's 73%.

China is expected to continue to lower tariffs on imported automobiles, to 25% in 2006, pursuant to China's WTO accession agreement, although many non-tariff barriers reportedly remain.[36]

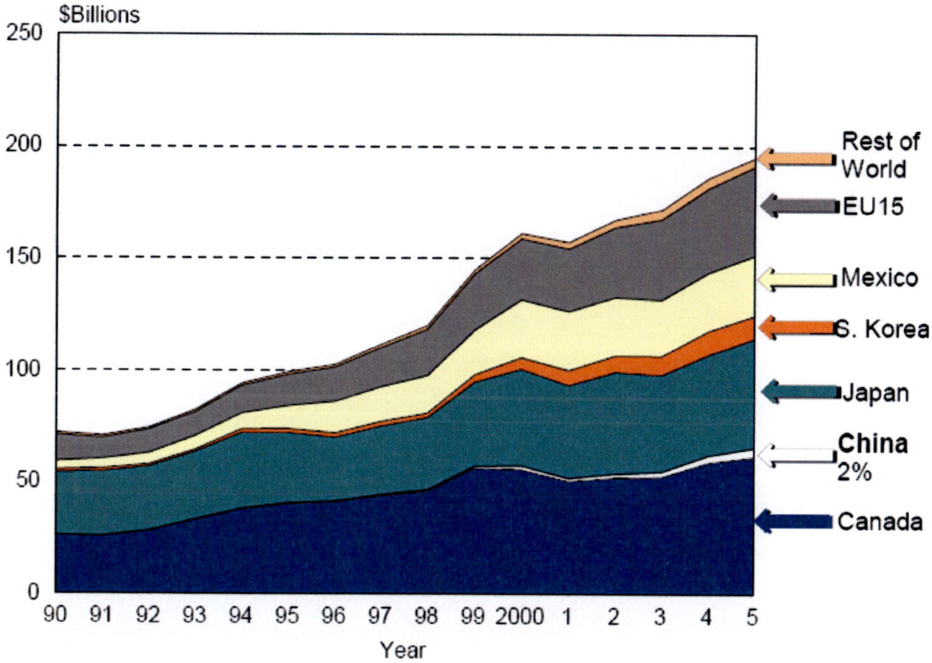

Source: U.S. Department of Commerce.

Figure 13. U.S. Imports of Road Motor Vehicles (SITC 78) by Country and Group, 1990-2005.

Table 10. U.S. Imports of Road Motor Vehicles (SITC 78) from Selected Countries and Country Groups, 1990, 2001-2005 (millions of dollars)

	1990	2001	2002	2003	2004	2005
Canada	26,094	50,477	52,050	52,448	58,832	61,332
Japan	29,839	41,429	45,449	43,178	45,033	48,867
EU15	12,270	28,022	31,043	35,975	37,813	39,958
Mexico	4,084	26,246	26,181	25,222	26,114	26,744
Korea	1,275	6,778	7,382	8,503	10,773	10,187
China	59	1,404	1,796	2,369	3,267	4,198
Taiwan	871	1,124	1,239	1,387	1,522	1,804
ASEAN	88	247	280	297	359	432
Hong Kong	7	13	14	38	43	39
Rest of World	930	2,892	3,338	4,271	4,412	3,853
World	75,517	158,632	168,772	173,688	188,168	197,414

Source: U.S. Department of Commerce.

Building and Lighting Products

In U.S. imports of prefabricated buildings, sanitary, plumbing, heating and lighting fixtures and fittings, China has surged to become a main factor. The PRC accounted for over half such imports in 2005, although total imports of such products from China amounted to only $4 billion, making it the 13th largest U.S. import from China.

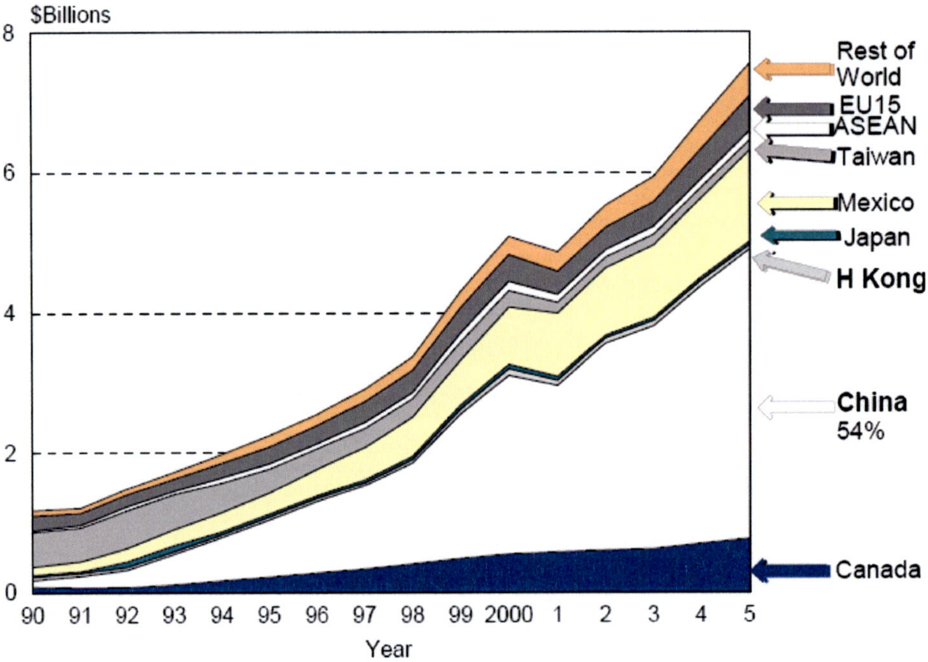

Source: U.S. Department of Commerce.

Figure 14. U.S. Imports of Building and Lighting Products (SITC 81) by Country and Group, 1990-2005.

Table 11. U.S. Imports of Prefabricated Buildings, Sanitary, Plumbing, Heating and Lighting Fixtures and Fittings (SITC 81) from Selected Countries and Country Groups, 1990, 2001-2005 (millions of dollars)

	1990	2001	2002	2003	2004	2005
China	94	2,383	2,962	3,199	3,697	4,146
Mexico	117	903	961	1,036	1,132	1,300
Canada	80	572	598	617	693	762
EU15	205	329	319	356	428	497
Taiwan	495	156	152	151	154	142
ASEAN	27	116	106	115	121	137
Hong Kong	47	70	77	80	73	59
Japan	28	59	36	41	49	52
Korea	61	32	36	42	37	37
Rest of World	78	275	319	362	422	464
World	1,232	4,895	5,566	5,999	6,806	7,596

Source: U.S. Department of Commerce.

Furniture

In U.S. imports of furniture and related parts, China has become a dominant supplier. The PRC accounted for over 43% of U.S. furniture imports in 2005. U.S. imports of furniture from China now exceed the combined U.S. imports from Canada and Mexico, which were the leading foreign suppliers of furniture until the late 1990s. In 2004, the Bush Administration imposed anti-dumping penalties on approximately 500 furniture manufacturers in China.

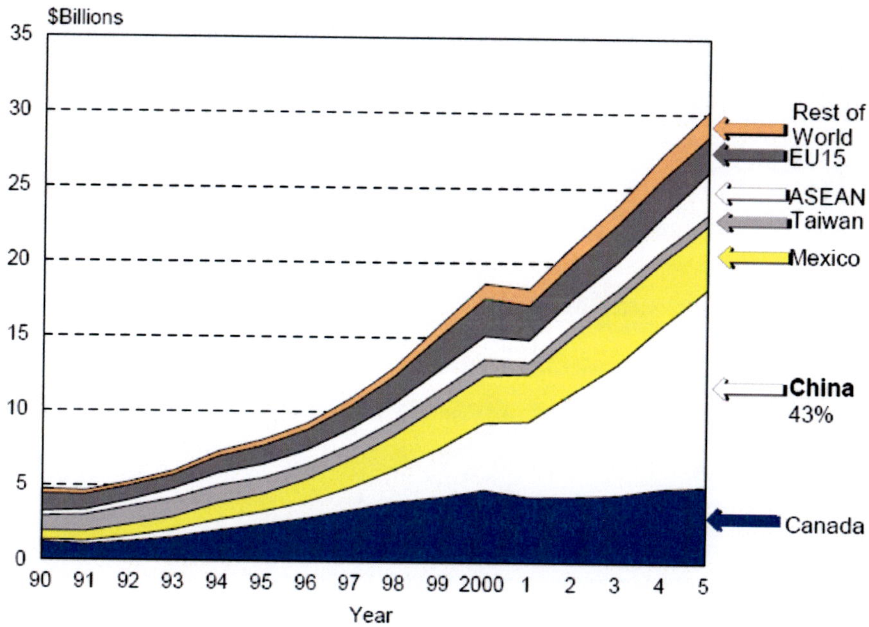

Source: U.S. Department of Commerce.

Figure 15. U.S. Imports of Furniture and Parts (SITC 82) by Country and Group, 1990-2005.

Table 12. U.S. Imports of Furniture and Parts (SITC 82) from Selected Countries and Country Groups, 1990, 2001-2005 (millions of dollars)

	1990	2001	2002	2003	2004	2005
China	145	5,017	6,954	8,742	10,905	13,179
Canada	1,209	4,411	4,423	4,551	5,007	5,126
Mexico	578	3,212	3,824	4,275	4,316	4,297
ASEAN	331	1,492	1,753	1,886	2,303	2,800
EU15	1,174	2,309	2,321	2,489	2,491	2,371
Taiwan	1,009	765	794	748	753	716
Japan	162	141	107	135	181	210
Korea	67	75	75	69	68	111
Hong Kong	29	98	90	109	97	82
Rest of World	299	1,081	1,219	1,289	1,557	1,691
World	5,003	18,601	21,560	24,293	27,678	30,583

Source: U.S. Department of Commerce.

Travel Goods and Handbags

China has become the principal supplier of imported travel goods, handbags, and similar items, accounting for nearly 75% of U.S. imports of such merchandise in 2005. The EU has become an important supplier while China appears to have taken market shares from South

Korea, Taiwan, and, more recently, ASEAN. This U.S. import category is ranked only 42st in total customs value.

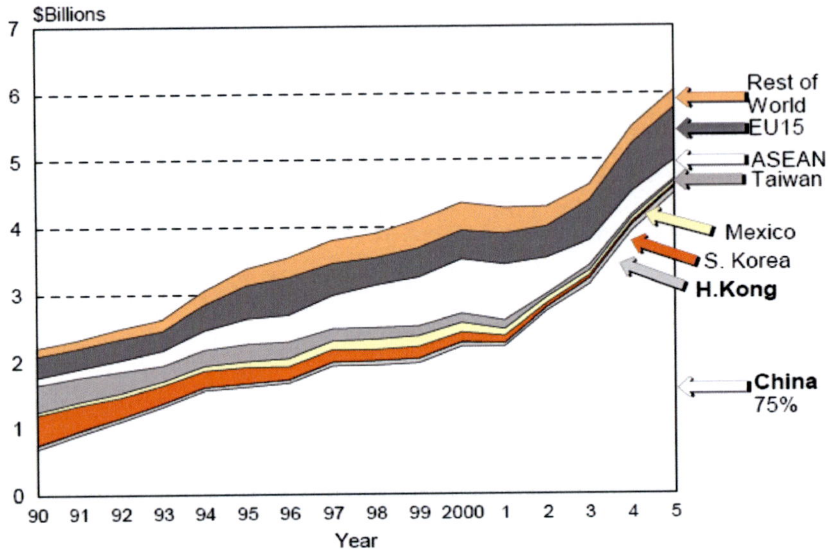

Source: U.S. Department of Commerce.

Figure 16. Imports of Travel Goods, Handbags, and Similar Products (SITC 83) by Country and Group, 1990-2005.

Table 13. U.S. Imports of Travel Goods, Handbags, (SITC 83) from Selected Countries and Country Groups, 1990, 2001-2005 (millions of dollars)

	1990	2001	2002	2003	2004	2005
China	692	2,211	2,741	3,136	3,936	4,504
EU15	270	463	476	602	715	790
ASEAN	114	836	538	372	340	275
Hong Kong	50	46	52	85	95	92
Mexico	46	104	87	69	63	54
Canada	17	39	35	37	35	36
Taiwan	406	129	52	79	47	32
Korea	446	106	56	39	31	21
Japan	9	7	7	8	12	12
Rest of World	121	384	292	233	248	262
World	2,171	4,325	4,336	4,660	5,522	6,078

Source: U.S. Department of Commerce.

Apparel and Clothing

U.S. imports of apparel and clothing accessories from China have been rising, reaching 26% of U.S. imports in 2005. According to some estimates, more than 80% of Chinese apparel exports are produced by joint ventures, many of them involving East Asian investment.[37] Global quotas on imported textiles and apparel expired on January 1, 2005, pursuant to the Multi-Fiber Agreement, resulting in a surge in U.S. garment imports from China, which increased by 46% in 2005. Other nations with large gains in the U.S. apparel market were India (up 33%), Indonesia (20%) Bangladesh (20%), and Cambodia (20%). Although wages for low skill labor in China reportedly are rising relative to other developing countries, China's clothing manufacturers retain competitive advantages such as high labor productivity, "vertical integration" — the ability to produce all manufacturing inputs domestically — and developed infrastructure. In November 2005, the United States and the PRC signed a three-year agreement on textiles trade which imposes quotas on 21 types of Chinese textiles and clothing but which allows for a progressive increase in U.S. imports of apparel products from China through 2008.

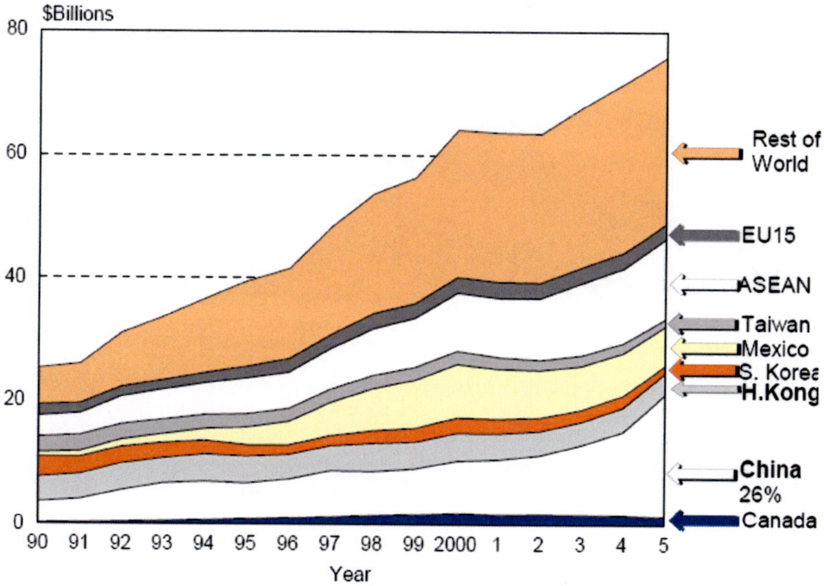

Source: U.S. Department of Commerce.

Figure 17. U.S. Imports of Apparel and Clothing Accessories (SITC 84) by Country and Group, 1990-2005.

Table 14. U.S. Imports of Apparel and Clothing Accessories (SITC 84) from Selected Countries and Country Groups, 1990, 2001-2005 (millions of dollars)

	1990	2001	2002	2003	2004	2005
China	3,422	8,852	9,538	11,341	13,567	19,888
ASEAN	3,404	9,581	10,020	11,773	12,157	13,043
Mexico	709	8,127	7,731	7,199	6,943	6,321
Hong Kong	3,974	4,282	3,928	3,760	3,919	3,553
EU15	1,790	2,584	2,473	2,564	2,586	2,444
Canada	247	1,764	1,799	1,740	1,692	1,468
Korea	3,244	2,354	2,206	1,925	1,936	1,253
Taiwan	2,475	1,907	1,664	1,690	1,626	1,203
Japan	158	170	205	252	325	121
Rest of World	5,891	24,168	24,150	25,907	27,438	26,983
World	25,314	63,789	63,714	68,060	72,189	76,277

Source: U.S. Department of Commerce.

Footwear

U.S. imports of footwear from China surged during the 1990s. From $1.5 billion in 1990, they rose to over $10 billion in 2002 or two-thirds of all such imports. China has largely replaced South Korea and Taiwan as the main source of Asian-produced footwear in the United States. Other large suppliers are Italy, Brazil, and Vietnam.

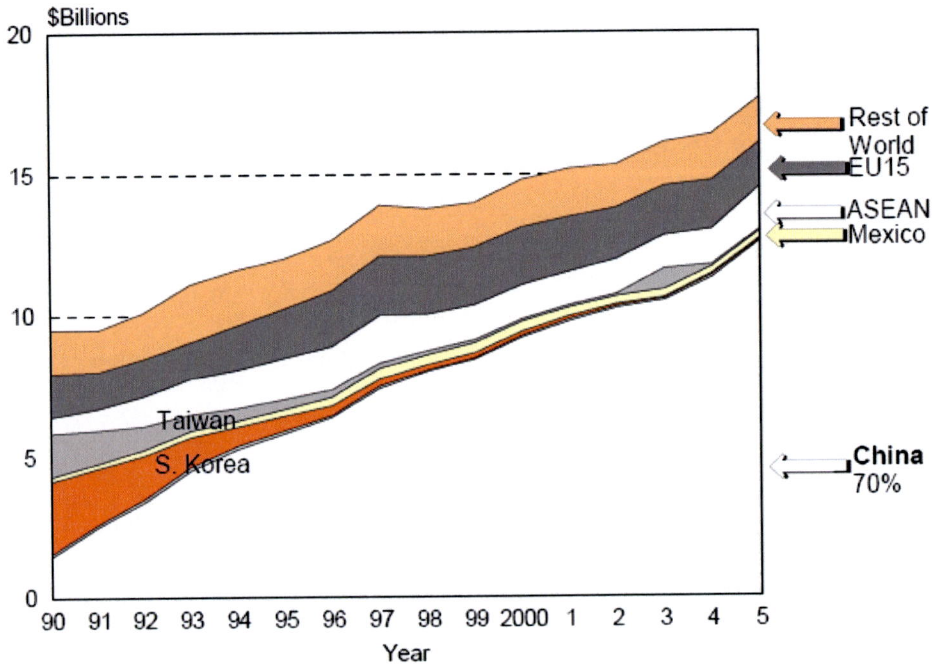

Source: U.S. Department of Commerce.

Figure 18. U.S. Imports of Footwear (SITC 85) by Country and Group, 1990-2005.

Table 15. U.S. Imports of Footwear (SITC 85) from Selected Countries and Country Groups, 1990, 2001-2005 (millions of dollars)

	1990	2001	2002	2003	2004	2005
China	1,475	9,766	10,241	10,546	11,347	12,654
EU15	1,523	1,950	1,826	1,763	1,722	1,558
ASEAN	579	1,185	1,237	1,184	1,259	1,525
Mexico	165	311	278	275	242	247
Canada	53	78	67	64	76	93
Taiwan	1,528	75	73	73	80	69
Hong Kong	109	81	67	60	86	52
Korea	2,558	103	65	50	51	45
Japan	5	2	2	2	2	3
Rest of World	1,543	1,698	1,523	1,542	1,632	1,588
World	9,538	15,249	15,379	15,559	16,497	17,834

Source: U.S. Department of Commerce.

Professional, Scientific, and Controlling Instruments

China is a minor supplier of U.S. imports of professional, scientific and controlling instruments, supplying 8% of U.S. imports in this category in 2005. Over two-thirds of such imports originate in the European Union, Mexico, and Japan.

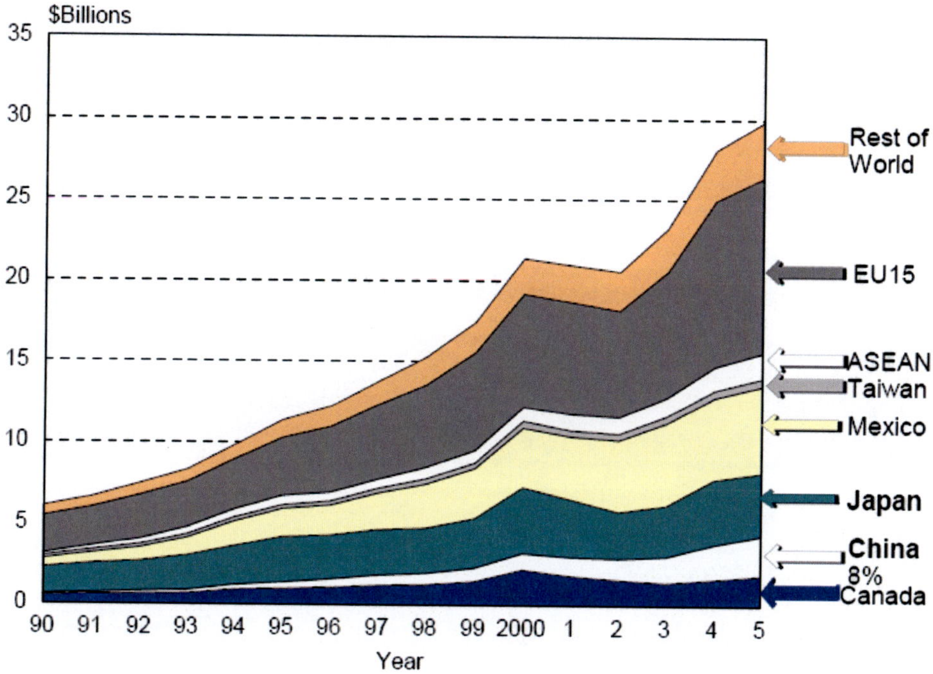

Source: U.S. Department of Commerce.

Figure 19. U.S. Imports of Professional, Scientific, and Controlling Instruments (SITC 87) by Country and Group, 1990-2005.

Table 16. U.S. Imports of Professional, Scientific and Controlling Instruments and Apparatus (SITC 87) from Selected Countries and Country Groups, 1990, 2001-2005 (millions of dollars)

	1990	2001	2002	2003	2004	2005
EU15	2,310	6,887	6,543	7,744	10,225	10,802
Mexico	513	3,895	4,436	5,090	5,082	5,371
Japan	1,494	3,561	2,902	3,177	4,016	3,887
China	74	1,172	1,301	1,660	2,176	2,483
Canada	527	1,793	1,575	1,406	1,611	1,833
ASEAN	152	1,027	1,037	1,139	1,448	1,571
Taiwan	176	372	393	450	458	472
Korea	89	152	156	153	177	230
Hong Kong	82	55	67	70	67	79
Rest of World	604	2,287	2,400	2,675	3,101	3,433
World	6,021	21,201	20,810	23,564	28,361	30,161

Source: U.S. Department of Commerce.

Photographic and Optical Equipment and Timepieces

China is a rising supplier of photographic apparatus, equipment and supplies and optical goods as well as watches and clocks. In 2005, China accounted for 17.5% of U.S. imports of such products. Japan and the European Union still dominate U.S. imports. By country, the top three suppliers of such imports for the United States are Japan, China, and Switzerland.

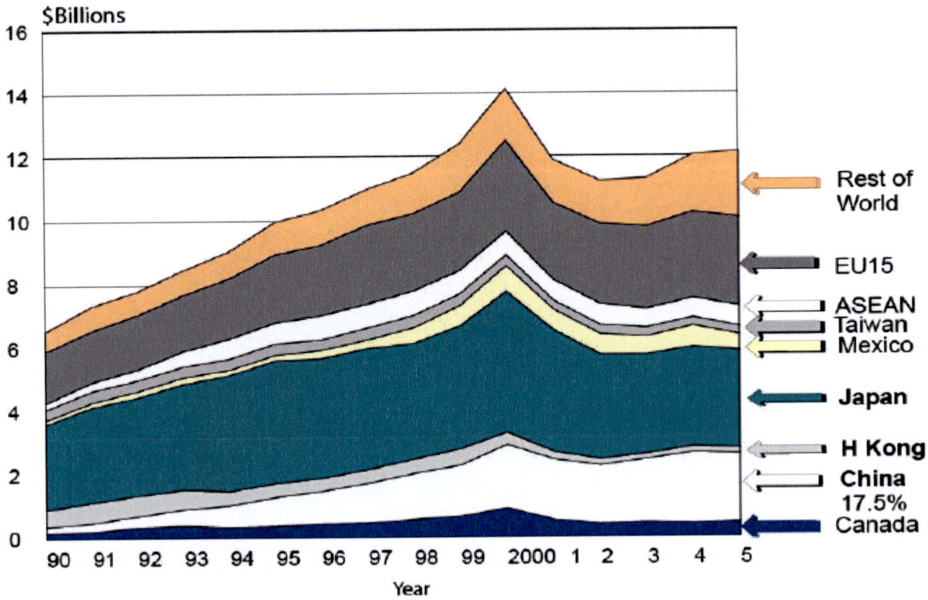

Source: U.S. Department of Commerce.

Figure 20. U.S. Imports of Photographic Equipment, Optical Goods, Watches and Clocks (SITC 88) by Country and Group, 1990-2005.

Table 17. U.S. Imports of Photographic Apparatus, Equipment and Supplies and Optical Goods; Watches and Clocks (SITC 88) from Selected Countries and Country Groups, 1990, 2001-2005 (millions of dollars)

	1990	2001	2002	2003	2004	2005
Japan	2,668	3,848	3,309	3,138	3,140	3,082
EU15	1,619	2,439	2,535	2,612	2,716	2,807
China	191	1,908	1,842	2,001	2,239	2,153
ASEAN	199	650	664	587	614	646
Mexico	128	648	634	555	665	494
Canada	180	545	414	461	428	469
Taiwan	334	282	288	280	265	258
Hong Kong	526	236	200	164	182	178
Korea	127	168	150	134	124	127
Rest of World	574	1,348	1,353	1,510	1,797	2,072
World	6,546	12,072	11,389	11,442	12,170	12,286

Source: U.S. Department of Commerce.

FOREIGN DIRECT INVESTMENT IN CHINA

Fueling China's export boom is an unprecedented infusion of foreign capital in the manufacturing sector.[38] Foreign direct investment (FDI) is directed toward investments in companies in which the foreign investor has a controlling interest. It is primarily for physical plant and equipment and for the costs of establishing enterprises in China. It is not for portfolio investment on China's stock exchanges. In 2002, China overtook the United States as the world's largest recipient of foreign direct investment. In 2005, China remained in that position, despite a slight decrease from a year earlier, with $60 billion in utilized FDI. The United States is one of the largest sources of utilized FDI in China, investing $3.1 billion in 2005. (See table 18.) China relies heavily upon investment from Hong Kong and other East Asian countries and regions. A significant amount of FDI from Hong Kong comes from Taiwan or from mainland Chinese companies via their subsidiaries in Hong Kong.[39] Annual or utilized FDI from Japan and South Korea surpassed that of the United States in 2003. In 2004, South Korea surpassed Japan to be the third largest source of FDI in China. The United States remains the second largest source of cumulative FDI after Hong Kong. China's WTO commitments include allowing more foreign investment in sectors such as telecommunications, energy, banking, and insurance.

Table 18. China's Utilized Foreign Direct Investment Inflows, Top Foreign Investors, 2000-2005 (billions of dollars)

Country or Region	2001	2002	2003	2004	2005
Hong Kong	16.7	17.8	17.7	18.9	17.1
Virgin Islands[40]	5.0	6.1	5.7	6.7	9.0
Japan	4.3	4.2	5.0	5.4	6.5
South Korea	2.1	2.7	4.5	6.2	5.2
United States	4.4	5.4	4.2	3.9	3.1
Singapore	2.1	2.3	2.0	2	2.2
Taiwan	2.9	3.9	3.4	3.1	2.1
Germany	1.2	0.9	0.8	1	1.5
All Sources	46.9	52.7	53.5	64	60.3

Source: U.S. and Foreign Commercial Service and U.S. Department of State, "Doing Business in China: A Country Commercial Guide for U.S. Companies," 2006.

APPENDIX

Table A1. China's Merchandise Trade with the World, 1984-2005 (millions of dollars)

Year	China's Trade with the World (Chinese data)			World Trade with China (Partner Country Data)		
	China Exports	China Imports	China Balance	World Exports	World Imports	World Balance
1984	24,824	25,953	-1,129	24,640	26,904	-2,264
1985	27,329	42,534	-15,205	38,355	30,867	7,488
1986	31,367	43,247	-11,880	36,152	35,310	842
1987	39,464	43,222	-3,758	39,250	46,654	-7,404
1988	47,663	55,352	-7,689	51,794	59,748	-7,954
1989	52,916	59,131	-6,215	51,666	72,810	-21,144
1990	62,876	53,915	8,961	49,036	88,692	-39,656
1991	71,940	63,855	8,085	61,732	112,372	-50,640
1992	85,492	81,843	3,649	81,996	136,853	-54,857
1993	91,611	103,552	-11,941	108,406	156,896	-48,490
1994	120,822	115,629	5,193	120,634	191,663	-71,029
1995	148,892	132,063	16,829	145,897	233,614	-87,717
1996	151,093	138,949	12,144	156,200	254,440	-98,240
1997	182,917	142,163	40,754	165,230	286,540	-121,310
1998	183,744	140,385	43,359	152,890	289,620	-136,730
1999	194,932	165,717	29,215	162,650	322,080	-159,430
2000	249,212	225,097	24,115	212,060	398,060	-186,000
2001	266,200	243,600	22,600	221,450	413,280	-191,830
2002	325,642	295,302	30,339	270,930	483,610	-212,680
2003	438,472	413,095	25,377	422,590	601,920	-179,330
2004	593,647	560,811	32,831	527,370	794,480	-267,110
2005	762,326	660,221	102,105	647,690	989,880	-342,190

Note: Summation of data reported by 109 of China's trading partner countries in 1983 growing to 156 countries reporting in 2005.

Sources: Chinese data: PRC General Administration of Customs and *Global Trade Atlas*. World Data: International Monetary Fund, *Direction of Trade Statistics Yearbook* and *Direction of Trade Statistics Quarterly*.

Table A2. U.S. Merchandise Trade with China and China's Merchandise Trade with the United States, 1984-2005 (millions of dollars)

Year	U.S. Trade with China (U.S. data)			China's Trade with U.S. (Chinese data)		
	U.S. Exports	U.S. Imports	U.S. Balance	China Exports	China Imports	China Balance
1984	3,004	3,381	-377	2,313	3,837	-1,524
1985	3,856	4,224	-368	2,336	5,199	-2,863
1986	3,106	5,241	-2,135	2,633	4,718	-2,085
1987	3,497	6,910	-3,413	3,030	4,836	-1,806
1988	5,017	9,261	-4,244	3,399	6,633	-3,234
1989	5,807	12,901	-7,094	4,414	7,864	-3,450
1990	4,807	16,296	-11,489	5,314	6,591	-1,277
1991	6,287	20,305	-14,018	6,198	8,010	-1,812
1992	7,470	27,413	-19,943	8,599	8,903	-304
1993	8,767	31,183	-22,416	16,976	10,633	6,343
1994	9,287	41,362	-32,075	21,421	13,977	7,444

Table A2. Continued

Year	U.S. Trade with China (U.S. data)			China's Trade with U.S. (Chinese data)		
	U.S. Exports	U.S. Imports	U.S. Balance	China Exports	China Imports	China Balance
1995	11,749	48,521	-36,772	24,744	16,123	8,621
1996	11,978	54,409	-42,431	26,731	16,179	10,552
1997	12,805	65,832	-53,027	32,744	16,290	16,454
1998	14,258	75,109	-60,851	38,001	16,997	21,004
1999	13,118	81,786	-68,668	41,946	19,480	22,466
2000	16,253	100,063	-83,810	52,104	22,363	29,741
2001	19,234	102,280	-83,046	54,300	26,200	28,100
2002	22,053	125,167	-103,115	69,959	27,227	42,731
2003	26,806	151,620	-123,960	92,510	33,882	58,628
2004	34,721	196,699	-161,978	124,973	44,652	80,321
2005	41,836	243,462	-201,626	162,938	48,734	114,204

Sources: U.S. data from U.S. Department of Commerce. Chinese data from PRC General Administration of Customs and *Global Trade Atlas.*

Table A3. Japan's Merchandise Trade with China and China's Merchandise Trade with Japan, 1984-2005 (millions of dollars)

Year	Japan's Trade with China (Japanese Data)			China's Trade with Japan (Chinese Data)		
	Japan Exports	Japan Imports	Japan Balance	China Exports	China Imports	China Balance
1984	7,199	5,943	1,256	5,155	8,057	-2,902
1985	12,590	6,534	6,056	6,091	15,178	-9,087
1986	9,936	5,727	4,209	5,079	12,463	-7,384
1987	8,337	7,478	859	6,392	10,087	-3,695
1988	9,486	9,861	-375	8,046	11,062	-3,016
1989	8,477	11,083	-2,606	8,395	10,534	-2,139
1990	6,145	12,057	-5,912	9,210	7,656	1,554
1991	8,605	14,248	-5,643	10,252	10,032	220
1992	11,967	16,972	-5,005	11,699	13,686	-1,987
1993	17,353	20,651	-3,298	15,782	23,303	-7,521
1994	18,687	27,569	-8,882	21,490	26,319	-4,829
1995	21,934	35,922	-13,988	28,466	29,007	-541
1996	21,827	40,405	-18,578	30,888	29,190	1,698
1997	21,692	41,827	-20,135	31,820	28,990	2,830
1998	20,182	37,079	-16,897	29,718	28,307	1,411
1999	23,450	43,070	-19,620	32,400	33,768	-1,368
2000	30,440	55,340	-24,900	41,611	41,520	90
2001	30,941	57,795	-26,558	45,078	42,810	2,267
2002	40,001	61,882	-21,881	48,483	53,489	-5,006
2003	57,474	75,579	-18,105	59,453	74,204	-14,751
2004	73,971	94,446	-20,475	73,536	94,191	-20,655
2005	79,972	108,515	-28,543	84,097	100,467	-16,370

Sources: IMF, Direction of Trade Statistics Quarterly; Global Trade Atlas; PRC, General Administration of Customs.

Table A4. European Merchandise Trade with China and China's Merchandise Trade with the European Union, 1984-2005 (millions of dollars)

Year	EU-15 Trade with China (EU data)			China's Trade with the EU-15 (Chinese Data)		
	EU Exports	EU Imports	EU Balance	China Exports	China Imports	China Balance
1984	2,929	2,639	290	2,232	3,323	-1,091
1985	5,484	2,971	2,513	2,283	6,157	-3,874
1986	6,403	4,106	2,297	4,017	7,757	-3,740
1987	6,430	5,945	485	3,916	7,274	-3,358
1988	6,772	7,719	-947	4,746	8,176	-3,430
1989	7,360	9,877	-2,517	5,114	9,785	-4,671
1990	7,373	13,289	-5,916	6,275	9,147	-2,872
1991	7,719	18,160	-10,441	7,127	9,297	-2,170
1992	9,604	20,995	-11,391	8,004	10,863	-2,859
1993	14,301	23,730	-9,429	12,258	15,739	-3,481
1994	16,246	27,644	-11,398	15,418	18,604	-3,186
1995	19,327	32,333	-13,006	19,258	21,313	-2,055
1996	18,387	35,440	-17,053	19,868	19,883	-15
1997	18,054	42,172	-24,118	23,865	19,205	4,660
1998	19,298	47,005	-27,707	28,148	20,715	7,433
1999	20,326	52,573	-32,247	30,207	25,463	4,744
2000	23,063	64,022	-40,958	38,193	30,845	7,348
2001	26,620	67,634	-41,025	40,904	35,723	5,181
2002	32,208	77,495	-45,227	48,184	38,552	9,632
2003	44,217	108,562	-64,345	72,457	53,112	19,345
2004	57,773	147,111	-89,338	99,843	68,011	31,832
2005	61,894	183,734	-121,840	134,872	71,694	63,178

Note: From 1980-88, data are for the 12 nations of the European Economic Community and after 1988 for the 15 nations of the EU (addition of Austria, Finland, and Sweden).

Sources: IMF. *Direction of Trade Statistics Yearbook* and *Direction of Trade Statistics Quarterly*; *Global Trade Atlas*; PRC. General Administration of Customs.

Table A5. Major Country Merchandise Exports to China, Imports from China, and Trade Balances with China, 2004 and 2005 (billions of dollars)

Partner	Trading Partner Data						Chinese Data					
	2004			2005			2004			2005		
	Exp	Imp	Bal	Exp	Imp	Bal	Exp	Imp	Bal	Exp	Imp	Bal
U.S.	34.7	196.6	-161.9	41.8	243.4	-201.6	44.6	124.9	-80.3	48.7	162.9	-114.2
Japan	73.9	94.4	-20.5	79.9	108.5	-28.5	94.2	73.5	20.7	100.4	84.1	16.3
EU-15	57.7	146.7	-89.0	61.9	183.7	-121.8	68.0	99.8	-31.8	71.7	134.8	-63.1
Hong Kong	114.2	118.0	-3.8	130.3	135.1	-4.8	11.8	101.0	-89.2	12.2	124.5	-112.3
Taiwan	44.9	16.7	28.2	51.8	19.9	31.9	64.7	13.5	51.2	74.6	16.7	57.9
S. Korea	54.9	29.2	25.7	69.8	38.6	31.2	62.0	27.8	34.2	76.8	35.1	41.7
Germany	26.0	38.4	-12.4	26.4	49.4	-23.0	30.0	23.7	6.3	30.6	32.5	-1.9
Singapore	15.4	16.2	-0.8	19.7	20.5	-0.8	14.0	12.6	1.4	16.5	16.7	-0.2
U.K.	4.3	19.1	-14.8	5.1	23.9	-18.8	4.7	14.9	-10.2	5.5	18.9	-13.4
France	6.7	14.5	-7.8	8.0	17.9	-9.9	7.6	9.9	-2.3	9.0	11.6	-2.6

Sources: IMF. *Direction of Trade Statistics Yearbook* and *Direction of Trade Statistics Quarterly*; *Global Trade Atlas*; Hong Kong Trade Development Council; Ministry of Economic Affairs, Board of Foreign Trade (Taiwan).

Table A6. U.S. Merchandise Trade Balances with Selected Asian Developing Nations, 1984-2005 (millions of dollars)

Year	China	Indonesia	S. Korea	Malaysia	Philippines	Taiwan	Thailand
1984	-377	-4,674	-4,188	-9983	-913	-11,266	-381
1985	-373	-4,152	-4,992	-936	-959	-13,295	-804
1986	-2,135	-2,757	-7,588	-807	-805	-16,069	-1,018
1987	-3,422	-2,955	-10,326	-1,159	-898	-19,221	-904
1988	-4,237	-2,438	-10,578	-1,715	-1,069	-14,314	-1,739
1989	-7,094	-2,618	-7,115	-2,052	-1,102	-14,305	-2,343
1990	-11,488	-1,785	-4,888	-2,071	-1,151	-12,347	-2,597
1991	-14,018	-1,675	-2,224	-2,446	-1,439	-11,038	-2,693
1992	-19,943	-1,927	-2,732	-4,144	-1,870	-10,601	-3,944
1993	-24,927	-3,117	-3,003	-4,858	-1,646	-10,050	-5,214
1994	-32,076	-4,209	-2,346	-7,454	-2,137	-10,864	-5,938
1995	-36,772	-4,599	523	-9,162	-2,070	-10,863	-5,452
1996	-42,431	-4,778	3,286	-9,809	-2,372	-12,610	-4,587
1997	-53,026	-5,222	1,269	-7,695	-3,370	-13,331	-5,699
1998	-56,927	-7,042	-7,456	-10,043	-5,211	-14,960	-8,198
1999	-68,668	-7,575	-8,308	-12,349	-5,153	-16,077	-9,340
2000	-83,810	-7,839	-12,398	-14,573	-5,147	-16,134	-9,747
2001	-83,045	-7,605	-12,988	-12,956	-3,666	-15,239	-8,733
2002	-103,115	-7,062	-12,979	-13,661	-3,715	-13,805	-9,939
2003	-123,960	-6,999	-12,864	-14,517	-2,068	-14,111	-9,338
2004	-161,977	-8,142	-19,829	-17,288	-2,072	-12,866	-11,214
2005	-201,625	-8,971	-16,109	-23,252	-2,355	-12,788	-12,569

Source: U.S. Department of Commerce, International Trade Commission.

References

[1] The White House, *The National Security Strategy of the United States of America* (March 2006), available at [http://www.whitehouse.gov/nsc/nss/2006].

[2] See Sections 201 to 204 of the Trade Act of 1974 (19 U.S.C. §§ 2251-2254).

[3] Unfair competition includes dumping (sales in the United States of an imported product at less than fair value), countervailable subsidies (excessive government subsidies of exporting industries) (see Subtitles A and B of Title VII of the Tariff Act of 1930, as added by the Trade Agreements Act of 1979 (19 U.S.C. §§ 1673 et seq.), and imports that infringe on intellectual property rights (see Section 337 of the Tariff Act of 1930, 19 U.S.C. § 1337).

[4] See CRS Report RL33602, *Global Climate Change: Major Scientific and Policy Issues*, by John R. Justus and Susan R. Fletcher.

[5] For further discussion of U.S. trade, U.S. -China trade, and U.S. trade policies toward China, see CRS Report RL33577, *U.S. International Trade: Trends and Forecasts*, by Dick Nanto; CRS Report RL33536, *China-U.S. Trade Issues*, by Wayne M. Morrison; and CRS Report RL32165, *China's Currency: Economic Issues and Options for U.S. Trade Policy*, by Wayne Morrison and Marc Labonte.

[6] Office of the United States Trade Representative. "USTR Portman Announces US-China Broad Textile Agreement." USTR Press Release, November 8, 2005.

[7] The yuan can fluctuate within a band of 0.3% per day. The exchange rate as of December 2006 was 7.8 yuan to 1.0 U.S. dollar.

[8] Doug Palmer, "U.S. Sets Duty of up to 198 Pct on Chinese Furniture," *Reuters News*, November 9, 2004.

[9] Chris Buckley, "China on Unfamiliar Ground in Trade Fight with U.S.," *New York Times*, March 23, 2004.

[10] "Levin Says Bernanke Comments Justify CVD Action Against China," *Inside US-China Trade*, December 20, 2005; Doug Palmer, "U.S. Lawmakers Urge Action after China Meeting," *Washington Post*, December 15, 2006.

[11] In 2005, U.S.-China trade ($285 billion) nearly reached the value of U.S.-Mexico trade ($290 billion). U.S. Census Bureau, *Foreign Trade Statistics*.

[12] "EU Becomes China's Biggest Trading Partner — USDA Attache," *Reuters News*, February 25, 2005.

[13] PRC data. "China 2005 Trade Surplus Jumps to Record High," *Yahoo! Asia News*, January 11, 2006.

[14] U.S. Department of Commerce, International Trade Commission.

[15] *Global Trade Atlas*; "Economy Increasingly Dependent on Mainland Ties," *Nikkei Weekly*, June 14, 2004.

[16] Jonathan Anderson, "China, Asia's Paper Tiger?" *The Asian Wall Street Journal*, August 15, 2002.

[17] "China to Become 2nd Largest Automaker by 2010," *Asia Times Online* [http://www.atimes.com], August 25, 2005; *Xinhua News Agency*, April 11, 2005.

[18] According to the Hong Kong Trade Development Council, 55% of Hong Kong's total exports involve re-exports of Chinese (mainland) goods to markets other than China.

[19] U.S.-China Business Council, "Understanding the U.S.-China Balance of Trade," May 2003.

[20] Global Trade Atlas.

[21] Global Insight, "China: Interim Forecast Analysis," June 2006, and "China: Economic: Current Situation: Highlights," August 2006.

[22] U.S. Department of Commerce, International Trade Commission; Global Trade Atlas; International Monetary Fund, *Direction of Trade Statistics Quarterly*, June 2006.

[23] Robert J. Samuelson, "The World's Powerhouse," *Newsweek*, May 31, 2004.

[24] Taiwan's major exports to China include telecommunications products, computers, plastic products, steel, man-made fibers, industrial-use textiles, organic chemical products, optical and photo-taking instruments and parts, copper products, and polyester. Hong Kong Trade Development Council.

[25] When Hong Kong is included, China is the largest trading partner of both Taiwan and Japan. Directorate General of Customs, Ministry of Finance, Republic of China; Korean International Trade Association; *Global Trade Atlas*.

[26] Sadanand Dhume, "Buying Fast into Southeast Asia," *Far Eastern Economic Review*, March 28, 2002.

[27] Global Trade Atlas

[28] "China-ASEAN Trade Surges over 40 Percent in 2003," *Thai News Service*, February 11, 2004.

[29] Keith Bradsher and David Barboza, "As Exports Boom, China Risks Global Backlash," International Herald Tribune, April 9, 2005.

[30] Council of Economic Advisors, *Economic Report of the President*, February 2004.

[31] U.S. Imports for Consumption, U.S. International Trade Commission.

[32] NICS — Hong Kong, Taiwan, and South Korea (Singapore is counted in ASEAN).

[33] Global Trade Atlas.

[34] In 2005, GM sold more than 650,000 vehicles in China compared to Volkswagen, with sales of 500,000 cars, and Toyota, with 179,000 units. "Toyota in China: Full Speed Ahead," *BusinessWeek Online*, March 9, 2006.

[35] "Chinese Automaker Geely Sets Sights on Exports to U.S." *Associated Press Newswires*, January 11, 2006.

[36] "MOC: Tariff Cut to Put Little Effect on Imported Car Price next Year," *Xinhua News Agency*, December 19, 2005.

[37] Jiang Jingjin, "China Not the Only Beneficiary," *China Daily (China Business Weekly)*, April 5, 2004.

[38] For further discussion of China's economy and foreign investment, see CRS Report RL33534, *China's Economic Conditions*, by Wayne M. Morrison.

[39] Mainland subsidiaries in Hong Kong and Macao can take advantage of investment incentives for foreign companies on the PRC mainland.

[40] Many foreign firms, including U.S. companies, are registered in the Virgin Islands, Cayman Islands, and Western Samoa for tax purposes.

In: Trade Policies and Agreements in the Era of Globalization ISBN: 978-1-60021-836-1
Editor: Paul B. Lucus, pp. 73-94

Chapter 3

TRADE AGREEMENTS: IMPACT ON THE U.S. ECONOMY*

James K. Jackson

ABSTRACT

The United States is negotiating an unprecedented number of trade agreements. These agreements range from bilateral trade agreements with countries that account for meager shares of U.S. trade to multilateral negotiations that could affect large numbers of U.S. workers and businesses. During this process, Congress likely will be presented with an array of data estimating the impact of trade agreements on the economy, or on a particular segment of the economy.

An important policy tool that can assist Congress in assessing the value and the impact of trade agreements is represented by sophisticated models of the economy that are capable of simulating changes in economic conditions. These models are particularly helpful in estimating the effects of trade liberalization in such sectors as agriculture and manufacturing where the barriers to trade are identifiable and subject to some quantifiable estimation. Barriers to trade in services, however, are proving to be more difficult to identify and, therefore, to quantify in an economic model. In addition, the models are highly sensitive to the assumptions that are used to establish the parameters of the model and they are hampered by a serious lack of comprehensive data in the services sector. Nevertheless, the models do provide insight into the magnitude of the economic effects that may occur across economic sectors as a result of trade liberalization. These insights are especially helpful in identifying sectors expected to experience the greatest adjustment costs and, therefore, where opposition to trade agreements is likely to occur.

This report examines the major features of economic models being used to estimate the effects of trade agreements. It assesses the strengths and weaknesses of the models as an aid in helping Congress evaluate the economic impact of trade agreements on the U.S. economy. In addition, this report identifies and assesses some of the assumptions used in the economic models and how these assumptions affect the data generated by the models. Finally, this report evaluates the implications for Congress of various options it may consider as it assesses trade agreements.

---

* Excerpted from CRS Report RL31932, dated March 15, 2007.

BACKGROUND

Congress plays a direct role in formulating and implementing U.S. international trade policies. During the 108th and 109th Congresses, this role gained increased importance as the United States continues to negotiate an unprecedented number of trade agreements. Currently, the United States is involved in multilateral negotiations in the Doha Development Agenda under the auspices of the World Trade Organization (WTO). On a regional level, the United States is involved in negotiations on a Free Trade Area of the Americas (FTAA) and with countries in southern Africa. In addition, the United States is pursuing bilateral trade agreements with Malaysia, Oman and the United Arab Emirates, Thailand, and South Korea. It has concluded agreements with Australia, Bahrain, Chile, Morocco, Singapore, the Dominican Republic, and the five countries of the Central American Common Market (Guatemala, Honduras, Nicaragua, El Salvador, and Costa Rica) and Congress has approved them.[1] The Bush Administration has also concluded agreements with Panama, Peru and Colombia, separately from Ecuador and Bolivia, the other members of the proposed Andean-U.S. Free Trade Agreement.

Building a broad-based public consensus on international trade issues often has proved to be difficult, especially as certain industries and labor groups within the economy have been adversely affected by international competition. Based on previous experiences with international trade agreements, Members of Congress and the public may view these agreements with varying degrees of support and opposition. While few critics are likely to oppose outright all of the trade agreements being negotiated, critics will oppose some aspects of the agreements, because certain groups within the economy will incur a disproportionate share of the adjustment costs associated with each trade agreement. Economists and others have developed economic models that utilize advanced techniques to assess the economic impact of trade agreements on the economy as a whole and on specific sectors within the economy. To help Congress evaluate the potential economic effects, this report examines a sampling of these studies and offers an assessment of the estimates they have generated.

CRS Products on Trade Issues

CRS Report RS20529; *United States-Israel Free Trade Area*, by Joshua Ruebner.
CRS Report RS20864; A Free Trade Area of the Americas: Status of Negotiations and Major Policy Issues, by J. F. Hornbeck.
CRS Report RS20909; Trade Agreements: A Pro-Con Analysis of Including Core Labor Standards, by Gary J. Wells.
CRS Report RS21387; United States - Southern African Customs Union Free Trade Agreement Negotiations, by Danielle Langton.
CRS Report RS21464; *Morocco - U.S. Free Trade Agreement*, by Raymond J. Ahearn.
CRS Report RS21846; *U.S.-Bahrain Free Trade Agreement*, by Martin A. Weiss.
CRS Report RS21868; U.S.-Dominican Republic Free-Trade Agreement, by Lenore Sek.
CRS Report RS22391; *U.S.-Peru Trade Promotion Agreement*, by M. Angeles Villarreal.
CRS Report RS22419; *U.S.-Colombia Trade Promotion Agreement*, by M. Angeles Villarreal.
CRS Report RL30416; The Vietnam-U.S. Bilateral Trade Agreement, by Mark E. Manyin
CRS Report RL30652; *U.S.-Jordan Free Trade Agreement*, by Mary Jane Bolle.
CRS Report RL31144; The U.S.-Chile Free Trade Agreement; Economic and Trade Policy Issues, by J. F. Hornbeck.
CRS Report RL31356; Free Trade Agreements: Impact on U.S. Trade and Implications for U.S. Trade Policy, by William H. Cooper.

CRS Report RL31789; *The U.S.-Singapore Free Trade Agreement*, by Dick K. Nanto.
CRS Report RL31870; The Dominican Republic-Central America-United States Free Trade Agreement (CAFTA-DR), by J. F. Hornbeck.
CRS Report RL32060; World Trade Organization Negotiations: The Doha Development Agenda, by Ian F. Fergusson.
CRS Report RL32314; *U.S.-Thailand Free Trade Agreement Negotiations*, by Raymond J. Ahearn and Wayne M. Morrison.
CRS Report RL32322; Central America and the Dominican Republic in the Context of the Free Trade Agreement (DR-CAFTA) with the United States, coordinated by K. Larry Storrs.
CRS Report RL32375; The U.S. Australian Free Trade Agreement: Provisions and Implications, William H. Cooper.
CRS Report RL32540; The Proposed U.S.-Panama Free Trade Agreement, by J. F. Hornbeck.
CRS Report RL32770; *Andean-U.S. Free-Trade Agreement Negotiations*, by M. Angeles Villarreal.
CRS Report RL32829; Trade Issues in the 109th Congress: Policy Challenges and Opportunities, by William H. Cooper.
CRS Report RL33328; *Proposed U.S.-Oman Free Trade Agreement*, by Mary Jane Bolle.
CRS Report RL33435; *The Proposed South Korea-U.S. Free Trade Agreement*, by William H. Cooper and Mark E. Manyin.
CRS Report RL33445; The Proposed U.S.-Malaysia Free Trade Agreement, by Michael F. Martin

AN OVERVIEW OF THE MAJOR AGREEMENTS

Multilateral Agreements

In November 2001, trade ministers from 142 member countries of the World Trade Organization met in Doha, Qatar to launch the 4th WTO ministerial. The Doha meeting succeeded primarily by agreeing to begin a new round of multilateral trade negotiations.[2] These negotiations are intended to build on agreements reached under the Uruguay Round of negotiations on trade in agriculture and trade in services, part of the WTO's already-established work program. For the United States, the chief goal of the negotiations is to improve market access in agricultural trade, primarily by eliminating agricultural export subsidies; easing tariffs and quotas; and reducing other forms of trade-distorting domestic support. In addition, the United States hopes to expand negotiations on trade in services and to reduce tariffs on industrial goods.

A framework agreement on future negotiations was concluded in Geneva on August 1, 2004, but a new deadline for the completion of the talks was not set and the talks stalled in 2005. This framework was viewed hopefully, because it provides a blueprint for future negotiations on agriculture, non-agricultural market access, services and trade facilitation. The 6th Ministerial, which occurred in Hong Kong in December 2005, was seen by many as the last opportunity to settle key negotiating issues that could produce an agreement by 2007, the de facto deadline for the negotiations before the U.S. trade promotion authority expires. On April 21, 2006, WTO Director-General Pascal Lamy announced that WTO negotiators would not meet the April 30, 2006 deadline for reaching an agreement on a framework for further negotiations and that he had committed negotiators to six weeks of continuous talks to reach an agreement. It seems unlikely that, even if the talks do move the issue forward, a final schedule for tariffs on agriculture, market access, offers on services issues, texts on rules and trade facilitation, and recommendations to implement the 'aid for trade" issue advanced in the Hong Kong declaration can be reached in such a short time-frame.

Regional Trade Agreements

Free Trade Area of the Americas (FTAA)

At the second Summit of the Americas in April 1998, 34 nations of the Western Hemisphere agreed to initiate formal negotiations to create a Free Trade Area of the Americas by 2005.[3] The negotiations initiated efforts in five areas: market access; agriculture; services; investment; and government procurement, but the negotiations have stalled. The United States and Brazil attempted to broker a compromise by moving the negotiations away from a comprehensive, single undertaking toward a two-tier framework comprising a set of "common rights and obligations" for all countries, combined with voluntary plurilateral arrangements with country benefits related to commitments. This approach, however has proved elusive and five of the participants — Brazil, Argentina, Uruguay, Paraguay, and Venezuela — have blocked an effort to restart the negotiations.

U.S.-Southern African Customs Union Free Trade Agreement

In November 2002, the Bush Administration announced that it was pursuing negotiations for a free trade agreement with the Southern African Customs Union, comprised of Botswana, Namibia, Lesotho, South Africa, and Swaziland.[4] These negotiations reflect congressional interest in strengthening U.S. trade with Africa as expressed in the African Growth and Opportunity Act (P.L. 106-200). U.S. negotiators hope to gain reductions in tariffs and in non-tariff barriers in such areas as telecommunications, financial services, legal services, and the movement of personnel. The Southern African members are pressing for increased market access for goods not already covered by the Africa Growth and Opportunity Act, especially for textiles and apparel, footwear, and agricultural products. After six rounds of talks, negotiations have stalled and the December 2004 deadline for concluding the talks has passed. The talks are deadlocked over differing views over the objectives of the talks and what sectors should be included for negotiation. Currently, there is no deadline for concluding the talks.

Enterprise for ASEAN

On October 26, 2002, President Bush announced that the United States would begin negotiations with the Association of Southeast Asian Nations (ASEAN) under the Enterprise for ASEAN Initiative.[5] The initiative offers the prospect of bilateral trade agreements with the 10 ASEAN members (Brunei, Cambodia, Indonesia, Laos, Malaysia, Myanmar (Burma), Philippines, Singapore, Thailand, and Vietnam). Under the agreement, the United States and each country will jointly determine when conditions are ripe for FTA negotiations. Two-way trade between the United States and ASEAN reached $120 billion in 2001.

U.S.-Andean Free Trade Agreement

The Bush Administration initiated talks with the four Andean countries — Colombia, Peru, Ecuador, and Bolivia — in November 2003 to reduce and eliminate barriers to trade and investment.[6] Negotiations began in May 2004, but the talks failed to reach a conclusion. As a result, Peru decided to continue negotiating with the United States without Colombia or Ecuador, and concluded a bilateral agreement in December 2005. Separate talks continued with Colombia and concluded successfully on February 27, 2006. Negotiations with Ecuador are stalemated. The agreements likely will be submitted to Congress as separate agreements, but they have not been submitted as of June 1, 2006.

Central American Free Trade Agreement-Dominican Republic

The Bush Administration signed an agreement with the five Central American Common Market nations — Costa Rica, El Salvador, Guatemala, Honduras, and Nicaragua —on August 5, 2004.[7] President Bush signed the agreement into law on August 2, 2005 (P.L. 109-53). All countries except Costa Rica and the Dominican Republic have ratified the agreement. As of July 1, 2006, the United States had implemented the agreement for El Salvador, Honduras, Nicaragua and Guatemala will do so for Costa Rica when it has adopted the necessary regulatory and legal framework.

Many supporters have viewed the Dominican Republic-Central American Free Trade Agreement (CAFTA) as a stepping stone toward completing a Free Trade Area of the Americas. U.S. negotiators hope to assist U.S. firms and workers by reducing tariffs on U.S. merchandise exports, and by reducing barriers to e-commerce, services, and intellectual property trade. The U.S. also hopes to use the agreement to improve the participants' commitment to the World Trade Organization's General Agreement on Trade in Services (GATS) and to define better the rules on transparency. The Central American participants are aiming to deepen their already strong trade relationship with the United States and to improve access for their textile and apparel products to the U.S. market.

Completed Bilateral Trade Agreements

U.S.-Australian Free Trade Agreement

The United States and Australia concluded a bilateral free trade agreement on February 8, 2004. The agreement was signed by the President on August 3, 2004 (P.L. 108-286) and took effect January 1, 2005. For the United States, the agreement lowered Australian tariffs on most U.S. exports of manufactured goods and agricultural products and will ensure nondiscriminatory treatment in most areas of bilateral trade in services, government procurement, foreign investment, and improved protection for intellectual property rights. For Australia, the agreement lowers tariffs on U.S. imports of Australian beef, dairy, cotton, and peanuts, but provides no change in access to sugar producers. Various U.S. agricultural interests, including beef, dairy, and sugar producers, opposed the negotiations, because of Australia's large, and competitive, agricultural sector. At $14 billion in 2004, Australia is the 15th largest market for U.S. exports and, at $7 billion, Australia is the 30th largest importer to the United States.

U.S.-Bahrain Free Trade Agreement

On September 14, 2004, the United States and Bahrain concluded negotiations for a free trade agreement.[8] The President signed the agreement into law on January 11, 2006 (P.L. 109-169). The Administration views the agreement as a first step toward an eventual Middle East Free Trade Area by 2013. Bahrain has a Bilateral Investment Treaty with the United

States and a Trade and Investment Framework Agreement. The agreement will eliminate tariffs on all consumer and industrial product exports to Bahrain and eliminate tariffs on 98% of all U.S. agricultural products with a 10-year phase out for the remaining items. Textiles and apparel trade will be duty free if the product contains either U.S. or Bahrainian yarn. U.S. services providers will have among the highest degree of access to service markets in Bahrain of any U.S. FTA to date in such areas as audiovisual, express delivery, telecommunications, computer and related services, distribution, healthcare, and services incidental to mining, construction, architecture, and engineering. U.S. financial services and life and medical insurance providers will also have access to Bahrain's economy.

U.S.-Chile Free Trade Agreement

On June 6, 2003, the United States and Chile signed a bilateral free trade agreement.[9] The agreement was signed by the President on September 3, 2003 (P.L. 108-77) and became effective on January 1, 2004. For the United States, trade with Chile accounts for less than one percent of U.S. overall trade, but the agreement is significant because it is the first such agreement with a South American country. The main U.S. objectives were accomplished by gaining market access and reduced tariff rates for U.S.-made goods. In time, all goods traded between the two countries will receive duty-free access. Under the agreement, 85% of bilateral trade in consumer and industrial products is eligible for duty-free treatment, with other product tariff rates being reduced over time. About 75% of U.S. agricultural exports will enter Chile duty-free within four years and all duties will be fully phased out within 12 years after implementation of the agreement. For Chile, 95% of its exports gain duty-free status immediately and only 1.2% fall into the longest 12 year phase out period. Other critical issues that were resolved include environment and labor provisions, more open government procurement rules, increased access for services trade, greater protection of U.S. investment and intellectual property.

U.S.-Colombia Free Trade Agreement

On February 6, 2006, the United States and Colombia announced that they had concluded negotiation of a free trade agreement. The agreement is comprehensive and would eliminate tariffs and other barriers in goods and services trade between the two countries.[10] Similar to the U.S.-Peru FTA, the U.S.-Colombia agreement would eliminate duties on 80% of U.S. exports of consumer and industrial products to Colombia immediately upon implementation. An additional 7% of U.S. exports would receive duty-free treatment within five years and all remaining tariffs would be eliminated within ten years of implementation. Implementing legislation has not been introduced in the Congress.

U.S.-Moroccan Free Trade Agreement

President Bush signed the United States-Morocco Free Trade Agreement (P.L. 108-302) on August 3, 2004. The agreement entered into force on January 1, 2006, after the Moroccan parliament ratified the agreement and King Mohammed VI signed it.[11] The agreement is intended to strengthen economic ties between the United States and Morocco and to show support for Morocco's position as a moderate Arab state. Morocco's agriculture sector is highly protected and should offer opportunities for U.S. business investment and U.S. exports. In particular, U.S. trade officials expect that reductions in Morocco's 20% tariff rate called for by the agreement should increase U.S. exports to the country, especially exports of such items as wheat, soybeans, feed grains, beef, and poultry. Business leaders also expect that the agreement will increase U.S. investment in Moroccan telecommunications and tourism as well as in the fields of energy, entertainment, transport, finance, and insurance. U.S. exports of information technology products, construction equipment, and chemicals are expected to benefit. Morocco is looking for increased access to the U.S. market, especially for Morocco's citrus products, textiles, and apparel goods.

U.S.-Panama Free Trade Agreement

The Bush Administration began formal negotiations with Panama on April 25, 2004, in Panama City, Panama.[12] The negotiations have progressed quickly. Negotiators met during the week of January 31-February 6, 2005, and could conclude their talks at a tenth, but yet unscheduled, round. The United States is seeking reductions in tariffs and other barriers to U.S. industrial, agricultural, and consumer goods, and define rules for services trade, investment, government procurement, intellectual property rights, and dispute resolution mechanisms. U.S. labor groups are challenging Panama's labor conditions, laws, enforcement efforts, and the language of the FTA. Panama is seeking to solidify its access to U.S. markets for agricultural goods, textiles and apparel, but already receives considerable benefits from the Caribbean Basin initiative's (CBI) unilateral trade preferences of the United States and is among the largest recipients of U.S. foreign direct investment in Latin America.

U.S.-Peru Free Trade Agreement

On December 7, 2005, the United States and Peru announced the conclusion of a bilateral free trade agreement. President Bush notified the Congress on January 6, 2006, that the United States intended to enter into an agreement. The agreement is comprehensive and would eliminate tariffs and barriers in goods and services trade between the two countries. Upon implementation, the agreement would eliminate duties on 80% of U.S. exports of consumer and industrial products to Peru. An additional 7% of U.S. exports would receive duty-free treatment within five years and all remaining tariffs would be eliminated within ten years of implementation. The Administration views the agreement as a building block in its strategy to advance free trade throughout the Americas.[13] Implementing legislation had not been introduced as of June 1, 2006.

U.S.-Singapore Free Trade Agreement

On September 4, 2003, President Bush signed the U.S.-Singapore Free Trade Agreement (P.L. 108-78) into law.[14] This agreement is the first of its kind for the United States with an Asian country and sparked a debate over whether the United States should pursue such bilateral agreements or pursue greater liberalization of trade relations through regional or multilateral forums. Both Singapore and the United States had few remaining restrictions on their overall trade activities, so the economic impact of this particular FTA is expected to be small for the United States. Nevertheless, the agreement eliminates, with a phase-in period, tariffs on all goods traded between the two countries; covers trade in services; and protects intellectual property rights.

The areas that are affected the most are U.S. exports of chewing gum and distilled spirits and imports of textiles and apparel. Industry analysts expect that U.S. textile and apparel producers will experience few direct economic effects from this agreement, but there has been a sharp division of views among industry representatives regarding the agreement's rules of origin governing trade in apparel goods. Apparel producers argue that the rules of origin on apparel are restrictive and have been made worse through the agreement by additional complications and burdens that discourage trade in apparel. The AFL-CIO opposed the agreement, because it argued that the agreement would not sufficiently protect core worker rights.

In the area of services, the agreement should improve U.S. market access across a broad range of sectors. U.S. banks, insurance companies, and securities and financial services companies are looking to expand in Singapore's market. The agreement also liberalizes controls over express delivery service and such professional service providers as lawyers, engineers, and architects. In addition, the agreement eases restrictions on telecommunications services, e-commerce, foreign investment, intellectual property rights, and government procurement.

Pending Bilateral Trade Agreements

U.S.-South Korea Free Trade Agreement

The Bush Administration notified Congress on February 3, 2006, of its intent to begin formal negotiations on a free trade agreement with South Korea.[15] On February 12, 2007, the negotiators had completed the seventh round of talks. For U.S. negotiators, the most difficult part of the talks is in contending with South Korea's well-protected agricultural sector, non-tariff barriers in the automotive and other manufacturing sectors, and status of products made at the Kaesong industrial complex, an industrial zone in North Korea set up by South Korean manufacturers. For the South Koreans, major sticking points are U.S. protection of textiles and apparel producers.

U.S.-Malaysia Free Trade Agreement

Negotiations with Malaysia began on March 8, 2006; the fifth round of the talks occurred during the week of February 5, 2007.[16] The United States is seeking the removal of import licensing restrictions on motor vehicles, removal of government procurement restrictions, increased protection for intellectual property rights (IPR), liberalized financial services, and negotiations on a broad range of services.

U.S.-Thailand Free Trade Agreement

The United States and Thailand began formal negotiations on a free trade agreement on June 28, 2004, in Hawaii. The Administration argues that the agreement will be comprehensive and seek to liberalize trade in goods, agriculture, services, investment, and intellectual property rights. In particular, the Administration said that the agreement will promote U.S. exports, primarily benefitting U.S. farmers and the auto and auto parts industries, will protect U.S. investment, and will advance the Enterprise for ASEAN Initiative. Other issues that likely will be negotiated include government procurement, competition policy, environment and labor standards, and customs procedures. The United States is Thailand's largest market, which accounts for 20% of Thailand's exports.

U.S.-United Arab Emirates-Oman Free Trade Agreement

The Bush Administration notified Congress in November 2004 that it would begin negotiations on a free trade agreement with the United Arab Emirates (UAE) and Oman. Talks began on March 8, 2005, with the UAE and on March 12, 2005, with Oman. The President signed an agreement with Oman on January 19, 2006, but implementing legislation has not yet been submitted to Congress. Negotiations with the UAE are continuing. Worker protection issues have presented a major hurdle. Both the UAE and Oman rely heavily on guest workers and place restrictions on the right to strike or organize. The Administration hopes that an agreement will build on agreements that have been signed with other nations in the area (Israel, Jordan, Morocco, and Bahrain) and will encourage a movement toward more open trade and more investment.

TRADE LIBERALIZATION AND THE GAINS FROM TRADE

Nations pursue trade liberalization to achieve a number of national objectives. Economists argue, however, that free trade, or the international trade of goods and services free from restrictions and barriers, provides nations with a broad group of economic benefits.[17] These benefits are categorized as one-time, or static, benefits, which include gains for consumers and gains for producers, and dynamic benefits that accrue over time and can positively affect the long-term rate of growth of a country. While it is not always possible to measure these effects precisely, most economists believe that the net effect of international trade on the national economy as a whole is positive, i.e., that the total gains exceed the total costs.

Production Gains

International trade is one among a number of forces that determine the complex makeup of jobs, industries, wages, and products in the economy. For an economy such as that in the United States, international trade alone does not determine economic expansions or contractions, the level of income, the level of national output, the overall wage rate, or even have much of an impact on the distribution of income.[18] Trade liberalization, however, by reducing foreign barriers to U.S. exports and by removing U.S. barriers to foreign goods and services, helps to strengthen those industries that are the most competitive and productive and to reinforce the shifting of labor and capital from less productive endeavors to more productive economic activities.

Adjustment Costs

Economists have long recognized that the long-term production gains associated with greater specialization in the economy create a wide range of short-term adjustment costs as labor and capital are shifted from less efficient industries and activities into more efficient industries and activities. These adjustment costs are difficult to measure, but they are potentially large over the short run and can entail significant dislocations for some segments of the labor force, for some companies, and for some communities. In negotiating trade agreements, governments are most mindful of the adjustment costs involved and, at times, are constrained in their ability to fashion such agreements because of opposition by groups within the economy that will bear heavy costs from trade liberalization. These costs are especially acute for labor groups within the economy that lack advanced education and training skills that provide them with the means necessary to be redeployed in other sectors of the economy.

Consumption Gains

Economists generally agree that consumption gains for consumers comprise the largest long-term gains for an economy that arise from international trade and, therefore, from any reduction of trade barriers. Trade models attempt to estimate these effects indirectly. A change in trade policies should lead to changes in prices for traded goods and, therefore, in consumers' real incomes, as well as to changes in the efficiency of production, which will also improve a nation's overall economic welfare. Consumption gains mean that consumers benefit from international trade by having a broader selection of goods and services available to them at lower prices than are available from purely domestic production. Also, the wider array of product selection likely enhances consumer well-being, because the competition that arises from international trade also affects the quality of the goods and services that are available. In some cases, this means that consumers have a choice of different levels of quality and that they can acquire not only the particular type of good they desire, but also the level of quality they desire. Since international trade encourages specialization, the production gains from trade also mean that consumers are offered a greater selection of prices for the goods they consume. If consumers choose lower-priced goods, their real incomes rise, which allows them to consume an even broader assortment of goods and services, and it expands national incomes.

Economic Growth

In addition to the "static" gains from trade described above, a growing body of research suggests that trade potentially plays a dynamic role in the economy. The full range of these effects are difficult for trade models to capture because they extend beyond the estimation time-frame of the models. Research into dynamic trade models concludes that there are important feedback effects and channels through which trade can alter the structure of markets and the rate of economic growth over the long run. By stimulating trade and investment, trade liberalization could add to these feedback effects. The literature on dynamic trade models concludes that free trade, or trade liberalization, alters all participants' rate of economic growth through a number of channels, including improved access to specialized capital goods; human capital accumulation, learning-by-doing, and the transfer of skills; and the introduction of new products.[19] These activities alter the rate of economic growth by changing the incentives for firms to invest in research and development — technical change — which, in turn, leads to permanent changes in the rate of economic growth. In assessing this body of research, a U.S. International Trade Commission study asserted that, "...formal empirical application of the new growth theory in a trade context has barely started," but that, "...the dynamic effects of trade policy changes can yield substantially larger estimates than those based on static models."[20]

ESTIMATING THE ECONOMIC IMPACT OF TRADE AGREEMENTS

Overview

Since the stakes involved in liberalizing trade are potentially very large, a number of economists has attempted to analyze the economic effects of removing barriers to trade in goods and services and to derive monetary values for those effects. Several different approaches are used to estimate the cost and effect of reducing barriers to trade in goods and services.[21] The most common approach uses sophisticated mathematical models of the U.S. economy to simulate the effects of trade liberalization. The three models used most often are: gravity models, partial equilibrium models, and general equilibrium models. Gravity models are based on the theory that large economies have a greater pull on trade flows than do smaller economies.[22] As a result, the size of an economy and its distance from trading partners are important factors in estimating the monetary value of changes in trading rules. Partial equilibrium models are used to measure the effects of trade restraints on a specific sector, rather then on the economy as a whole. Both gravity models and partial equilibrium models provide aggregate estimates of the effects of changes in trading rules and barriers, but they offer limited detailed information on the labor and sectoral effects of trade liberalization.

General equilibrium models, or computable general equilibrium (CGE) models, attempt to encompass all economic activity within an economy and attempt to estimate the economy-wide effects of changes in trade or economic policy. These models can offer comprehensive assessments of cross- and inter-industry linkages both worldwide and between regions of the world.[23] Such models attempt to mimic as closely as possible the real world economy through the use of an abstract mathematical representation of the environment in which relevant economic agents operate and of the decision-making process by which they make choices of consumption of goods, capital accumulation, etc.[24] These models incorporate assumptions about consumer behavior, market structure and organization, production technology, investment, and capital flows in the form of foreign direct investment. General equilibrium models use large sets of data that represent numerous countries and attempt to estimate economy-wide feedback effects from a change in trade policy in a given sector or industry and assess the impact of the change on employment, production, and economic welfare.

The Michigan Model and Estimates

One well-known and often-referenced general equilibrium model used frequently to analyze the economic effects of changes in trade policy is the model maintained by economists Drusilla Brown, Robert M. Stern, and Alan V. Deardorff at the University of Michigan.[25] In a recent study, Brown, Stern, and Deardorff used the model to estimate the economic effects on the United States of trade negotiations in the multi-country Doha Development Round and various proposed regional and bilateral trade agreements. In each scenario, the trio begin by using available data to develop a base estimate of the present level of trade. Next, they adjust the model to reflect some basic assumptions about how trade negotiations will reduce barriers to trade and then use these estimates to make an adjusted projection of major macroeconomic data. The difference between the initial set of data on the economy and the projected macroeconomic data that reflects anticipated changes in the economy as a result of trade negotiations gives rise to the numerical estimates of the effects of trade negotiations on trade, employment, industrial composition, and other macroeconomic data. One important drawback to the estimates derived by Brown, Deardorff, and Stern, and others is that the general equilibrium models used to derive most of the estimates of trade liberalization do not capture the adjustment costs that inevitably arise from trade liberalization. As a result, the data generated by the models represent the positive effects of changes in trade rules, but not the overall net effects — positive and negative — of trade liberalization.

Using the technique described above, Brown, Stern, and Deardorff developed estimates of the impact on the U.S. economy of reaching an agreement on the various components of the Doha Development round. They adopted a number of key assumptions, including an assumption that the negotiations will result in a 33% reduction in the barriers to trade in agriculture, manufactures, and services, which is projected to give rise to a combined increase in economic activity of $164 billion in the U.S. economy, as indicated in table1.[26] This and the other estimates used in this report that were derived by the Michigan model estimated a permanent change in economic activity between the "before" and "after" states of the economy and should not be considered either as an annual change in economic welfare or as an annual amount that can be accumulated over time. Brown, Stern, and Deardorff also projected the impact on the United States if all barriers to trade worldwide were removed unilaterally, which they estimate at $497 billion. With current U.S. gross domestic product (GDP) of over $13 trillion, the monetary gains for the U.S. economy associated with the above estimates of trade liberalization would be less than 1.5% and 4.5% of GDP, respectively.

A small decline in U.S. welfare in the agricultural sector reflects reductions in agricultural import tariffs, export subsidies, and production subsidies. In this formulation, these reductions produce offsetting effects in the agricultural sector itself,[27] but they induce slightly negative effects on other sectors in the economy as a result of changes in prices for agricultural goods and for the U.S. terms of trade (prices of exports relative to prices of imports). Gains in the manufacturing sector arise from reduced foreign tariffs on U.S. manufactured goods exports, which increases U.S. exports and domestic manufacturing output and improves production efficiency. These gains also represent a shift of capital within the economy from less productive activities into manufacturing areas that are more productive and capital flows from abroad in the form of foreign direct investment. The large gains indicated in the services sector reflect the relatively high level of foreign barriers U.S. exporters presently face in this sector and the high level of U.S. competitiveness in this sector.

Table 1. Estimated Economic Effects on the United States of a 33% Reduction in Barriers to Trade in Agriculture, Manufactures, and Services at the Doha Development Round (in $ U.S. billions)

Agricultural Protection	Manufactures Tariffs	Services Barriers	Combined
$-7.23	$36.52	$134.75	$164.04

Source: Brown, Drusilla K., Alan V. Deardorff, and Robert M. Stern, *Multilateral, Regional, and Bilateral Trade-Policy Options for the United States and Japan.* Research Seminar in International Economics, Discussion Paper No. 490, The University of Michigan, December 16, 2002. Table 1.

In a process similar to that described above, Brown, Stern, and Deardorff estimate the impact on the U.S. economy of various regional and bilateral trade agreements, as indicated in table 2. As expected, bilateral trade arrangements would produce modest gains for the U.S. economy as a whole, given the smaller value of a bilateral trade relationship for the U.S. cconomy. These arrangements are expected to be of greater importance to the trading partners because of the size of their trade with the United States relative to the size of their overall level of trade and the size of their respective economies. Trade agreements with Chile, Singapore, Australia, Morocco, and South Korea, for instance, are estimated to result in trade benefits for the U.S. economy of $4 billion, $17 billion, $19 billion, $6 billion and $30 billion, respectively. A free trade agreement with the 21 nations that comprise the Asia-Pacific Economic Association Cooperation is projected to offer economic benefits of $244 billion for the United States and surpass those of the Doha round, most likely because free trade agreements tend to be more comprehensive in terms of the number of industrial and services sectors that are involved compared with the WTO negotiations. An agreement with ASEAN is projected to yield benefits of $13 billion, while a Free Trade Agreement of the Americas (FTAA) would give rise to an estimated $68 billion in economic benefits.[28] An agreement with the Southern African Customs union would be expected to yield $12.6 billion in trade benefits to the United States.[29]

The Michigan model incorporates an input-output model for each economy in the model. Input-output accounts trace the flow of input commodities into the production processes of industries, the flow of intermediate goods between industries, and the flow of output from industries to final uses in the economy. This approach provides an estimate of the magnitude of employment effects that might be expected and a view of the possible job gains and losses across industrial sectors in the economy, as indicated in tables 3 and 4. In the approach used by Brown, Stern, and Deardorff, it is assumed that job losses will be perfectly offset by job gains, so that the data in tables 3 and 4 are not projections of the job losses and job gains for each sector. Instead, the model provides an estimate of the relative magnitude of employment effects that might be experienced in various industries, thereby identifying those industries that are most vulnerable to increased competition as a result of trade liberalization.

According to this approach, global free trade, or trade without restrictions, would add jobs to the U.S. agricultural sector, but reduce jobs in textiles, apparel, retail trade, and services.[30] Similarly, completing the liberalization schedule of the Uruguay round of trade talks was shown to result in the largest gains in jobs in agriculture, with losses in textiles and apparel, although there would be job gains in services due to the more limited schedule of liberalization. The Doha Round, with its focus on agriculture and services, would generate gains in the agricultural sector, but employment losses in textiles and apparel, retail trade, and services, although these losses would be one-third of those that might be experienced under global free trade. As expected, free trade agreements with APEC, ASEAN, and a Free Trade Agreement of the Americas yield smaller changes in employment than either global free trade, or the Doha round of trade talks. Furthermore, the model simulation indicates that each bilateral trade agreement the United States has negotiated can be expected to have a small impact on the U.S. economy.

Table 2. Estimated Economic Effects on the United States of Free Trade Agreements With Various Trading Partners (in $ U.S. billions)

APEC FTA	ASEAN FTA	Free Trade Agreement of the Americas (FTAA)	Chile FTA	Singapore FTA	Korea FTA
$244.25	$12.98	$67.59	$4.41	$17.5	$30.1
SACU FTA	CAFTA	Australia FTA	Morocco FTA		
$12.61	$17.26	$19.39	$5.97		

Source: Brown, Drusilla K., Alan V. Deardorff, and Robert M. Stern, *Multilateral, Regional, and Bilateral Trade-Policy Options for the United States and Japan*. Research Seminar in International Economics, Discussion Paper No. 490, The University of Michigan, December 16, 2002. Table 3. Updated estimates are from: Brown, Drusilla K, Kozo Kiyota, and Robert M. Stern, *Computational Analysis of the Free Trade Area of the Americas (FTAA)*. Research Seminar in International Economics, Discussion Paper No. 508, the University of Michigan, revised February 5, 2005. Brown, Drusilla K, and Kozo Kiyota, and Robert M. Stern, *Computational Analysis of the U.S. FTAs With Central America, Australia, and Morocco*. Research Seminar in International Economics, Discussion Paper No. 507, Revised January 31, 2005. Brown, Drusilla K., Kozo Kiyota, and Robert M. Stern, *Computational Analysis of the U.S. FTA With the Southern African Customs Union (SACU)*. Research Seminar in International Economics, Discussion Paper No. 545, May 31, 2006.

Investment and Capital Flows

One drawback to the present state of development of general equilibrium models is that they still do not compare in complexity with the real economy, nor do they capture all of the potential economic effects that could arise from trade agreements. For instance, the Michigan model incorporates investment flows that reflect a shift of resources within the economy from less productive to more productive economic activities and a shift of resources across national borders in the form of foreign investment in the economy.[31] As a result of trade liberalization, inflows of foreign capital would be expected to increase as U.S. industries become more productive and, therefore, more profitable and attractive to foreign investors. By the same token, U.S. direct investment abroad would increase as trade liberalization improved the prospects of foreign economies. In some estimates, the flows of foreign capital comprise a large part of the overall economic gains that are derived within the models. The models, however, do not reflect the corresponding appreciation or depreciation of the dollar's exchange rate that would accompany such flows. These corresponding changes in the dollar's value could blunt or reinforce the positive trade effects the model associates with trade liberalization policies.

Table 3. Projected Sectoral Employment Effects (Job Gains and Losses) in the United States of Various Trade Agreements (number of workers)

	Global free trade	Doha (one-third cut)	APEC FTA	ASEAN
Agriculture	278,658	91,966	394,420	27,259
Mining	5,794	1,912	-236	-68
Food	61,966	20,451	34,811	3,401
Textiles	-66,265	-21,870	-50,099	-19,570
Apparel	-157,229	-51,891	-107,610	-38,570
Leather	-28,829	-9,515	-24,769	-10,068
Wood	46,941	15,502	4,264	4,459
Chemicals	27,828	9,184	-545	-1,410
Mineral Prod.	-1,146	-378	-1,906	643
Metal	22,174	7,318	-1,483	5,261
Transp.	15,209	5,020	-1,587	1,518
Mach.	68,028	22,451	-10,699	-870
Other Manuf	30,096	9,933	-40,992	-23,864
Elec.	7,566	2,497	-419	846
Constr.	2,814	929	-11,377	2,876
Trade	-91,056	-30,051	-129,833	13,330
Services	-300,997	-99,339	105	18,333
Gov. Services	78,418	25,881	-52,047	16,495

Source: Brown, Drusilla K., Alan V. Deardorff, and Robert M. Stern, *Multilateral, Regional, and Bilateral Trade-Policy Options for the United States and Japan.* Research Seminar in International Economics, Discussion Paper No. 490, The University of Michigan, December 16, 2002. Tables 2and 4. Brown, Drusilla K., Kozo Kiyota, and Robert M. Stern, *Computational Analysis of the Free Trade Area of the Americas (FTAA).* Research Seminar in International Economics, Discussion Paper No. 508, the University of Michigan, Revised February 5, 2005. Tables 2 and 4.

Table 4. Projected Sectoral Employment Effects (Job Gains and Losses) in the United States of Various Trade Agreements (number of workers)

	FTAA	SACU	Australia	Morocco
Agriculture	-12,460	973	94	1,314
Mining	-3,251	27	504	-44
Food	-3,452	353	-756	542
Textiles	-6,028	-109	810	-32
Apparel	-16,804	-211	619	-129
Leather	620	202	207	-8
Wood	2,502	163	394	-10
Chemicals	2,883	127	1,555	-88
Mineral Prod.	957	76	539	29
Metal	2,024	33	1,957	-138
Transp.	2,970	369	1,741	-50
Mach.	21,830	1,230	6,229	-367
Other Manuf	2,148	77	653	-52
Elec.	-228	14	15	2
Constr.	-88	-13	-257	-57
Trade	1,991	-2101	-11,716	-1,140
Services	2,788	11	-2,188	-194
Gov. Services	1,597	-1221	-398	389

Source: Brown, Drusilla K., Alan V. Deardorff, and Robert M. Stern, *Multilateral, Regional, and Bilateral Trade-Policy Options for the United States and Japan.* Research Seminar in International Economics, Discussion Paper No. 490, The University of Michigan, December 16, 2002. Table 2 and 43. Brown, Drusilla K., Kozo Kiyota, and Robert M.Stern, *Computational Analysis of the Free Trade Area of the Americas (FTAA).* Research Seminar in International Economics, Discussion Paper No. 508, the University of Michigan, Revised February 5, 2005. Tables 2 and 4

Updated estimates are from: Brown, Drusilla K, Kozo Kiyota, and Robert M. Stern, *Computational Analysis of the Free Trade Area of the Americas (FTAA)*. Research Seminar in International Economics, Discussion Paper No. 508, the University of Michigan, Revised February 5, 2005. Table 2. Brown, Drusilla K, and Kozo Kiyota, and Robert M. Stern, *Computational Analysis of the U.S. FTAs With Central America, Australia, and Morocco.* Research Seminar in International Economics, Discussion Paper No. 507, Revised January 31, 2005. Tables 7b and 8b. Brown, Drusilla K., Kozo Kiyota, and Robert M. Stern, *Computational Analysis of the U.S. FTA With the Southern African Customs Union (SACU)*. Research Seminar in International Economics, Discussion paper No. 509, July 6, 2004. Table 3b.

Data on Barriers to Trade in Services

Another inherent problem associated with estimating the effects of trade liberalization is the dearth of information on barriers to trade in services. As table 1 shows, the Michigan model and other general equilibrium models estimate that the largest gains from trade liberalization likely would arise from the liberalization of trade in services. This result conforms well with most notions of where additional benefits from trade liberalization may reside and from the dominating role of services in the U.S. economy. In developing their estimates of the benefits of liberalizing trade in services, Brown, Deardorff, and Stern use estimates developed by Bernard Hoekman[32] on the average gross operating margins of firms listed on national stock exchanges in 18 countries as a proxy for estimating barriers to services trade. Hoekman bases his estimates on a standard economic assumption that the prices firms charge should reflect their marginal costs.

Market restrictions, or barriers to entry by foreign firms, however, drive a wedge between market price and marginal cost so that firms operating in protected markets will generate higher than expected profits, or experience higher than average rates of return. Hoekman considers this wedge to be indicative of the magnitude of domestic barriers in services sectors. According to Hoekman's data, all U.S. service sectors except construction had profit margins above average, which would imply that all U.S. service sectors except construction have erected relatively high barriers to entry by foreign firms. As a result, the model simulation estimates large employment losses in this sector under global free trade and the Doha development round of trade negotiations.

This conclusion, however, does not conform well with the estimates of most studies on market openness. For instance, the Organization for Economic Cooperation and Development (OECD) concluded after analyzing the services sectors of the 30 member countries of the OECD that the U.S. services sector was among the very least restrictive.[33] Hoekman also offered a caution in using the estimates because, "In general, a large number of factors will determine the ability of firms to generate high (gross operating) margins, including market size (number of firms), the business cycle, the state of competition policy enforcement, the substitutability of products, fixed costs, etc."[34] In addition, Hoekman's estimates do not differentiate between industries that have high profit margins as a result of barriers and those that have high profit margins because they possess some sort of economic competitive advantage. Without better data on the extent and nature of barriers to trade in the services sectors, it will continue to be difficult to develop monetary estimates of the costs of those barriers and, therefore, estimates of the economic benefits that could accrue as a result of market liberalization. After reviewing various studies that have attempted to assign values to national barriers to services trade, Hoekman concluded,

> Summing up, although the data situation is not very good, quite a bit can be done by analysts to quantify the relative magnitude and distribution of the gains of increasing competition on services markets...The research clearly suggests that potential gains from liberalization may be very large. While this work is important and useful, the state of the data on barriers is such that, in the near term, policymakers will have to continue to rely primarily on rules of thumb in determining negotiating priorities.[35]

Brown, Deardorff, and Stern make an assumption that the Doha Round of negotiations will result in a 33% reduction in barriers to trade in services, agriculture, and manufactured goods. While such an assumption is essential in order to run the economic model, it may not reflect realistically the outcome of the negotiations. In addition, it is not clear what a 33% reduction in the barriers to trade in services would look like, since the nature of this sector and the barriers it faces are substantially different from those that exist in the manufacturing and agricultural sectors and the barriers in the services sector do not lend themselves to a similar process of reciprocal exchange of market access.

Economic activities that comprise the services sector range from such business services as accounting, financial, and architectural activities to a broad range of consumer services that are not easily defined and categorized.[36] Anticipating the effects of liberalizing trade in these areas is difficult for most nations because they do not know the full extent of the barriers their exports face. In addition, nations are grappling with a subtle, but important, distinction in the services sector between liberalizing barriers to market access that involve eliminating discrimination in the treatment of foreign and domestic services providers and governmental activities that involve a range of regulatory and supervisory activities, especially in the areas of public health and safety, the environment, and clean water and air standards. Such issues become even more complicated in countries like the United States where regulatory responsibilities are shared by the federal, state, and local governments, and professional governing bodies.

Implications for Congress

The United States currently is involved in negotiating an assortment of trade agreements. These agreements range from bilateral agreements with trading partners that account for very small shares of total U.S. trade to multinational trade agreements that could have a significant effect on certain U.S. workers, industries, and businesses. At some point, Congress may well be asked to consider legislation that implements these agreements. In doing so, it may consider a number of different, and perhaps conflicting, objectives and it will be presented with data and information that emphasize differing viewpoints on how the agreements will affect the economy and the nation.

Econometric modeling, aided by recent advances, can assist policymakers in analyzing the economic effects of trade agreements. These models are particularly helpful in exploring the effects of trade liberalization in such sectors as agriculture and manufacturing where the barriers to trade are identifiable and subject to some quantifiable estimates. In most cases, these barriers are represented by tariffs or quotas that can be adjusted on a reciprocal basis. Barriers to trade in the services sector, however, are proving to be more difficult to identify and, therefore, to quantify in an econometric model. Although progress is being made, it likely will be some time before the models can provide realistic estimates of the effects of trade liberalization in this sector. The models, however, do provide a sense of the magnitude of economic effects that can be expected to occur across sectors in the economy. This is especially helpful in identifying which sectors likely will experience the greatest adjustment costs.

There are drawbacks to using the econometric models. Such modeling is highly sensitive to the assumptions that are used to establish the parameters of the model and are hampered by a serious lack of comprehensive data in the services sector. Such shortcomings likely will not be as apparent in analysis of bilateral trade agreements between the United States and another trading partner, but they likely will become important when the analysis involves a large number of countries, such as in a regional or multilateral trade agreement. In addition, these models likely understate the adjustment costs that are inevitably involved in liberalizing trade and they may well understate the positive effects of trade liberalization over the long run, because such effects are beyond the time-frame of the estimates. As a result, it is possible that trade liberalization may have a larger positive impact on the U.S. economy over the long term than most economic models indicate. Nevertheless, even if the derived benefits from multilateral negotiations were twice as great as the most optimistic estimates indicate, except for unilateral reductions in trade barriers in all countries, the overall impact on the U.S. economy is expected to be modest, at best. The effects on the economy from liberalizing trade on a bilateral basis through the proposed bilateral free trade arrangements will yield especially minor gains for the U.S. economy.

Congress may choose to reject any trade agreement in favor of maintaining the status quo, or it may choose to circumvent the arduous task of negotiating multilateral trade agreements and unilaterally remove all barriers to U.S. trade. While unilaterally removing all trade barriers would please economic purists, it is unlikely given the issues it would raise and the prospects that it would leave U.S. negotiators with few bargaining chips during trade negotiations. Such an action likely would engender a public backlash, particularly from those labor and trade groups that would be most directly affected by such a policy. In addition, the task of demonstrating the benefits of liberalizing trade is complicated by the fact that the short term adjustment costs associated with trade liberalization are difficult to equate clearly with the benefits that accrue slowly over time. This means that it is difficult to demonstrate conclusively at the early stages of negotiations that the long-term benefits of trade liberalization will outweigh the short-term adjustment costs.

Given these prospects, it seems likely to assume that policymakers will weigh the benefits of greater trade liberalization against the anticipated dislocations for workers and industries and determine whether to accept or reject each agreement on the basis of a broad set of factors. While such analyses cannot forecast every outcome, they can aid policymakers in assessing which industries and sectors likely will experience the highest adjustment costs and, therefore, which industries and groups may need assistance in receiving training or other assistance. Often, Congress has addressed trade-induced changes through trade adjustment assistance for workers and firms displaced as a result of trade agreements and trade liberalization. Such assistance has often been promoted as a principle of fairness by spreading out the adjustment costs beyond those most directly affected, and as a method for persuading those who are affected to buy into the changes by reallocating some of the gains from those who benefit to those who bare the greatest share of the adjustment costs. These adjustment costs likely will rise if the scope of trade agreements expand beyond single trading partner to incorporate large numbers of trading partners.

REFERENCES

[1] For additional information and status of the current negotiations, see CRS Report RL33463, *Trade Negotiations During the 110th Congress*, by Ian F. Fergusson.

[2] CRS Report RL32060, World Trade Organization Negotiations: The Doha Development Agenda, by Ian F. Fergusson.

[3] CRS Report RS20864, A Free Trade Area of the Americas: Status of Negotiations and Major Policy Issues, by J. F. Hornbeck.

[4] CRS Report RS21387, United States - Southern African Customs Union Free Trade Agreement Negotiations: Background and Potential, by Danielle Langton.

[5] See [http://www.whitehouse.gov/news/releases/2002/10/20021026-7.html].

[6] CRS Report RL32770, *Andean-U.S. Free Trade Agreement Negotiations*, by M. Angeles Villarreal.

[7] CRS Report RL31870, The U.S.-Central American Free Trade Agreement (CAFTA): Challenges for Sub-Regional Integration, by J.F. Hornbeck.

[8] CRS Report RS21846, Proposed U.S.-Bahrain Free Trade Agreement, by Martin A. Weiss.

[9] CRS Report RL31144, The U.S.-Chile Free Trade Agreement: Economic and Trade Policy Issues, by J.F. Hornbeck.

[10] CRS Report RS22419, *U.S.-Colombia Trade Promotion Agreement*, by M. Angeles Villarreal.

[11] CRS Report RS21464, *Morocco - U.S. Free Trade Agreement*, by Raymond J. Ahearn.

[12] CRS Report RL32540, The Proposed U.S.-Panama Free Trade Agreement, by J.F. Hornbeck.

[13] CRS Report RS22391, *U.S.-Peru Trade Promotion Agreement*, by M. Angeles Villarreal.

[14] CRS Report RL31789, *The U.S.-Singapore Free Trade Agreement*, by Dick K. Nanto.

[15] CRS Report RL33435, *The Proposed South Korea-U.S. Free Trade Agreement (KORUS FTA)*, by William H. Cooper and Mark E. Manyin.

[16] CRS Report RL33445, The Proposed U.S. -Malaysia Free Trade Agreement, by Michael F. Martin.

[17] Economic trade theory argues that natural resources, which serve as the building blocks of production within an economy, are limited at any one point in time, whereas demands for those resources are unlimited, creating a scarcity of resources. This scarcity of resources means that nations strive to use their resources in the most efficient way possible in order to maximize the goods and services that are available to their citizens, a common definition of a nation's standard of living. Nations then specialize in the production of certain goods and then trade with other nations for the goods they do not produce. These concepts of specialization and trade lead to the conclusion that a nation will find that it is in its economic self-interest to engage in trade with other nations even if it can produce all goods and services at a lower cost

than any other nation. By specializing in the production of those goods and services in which it is most efficient, or in which it has a comparative advantage, a nation maximizes its total productive capability and national income.

[18] Gottschalk, Peter, and Timothy M. Smeeding, Cross-National Comparisons of Earnings and Income Inequality. *Journal of Economic Literature*, June 1997. p. 645.

[19] Krugman, Paul R. *Rethinking International Trade*. Cambridge, The MIT Press, 1990; Romer, Paul M. Capital, Labor, and Productivity. *Brookings Papers on Economic Activity: Microeconomics 1990*. Washington, the Brookings Institution. p. 337-367; Romer, Paul M. Increasing Returns and Long-Run Growth. *Journal of Political Economy*, October 1986. p. 1002-1037; Grossman, Gene M., and Elhanan Helpman. *Endogenous Product Cycles*. Cambridge, National Bureau of Economic Research, March 1989. (Working Paper No. 2913).

[20] *The Dynamic Effects of Trade Liberalization: A Survey*. Washington, United States International Trade Commission. (USITC Publication 2608). February, 1993. p. 11.

[21] A compilation of studies can be found in: Brown, Drusilla K., and Robert M. Stern, Measurement and Modeling of the Economic Effects of Trade and Investment Barriers in Services. The *Review of International Economics*, May 2001; Hoekman, Bernard, the Next Round of Services Negotiations: Identifying Priorities and Options. *Review*, Federal Reserve Bank of St. Louis, July/August 2000; and Dihel, Nora, *Quantification of the Costs to National Welfare of Barriers to Trade in Services: Scoping Paper*. Paris, Organization for Economic Cooperation and Development, November 21, 2000.

[22] Gravity models have been used for 40 years to estimate trade flows between countries. They are based on the conclusion that the volume of exports between any two trading partners is an increasing function of their national incomes, and a decreasing function of the distance between them. Although the models have been criticized for lacking a strong theoretical basis, recent work has demonstrated that the model is consistent with the Ricardian and Heckscher-Ohlin models. An important drawback of the model is that it can estimate only the aggregate flows of goods, but it does not provide any information about the effects on labor or on individual sectors in the economy. See Wall, Howard, J., Using the Gravity Model to Estimate the Costs of Protection. *Review*, Federal Reserve Bank of St. Louis, January/February, 1999. p. 39.

[23] Rivera, Sandra A., Key Methods for Quantifying the Effects of Trade Liberalization. *International Economic Review*, January/February 2003. p. 2-5.

[24] Zarazaga, Carlos, E.J.M., Measuring the Benefits of Unilateral Trade Liberalization Part 1: Static Models. *Economic and Financial Review*, Federal Reserve Bank of Dallas, Third Quarter 1999. p. 15; also see Zarazaga, Carlos, E.J.M., Measuring the Benefits of Unilateral Trade Liberalization Part 2: Dynamic Models. *Economic and Financial Review*, Federal Reserve Bank of Dallas, First Quarter 2000.

[25] Now known as the Michigan Brown-Deardorff-Stern Model, the Michigan Model of World Production and Trade includes data on 29 industrial sectors for 18 industrialized countries and 16 newly industrialized and developing countries.

[26] Brown, Drusilla K., Alan V. Deardorff, and Robert M. Stern, *Multilateral, Regional, and Bilateral Trade-Policy Options for the United States and Japan*. Research Seminar in International Economics, Discussion Paper No. 490, The University of Michigan, December 16, 2002. Table 1; and Brown, Drusilla K., Alan V. Deardorff, and Robert M. Stern, *Computational Analysis of Multilateral Trade Liberalization in the Uruguay*

Round and Doha Development Round. Research Seminar in International Economics, Discussion Paper No. 489, The University of Michigan, December 8, 2002.

[27] Reducing agricultural import tariffs lowers import prices and spurs the substitution of imports for domestic production, causing the domestic industry to contract. The extent of this contraction would depend on whether the tariff reduction in the U.S. sector was more or less than in other countries. Reducing export subsidies lowers world prices; similarly, reducing production subsidies raises prices. The net of these effects depends on the extent of tariffs and subsidies in the domestic economy prior to reduction and on reductions in domestic tariffs and subsidies relative to similar reductions abroad.

[28] According to authors of the study, the estimated economic effects of the FTAA should be considered as the most positive effects that are possible under the proposed terms of the agreement. These effects are expected to accrue over a considerable period of time and that the process of negotiations could be hampered by less than full compliance on the part of some of the members of the FTAA.

[29] Brown, Drusilla K., Kozo Kiyota, and Robert M. Stern, *Computational Analysis of the U.S. FTA With the Southern African Customs Union (SACU).* Research Seminar in International Economics, Discussion Paper No. 545, May 31, 2006.

[30] The estimates for job losses in services is surprising and is a product of the particular estimating method used in the model. For a more complete explanation see page 14 of this report.

[31] Brown, and Stern, Measurement and Modeling of the Economic Effects of Trade and Investment Barriers in Services, p. 280.

[32] Hoekman, Bernard, The Next Round of Services Negotiations: Identifying Priorities and Options. *Review*, the Federal Reserve Bank of St. Louis, July/August 2000. p. 38.

[33] Nicoletti, Giuseppe, *The Economy-Wide Effects of Product Market Policies.* Paris, Organization for Economic Cooperation and Development, 4-5 March 2002.

[34] Hoekman, The Next Round of Services Negotiations: Identifying Priorities and Options, p. 37.

[35] Ibid., p. 41.

[36] For instance, see the scope of the U.S. services offer at the Doha round: CRS Report RS21492, *Services Negotiations in the WTO: An Overview of the U.S. Offer*, by James K. Jackson.

In: Trade Policies and Agreements in the Era of Globalization ISBN: 978-1-60021-836-1
Editor: Paul B. Lucus, pp. 95-114

Chapter 4

U.S. TRADE POLICY AND THE CARIBBEAN: FROM TRADE PREFERENCES TO FREE TRADE AGREEMENTS*

J. F. Hornbeck

ABSTRACT

For over 40 years, the United States has relied on unilateral trade preferences to promote export-led development in poor countries. Congressionally authorized trade preferences give market access to selected developing country goods, duty-free or at tariffs below normal rates, without requiring reciprocal trade concessions. The Caribbean Basin has benefitted from multiple preferential trade arrangements, the best known being those linked to the Caribbean Basin Initiative (CBI) begun in the mid-1980s. Since then, the growing number of reciprocal U.S. free trade agreements (FTAs) in the region have effectively replaced preferential trade arrangements, signaling a shift in U.S. trade policy and raising questions with respect to the future of those mostly smaller countries still relying on trade preferences. This report discusses the evolution of U.S. trade policy toward the Caribbean, focusing on the implications of moving from unilateral tariff preferences to reciprocal FTAs.

The U.S. Congress has approved multiple trade preference programs over the past three decades (production sharing, GSP, CBERA, CBI II, CBTPA, and HOPE Act of 2006). Each one amended trade rules and tariff preferences in ways designed to increase imports from CBI countries. Trade grew and many of the goals for development were supported. Evaluations of the benefits, however, suggested that they may not have been as robust as originally expected. Benefits tended to be concentrated in a few countries and products, often skirting industries with the greatest potential to stimulate exports. Also, the benefits of preferences are being eroded by multilateral trade liberalization and recently implemented FTAs.

A number of issues and circumstances are converging during the 110th Congress that will be a challenge for U.S. trade policy in the Caribbean region. Among these circumstances are the expiring trade preference programs, their limited use by remaining eligible countries, and the reluctance of these countries to make the transition to an FTA

* Excerpted from CRS Report RL33951, dated April 4, 2007.

with the United States without some guarantee of a "development component" to the agreement. These concerns persist, despite the promise of permanent market access and increased investment that an FTA holds out. The Caribbean countries, long accustomed to dependent economic relationships, appear content to take a cautious and leisurely path toward any new arrangement with the United States.

For U.S. trade policy, which is still committed to achieving regional integration, these circumstances present a special challenge. Broader integration may be difficult to reconcile with the needs of very small developing countries, which are highly vulnerable to the vicissitudes of global economic trends and may require new and creative solutions, particularly if U.S. policy is still driven by the historical focus on development and regional security issues in addition to trade liberalization. In the context of continuing with trade preferences in similar or altered form, or opting for an FTA, the solution is not immediately obvious.

For over 40 years, the United States has relied on unilateral trade preferences as an integral part of its foreign economic policy. Trade preferences give market access to selected developing country goods, duty-free or at tariffs below normal (NTR)[1] rates, without requiring reciprocal trade concessions. They come in many forms and are intended to promote economic growth and development in poor countries by stimulating export promotion and investment, and to encourage the use of U.S. inputs in foreign manufacturing. Trade preference programs must be authorized by Congress and are usually done so for specific periods of time.

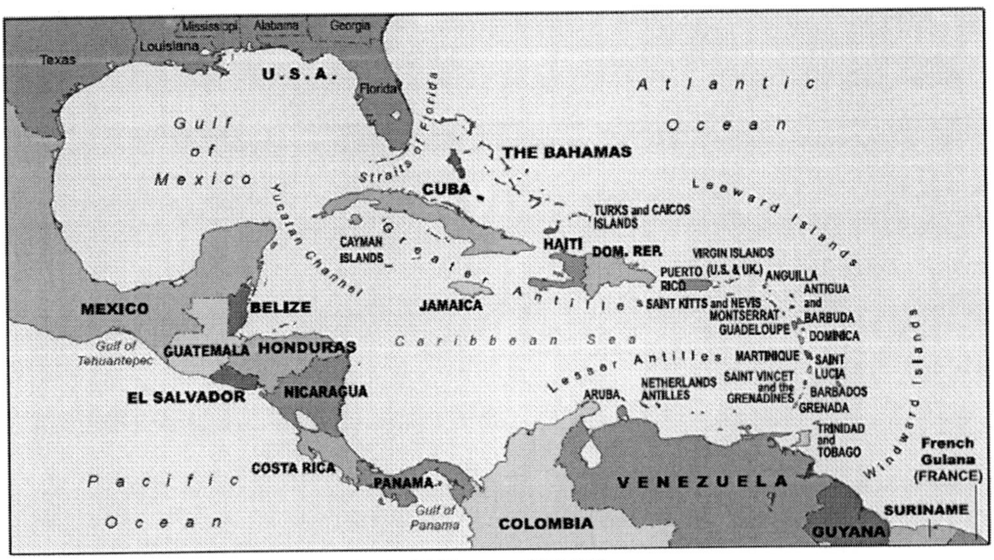

Source: Map Resources. Adapted by CRS. (K.Yancey 6/30/06).

Figure 1. Map of the Caribbean Basin Region.

The Caribbean Basin (see figure 1)[2] has benefitted from multiple preferential trade arrangements, the best known being those linked to the Caribbean Basin Initiative (CBI) begun in the mid-1980s. Since then, the growth of free trade agreements (FTAs) in the region has signaled a shift in U.S. trade policy, raising questions about the future path for those few countries still dependent on trade preferences. This report reviews the preference programs, discusses how they have been affected by FTAs in the region, and considers trade policy options for dealing with countries still relying on trade preferences, but that have yet to negotiate an FTA with the United States.

U.S. Preferential Trade Programs and the Caribbean Region

The United States has a long history of employing various types of trade incentives to encourage specific trade activities. Motivated by commercial, political, and security interests at times, the U.S. Congress has attempted to create trade preference programs that assist developing countries, while minimizing the negative economic impact on domestic producers and workers. Over time, bilateral, regional, and multilateral trade agreements have come to eclipse the importance of preference agreements, a trend that a review of these developments will show has been particularly visible in the Caribbean Basin.

Background: Early Trade Preference Programs

In 1964, the United States Government initiated a preferential tariff program based on production sharing. Production sharing is a cost-reducing business strategy that seeks competitive advantage by locating manufacturing processes in more than one country. U.S. firms specialize in the capital intensive, technology driven stages of production, and outsource assembly and other lower-skill processing to low-wage countries. Under the U.S. production-sharing program, foreign firms that import U.S. component parts and assemble or process them into finished or semi-finished products may then re-export them back to the United States, with duties levied only on the value added abroad (no tariff on U.S. content).[3]

U.S. firms benefit from production sharing by the required use of their inputs (to receive the tariff exemption) and in retaining a portion of the global market for goods that might otherwise go to lower-cost producers that do not use U.S. inputs. Foreign firms using U.S. inputs benefit from the tariff exemption, making their products more competitive in the U.S. market relative to those of other producers who face a duty on the full value of their exports. This type of production arrangement has been commonly used for automobile parts, electronics, and apparel, among other products.[4]

The Caribbean Basin and Mexico were early beneficiaries of the production sharing program, with proximity providing a major advantage at that time. Lower transportation costs and quicker turn around times have provided Mexican, Caribbean, and Central America producers with an additional competitive factor over their more distant, but lower cost Asian competitors. Many Caribbean countries developed their export processing zones around this program, particularly various niches in the apparel business.

By the 1970s, the concept of preference programs for developing countries shifted. Whereas production sharing was based on a mutually beneficial competitive business strategy, developing countries had long advocated unilateral trade preferences as a form of development assistance. Under the auspices of the General Agreement on Tariffs and Trade

(GATT), the Generalized System of Preferences (GSP) was conceived as a way for developed countries to respond to this expressed need. The GSP permits developed countries to grant unilateral tariff preferences for selected imports from developing countries to promote export-led growth. The U.S. program provides limited tariff incentives for many, but not all products. The Caribbean region has availed itself of both the GSP and production sharing incentives for many years. The U.S. GSP program requires periodic renewal by Congress and was last reauthorized through December 31, 2008.[5]

The tariff preference model as development strategy continued to evolve in the 1980s. The next step targeted specific regions of the world for deeper preferences, a strategy driven by security, as well as economic and political interests of the United States. Congress enacted the first such geographically targeted program for the Caribbean region in 1983.[6]

The Caribbean Basin Economic Recovery Act of 1983

The impetus to create a Caribbean trade preference program arose from concern over the region's economic collapse and concomitant political radicalization that materialized in the early 1980s. The Caribbean's Basin's "proximity, vulnerability, and instability" has long made it of particular strategic interest to the United States, a notion well established in U.S. political history dating to the Monroe Doctrine.[7] In light of this reasoning, President Reagan and many Members of Congress agreed to consider a comprehensive response to the Caribbean Basin's troubles. Trade preferences would emerge as the primary economic component.

President Reagan unveiled the CBI in a speech before the Organization of American States on February 24, 1982, arguing that ensuring economic and political stability in the Caribbean region was vital to U.S. security interests. He proposed a controversial mix of tax incentives, aid, and trade preferences. The idea was rejected by many, however, particularly import-competing firms and workers. As a consequence, the first bill died in the 97th Congress.[8] In the 98th Congress, however, Congress acted promptly on the Caribbean Basin Economic Recovery Act (CBERA).[9] Although it again drew stiff resistence from labor interests, once scaled back to modest duty-free treatment for only 10% of Caribbean imports, it passed with overwhelming support in both the House (392-12) and the Senate (90-7).[10] President Reagan signed it into law on August 5, 1983 (P.L. 98-67) and the preferences went into effect on January 1, 1984.

The CBERA stipulated that 27 countries could be designated by the President as beneficiary countries (24 eventually were — see Appendix 1) to receive duty-free or reduced-duty access for selected exports provided the countries meet specific conditions. Designation is prohibited if the country: 1) is a Communist country; 2) has seized U.S. property without compensation; 3) fails to recognize or enforce awards arbitrated in favor of U.S. citizens; 4) affords preferential treatment to goods from other countries to the detriment of U.S. commerce; 5) broadcasts U.S. copyrighted material without permission; 6) has not signed an extradition agreement with the United States, or 7) is not taking steps to afford internationally recognized worker rights. Eligibility can be suspended if a country fails to meet these criteria. Thus, the unilateral nature of the arrangement is clear: meet U.S.-defined eligibility criteria and selective imports will be granted trade preferences. No negotiation is involved.[11]

Provided a good is wholly the "growth, product, or manufacture" of, and imported directly from, a beneficiary country, it may enter the United States duty free or at a reduced rate of duty. There were, however, significant exceptions for articles defined by Congress as "import sensitive." These included textiles and apparel subject to textile agreements under the Multi-Fiber Arrangement (MFA),[12] a sector that has seen diminished employment from foreign competition, petroleum products, footwear, handbags, luggage, flat goods, work gloves, leather wearing apparel, canned tuna, and watches or watch parts. Under the rules of origin, 35% of the article's value of labor and parts had to originate in a beneficiary country, although some 15% of the 35% could be of U.S. origin.[13]

A number of special provisions also applied. First, all Caribbean imports were still subject to safeguard measures (resumption of tariffs) if the imports were shown to increase quantities to a level that would hurt U.S. producers. Also, special treatment was afforded to some import-sensitive goods. CBERA gave ethanol imports duty-free entry if produced under certain conditions[14] and sugar imports from the region entered under a tariff rate quota (TRQ) — duty free up to a specified quota and then taxed at prohibitively high levels.

Congress also required that the United States International Trade Commission (USITC) produce regular reports on the effects of the preference program. The USITC found that for the first five years, the impact was relatively small, with imports from beneficiary countries expanding at slower rates than imports from the rest of the world. CBERA eligible products, nonetheless, grew from 6.7% of total imports from CBERA beneficiary countries in 1984, to 7.4% in 1985, 11.1% in 1986, 12.7% in 1987, and 13.0% in 1988. Even these numbers overstate the effects because there was an increasing shift from use of duty-free access under GSP to CBERA, so the total value of duty-free goods entering from the CBERA beneficiary countries was nearly steady, rather than expanding.

Special Access Program

Under CBERA, textile and apparel products were excluded from receiving tariff reductions, despite the fact that they are a major manufacturing export (and job creating) sector for the region. Textile and apparel articles are considered highly import sensitive in the United States and elsewhere, and their trade was controlled by quotas defined in bilateral textile agreements permitted under the MFA. In 1986, President Reagan, by executive order, established a Special Access Program (SAP) that granted guaranteed access levels (GALs) for apparel from eligible CBERA countries, provided it was assembled from fabric formed and cut in the United States.[15]

Following implementation of the SAP, there was an immediate large increase in apparel imports from CBI countries. It is important to recognize, however, that this increase occurred because of changes in U.S. textile policy, not the CBERA, which did not provide preferential tariff rates for imports from Caribbean producers. The increase in demand for Caribbean apparel articles at this time was evident nonetheless, driven by their relatively low cost, production proximity, and the higher quota levels that Asian producers still faced. Tariffs on textile and apparel goods from the CBI countries, however, remained a significant barrier and would not be addressed in legislation until 2000.[16]

The Caribbean Basin Economic Recovery Expansion Act of 1990

Soon after the original CBERA went into force, concern over the effectiveness of its trade preferences surfaced. Two issues stood out: 1) expanding the program to include a greater number of Caribbean goods, and 2) making the program permanent. The legislation as initially proposed would have extended additional tariff benefits to textiles, apparel, sugar, petroleum, leather goods, and other items left out of the 1983 legislation. It also would have repealed the September 30, 1995 termination date, making the duty preferences permanent.

As the initiative made its way through the legislative process, however, many of the preferences that might have had the greatest economic impact on the Caribbean, like the textiles and apparel provisions, were stripped from the bill. This change allowed the Caribbean Basin Economic Expansion Act of 1990 (referred to as "CBI II") to be passed as Title II of the Customs and Trade Act (P.L. 101-382). It made permanent the existing CBI preferences for beneficiary countries, but extended them only to a few new products. Changes included a limited phased-in tariff reduction for handbags, luggage, flat goods, work gloves, and leather goods not eligible for GSP treatment, and duty-free and quota-free treatment for articles other than textiles, apparel, and petroleum products that are assembled or processed from U.S. components. There were also new limited benefits for ethanol imports and a few non-trade incentives. CBI imports were also given an exception from antidumping (AD) and countervailing duty (CVD) cumulation rules, making it harder to show that U.S. firms had experienced material injury from those imports.

The Caribbean Basin Trade Partnership Act and NAFTA Parity

On January 1, 1994, NAFTA took effect, altering the relative tariff situation in the region, thereby igniting a debate over parity issues among competing trade agreements and arrangements. Imports from Mexico received much reduced tariffs or duty-free treatment under NAFTA, which as it phased in over 14 years, would make for an increasingly large benefit to Mexico. Preferential access for textile and apparel goods would be applied not only to the value of U.S. content, but importantly, to the value added in Mexican production. Imports were subject to detailed rules of origin generally limiting content of traded goods to materials made in the NAFTA countries, thus excluding CBI countries. The effects seemed apparent; two-way trade in textiles and apparel between the United States and Mexico rose 218% from 1993 to 2002.[17]

NAFTA eliminated much of the relative trade advantage that the CBI countries had enjoyed over Mexico since 1984, and gave Mexico a distinct advantage in apparel production, which was a dominant export sector for the Caribbean countries as well. Mexico's much larger economy and production capacity for textiles and apparel became an immediate threat to income and employment in the CBI countries, which began to lobby for U.S. trade preferences equal to those of Mexico. This became known as the CBI/NAFTA parity issue.[18]

While some in Congress were sympathetic to CBI country claims, particularly after region's devastation from Hurricanes Georges and Mitch in 1998, it took years to gather the support to pass legislation. The idea was to provide the CBI countries with NAFTA-equivalent preferences until such a time that they could either accede to NAFTA, or enter into a similar reciprocal FTA with the United States. Because textile and apparel trade was at the heart of the program, the legislation had to overcome resistence from import-competing U.S. manufacturers. Nonetheless, on May 18, 2000, following Congressional passage, the Caribbean Basin Trade Partnership Act (CBTPA — P.L. 106-200) was signed into law, extending additional benefits for a "transition period" of eight years ending September 30, 2008, or until a beneficiary country signs an FTA with the United States.[19]

Eligibility for CBTPA benefits include all those under CBERA, plus an additional emphasis on countries meeting their trade obligations under the World Trade Organization (WTO) and making progress toward some type of FTA with the United States.[20] The most important provisions provide that certain articles excluded from CBERA that meet NAFTA rules of origin may receive NAFTA tariff treatment, specifically: canned tuna, petroleum products, footwear, handbags, luggage, flat goods, work gloves, and leather-wearing apparel.

Textile and apparel articles were also given essentially NAFTA-equivalent treatment. Those assembled in beneficiary countries are eligible for duty-free and quota-free treatment subject to rules of origin, provided they are assembled from fabrics made and cut from U.S. yarns.[21] However, articles in which the fabric is also cut in the CBTPA country may also enter duty free, if the parts are sewn together with U.S. thread. Limited amounts of knit apparel (not socks) using U.S. yarns are also given duty-free treatment, as are certain brassieres, handloomed, handmade, and folklore articles, textile luggage, and articles made from materials not available, or materials demonstrated not to be available in commercial quantities, in the United States. The apparel duty preferences were later modified in the Trade Act of 2002, requiring that imported knit and woven garments using U.S. fabric be dyed, printed, and finished in the United States.[22] The CBTPA also prohibits illegal transshipment of textile and apparel products and directs the President to have the USTR convene meetings with CBTPA beneficiary countries to encourage movement toward a free trade agreement with the United States.

CAFTA-DR and New Parity Issues

When the Dominican Republic-Central America-United States Free Trade Agreement (CAFTA-DR) was implemented on March 1, 2006 (P.L. 109-53), the trade preference landscape shifted again.[23] CAFTA-DR leads to nearly full free trade between the United States and member countries when it is fully implemented. Provisions covering textile and apparel, the largest import category from the region, were enhanced from those offered under CBTPA and made permanent.[24] They provide for immediate elimination of duties on textiles and apparel that meet rules of origin. These rules are even more relaxed than in other preferential agreements and FTAs, including the CBTPA. Stated briefly, provided components are sourced in any one of the member countries (the cumulation rule), the finished assembled product may be exported to the United States duty free. Generally, the intent of the agreement is to build on the history of increasingly flexible CBI programs that allow apparel producers in the region to combine materials and production in various ways and still receive duty-free access to the U.S. market.[25]

CAFTA-DR, much like NAFTA a decade earlier, created parity problems for other producers in the region that cannot export under these relaxed rules of origin or reduced tariffs. Mexico was one, but the United States agreed in January 2007 to harmonize the rules of origin as applied to NAFTA and CAFTA, which will allow Mexican and Central American producers to use each other's inputs without penalty, further integrating the region's apparel production.[26] Haiti was not included in this deal, which caused Congress subsequently to pass separate legislation covering Haitian apparel imports (see below). The rest of the CBI countries, however, are at a disadvantage relative to NAFTA, CAFTA-DR, and Haiti with respect to trade preferences in general, and apparel trade in particular.

The HOPE Act of 2006: New Haiti Trade Preferences

In part to respond to concerns over Haiti's apparel parity issue, Congress made the latest change to the CBI programs with passage of the Haitian Hemispheric Opportunity through Partnership Encouragement (HOPE) Act of 2006, Title V of the Tax Relief and Health Care Act of 2006 (P.L. 109-432). It was implemented on March 19, 2007. Congress provided the poorest country in the hemisphere with trade preferences in addition to those already available under the GSP, CBERA, and CBTPA. Eligibility criteria includes making progress toward achieving a market-based economy, enhancing the rule of law, eliminating barriers to U.S. trade, combating corruption, and protecting internationally recognized human and worker rights, among other institutional goals that have historically proven difficult for Haiti to achieve.[27]

The major benefits are tariff preferences for Haitian produced textile and apparel goods, including more flexible rules of origin than those applied to apparel imports from other countries. Apparel goods wholly assembled or knit to shape in, and imported directly from, Haiti receive duty-free treatment. The major difference is that Haitian firms may use components from third countries. This benefit, however, is limited. A certain percentage of material and processing cost, rising from 50% in year one to 60% in year five, must originate in Haiti, the United States, or a country that has a preference program or FTA with the United States. There are also quantitative restrictions. The Haiti program is set to expire in 2012.

Because 90% of Haiti's exports to the United States are woven and knit apparel, the HOPE Act potentially provides an important competitive advantage to Haitian garment producers over others in the region. Textile and apparel interests in the United States lobbied against the more generous rules of origin precisely because they would encourage apparel producers to move to Haiti from other locations in the region in order to use less expensive Asian inputs, to the possible detriment of U.S. producers.[28] Two issues currently dominate the implementation of the HOPE Act, administering the very complex rules of origin and making a realistic assessment of Haiti's ability to meet the eligibility criteria.

Trade Effects of Tariff Preferences

To promote export-led growth in CBI countries, the U.S. Congress has approved multiple trade preference programs over the past three decades (production sharing, GSP, CBERA, CBI II, CBTPA, and HOPE Act of 2006), as well as two free trade agreements (NAFTA and CAFTA-DR). Each one amended trade rules and tariff preferences in ways designed to increase U.S. imports from CBI countries. Although legislative action at the close of the 109th

Congress focused on enhancing Haiti trade preferences, there has been a longer term trend toward the use of free trade agreements in the region. Before considering this change, this section assesses the effects of unilateral trade preference programs by identifying changing trends in U.S. imports from the CBI countries.[29]

Imports by Duty Category

Table 1 displays trends in U.S. imports from CBI countries since the CBTPA program began. Imports are presented as entering either as dutiable or duty free under various preference programs.[30] It is important to distinguish between two types of trends in the tariff preference programs: those that allow new categories of goods to enter the United States duty free, counted as increased trade because of trade preferences, and those that merely switch goods from one preference category to another (e.g. from GSP to CBTPA), accounting for no real preferential trade growth. As may be seen in the top three rows of the table, the dutiable value, calculated duty, and average duty applied to CBI imports all show a downward trend from 2000 to 2004, reinforcing the corresponding percentage increase in the value of duty-free imports entering the United States shown in the seventh row.

In the second section of the table, note that the dutiable value of total imports has fallen from 35% to 21%, reflecting two trends: final implementation of the WTO Uruguay Round commitments, which shifted some imports from the CBERA to the NTR (other) duty-free category, and more significantly, the implementation of CBTPA for textile and apparel articles. Note that by 2004, most goods with duties entered the United States under the "other dutiable" category or NTR rates.[31]

The real story can be seen in the duty-free categories. The duty-free portion of U.S. imports of CBI goods has grown from 65% to 79% in the four years ending 2004. Note, however, that there has been no significant change in the percentage of duty-free goods entering under the CBERA, GSP, or "other duty free" categories. Articles coming in under the older production sharing program, by contrast, have fallen sharply. There has also been a slight increase in the portion of goods coming in NTR duty-free, while those entering under CBTPA grew suddenly once it was fully implemented. Taken together, these trends point to both a switch in apparel goods entering under the CBTPA that previously entered under production sharing preferences, and modest increase in the value of new imports eligible for duty-free treatment.[32]

The last two rows of table 1 highlight that the total imports entering under the combined CBERA and CBTPA provisions rose from 12.6% of total CBI imports in 2000 to 39.7% in 2004. In addition, the amount that entered exclusively from these preferences, that is, could not have entered under any other program such as GSP, rose from 6.8% of total imports to 30.1%. This trend reinforces the fact that the original CBERA program seemed to have had limited effect, whereas the CBTPA textile and apparel preferences appeared to have provided a more robust response.[33]

Nearly all these trends are consistent with the intent, expectations, and evolution of the preferences programs, but demonstrate that for nearly 17 years the effects of preference programs were less than might have been expected, until the CBTPA was implemented. The CBTPA trade appeared quickly, but stabilized by 2002. The increase in the NTR duty-free category is the one possible anomaly, which along with understanding the specific effects of each preference program, requires a more detailed analysis at the product level.

Table 1. U.S. Imports from CBI Countries by Dutiable Category, 2000-2004

Duty Import Category:	2000	2001	2002	2003	2004
- Dutiable Value, all imports ($ mil)	7,778	5,590	5,462	4,902	5,770
- Calculated Duty ($ thousands)	915	578	496	513	457
- Average Duty (%)	11.8	10.3	9.1	10.5	7.9
Dutiable Value — All Imports: (%)	35.2	27.2	25.8	20.2	21.0
- Production sharing	12.7	6.8	4.7	3.8	3.8
- Other dutiable	22.5	20.4	21.1	16.4	17.2
Duty-free Value — All Imports: (%)	64.7	72.9	74.2	79.8	79.0
- NTR	30.1	27.3	27.5	33.2	35.4
- Production sharing	21.0	6.7	3.6	2.1	2.2
- CBERA	11.7	12.7	13.7	12.2	11.0
- CBTPA	0.7	24.9	28.6	30.7	28.8
- GSP	0.9	0.9	0.4	1.0	1.3
- Other duty-free	0.3	0.4	0.4	0.5	0.3
Imports entering CBERA/CBTPA (%)	12.6	40.2	47.1	42.6	39.7
Exclusively under CBERA/CBTPA*(%)	6.8	22.9	31.5	30.2	30.1

Data source: USITC. The Impact of the Caribbean Basin Economic Recovery Act. Seventeenth Report, 2003-2004. September 2005. pp. 2-10, 2-11, and 3-4.

* Means goods would not have entered duty free under any other program.

Product Trends

Not all CBI exports were affected equally by the various tariff preference programs. Major product categories are shown in figure 2, three of which stand out: knit apparel, woven apparel, and mineral fuels. In 2006, mineral fuels, knitted, and non-knitted apparel composed 57% of U.S. imports from CBI countries. The mineral fuels group stands apart as a combination of products that received new benefits under CBTPA or entered NTR duty free when the final Uruguay Round commitments phased in, and were therefore, switched out of the CBERA category. The percentage increase also reflects recent increases in energy prices. Liquified natural gas, anhydrous ammonia, heavy fuel oil, and light fuel oil have NTR rates of 0.1% or less, and account for the increase in the portion of duty-free NTR goods.[34]

Trends in the apparel industry are more germane to this report as the key value-added export industry targeted at the United States market, and as a main focus of CBTPA. Table 1 indicates that there has been an increase in the value of duty-free apparel goods that entered under CBTPA as discussed above, largely attributable to preferences that encouraged a shift in content mix of apparel that for the first time allows fabrics to be cut in the region. Yet, as the USITC has noted, from 2000 to 2004, U.S. imports of apparel goods from the CBI countries were unchanged at 12%-13% of total apparel imports worldwide,[35] implying that even with growth in imports from these preferences, the CBI countries have only been able to maintain market share relative to the world's other apparel producers.

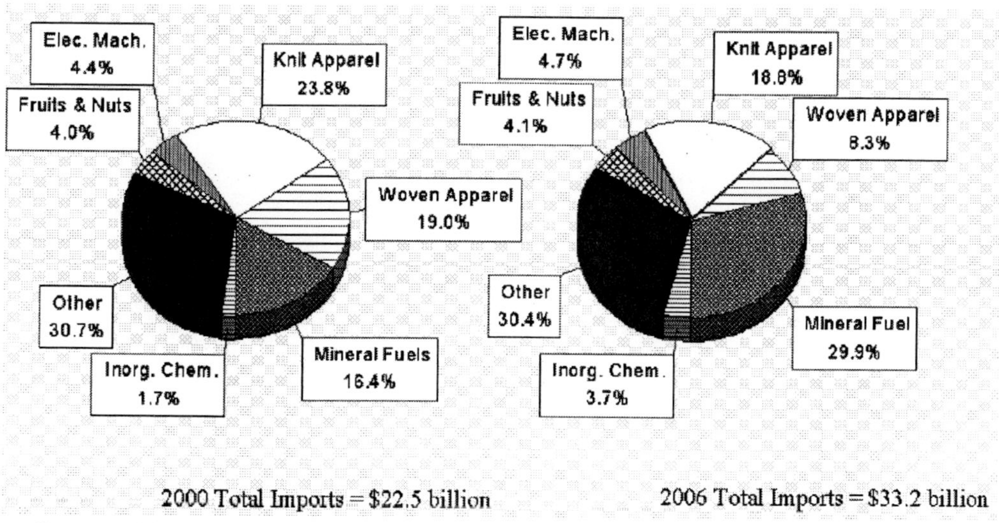

Data Sources: U.S. Department of Commerce.

Figure 2. U.S. Imports from CBI Countries, 2000 and 2006 (by major product category).

Country Trends

There were 24 countries in the original CBERA group until the CAFTA-DR took effect (see Appendix 1). Once implemented, the CAFTA-DR benefits replaced those under CBERA and the CBTPA. U.S. imports from all 24 countries from 2000 to 2006 are presented in table 2 and by product in figure 2. Among the most noticeable trends for 2005, the last year all 24 countries received CBI preferences, are:

- 51% of U.S. imports originated in only three CBI countries; 90% in the top eight;
- the number one exporter by value is Trinidad and Tobago, which with Aruba's high trade value, is explained by energy exports (see also figure 2);
- the other top exporters to the United States (Dominican Republic, Costa Rica, Guatemala, Honduras, El Salvador) are all major apparel manufacturers, with Costa Rica's trade increasingly dominated by semiconductors, which enter NTR duty free (details not shown);
- the top six CBI exporting countries, not including energy producers Trinidad and Tobago and Aruba, accounted for 95.6% of textile and apparel exports to the United States;
- For 2006, the first year that CAFTA-DR was in effect, imports from the five countries that have so far implemented the agreement (bolded in table 2) were valued at $14.7 billion, or 44% of total imports from the CBI countries. With the inclusion of Costa Rica (a presumed future CAFTA-DR country), this total becomes $18.6 billion, or 56% of total imports from the CBI countries;
- If imports from CAFTA-DR and energy exporting countries are not included, the remaining U.S. imports from the region amount to only 10% of the current total from beneficiary countries, and only a portion of that amount would be eligible for tariff preferences.

To summarize, benefits have been concentrated only in a few key beneficiary countries because of their well-endowed energy related products. The non-energy exports appear to support the conclusion that the CBTPA has had some influence on the export patterns of CBI countries, but the data trends also highlight a shift in duty category (from HTS9802 production sharing to CBTPA), as well as an increase in trade value or volume. As mentioned earlier, total U.S. imports of textile and apparel goods from the CBI countries as a percent of the world import total has remained fairly constant (13%-14%) from 2000 to 2004, and when CAFTA-DR is fully implemented, over half of the exports from eligible countries that account for most of the apparel manufacturing will no longer enter under a CBTPA program.[36] The preferences are effectively being phased out in favor of reciprocal FTAs.

Table 2. U.S. Imports by CBI Country, 2000-2006 ($ millions)

Country	2000	2001	2002	2003	2004	2005	2006#
Trinidad and Tobago	2,228	2,380	2,440	4,334	5,842	7,891	8,370
Dom. Rep.	4,383	4,183	4,169	4,455	4,527	4,604	4,529
Costa Rica	3,539	2,886	3,142	3,364	3,333	3,415	3,844
Honduras	3,090	3,126	3,261	3,313	3,640	3,749	3,718
Guatemala	2,607	2,589	2,796	2,947	3,154	3,137	3,100
Aruba	1,536	1,034	774	955	1,776	2,920	2,845
El Salvador	1,933	1,880	1,982	2,020	2,052	1,989	1,856
Nicaragua	588	604	680	770	990	1,181	1,526
Neth. Antilles	719	485	362	632	435	922	1,119
Jamaica	648	461	396	423	320	376	520
Haiti	297	263	255	332	371	447	496
Bahamas	275	314	450	479	638	700	453
Panama	307	291	303	302	316	327	378
Belize	94	97	78	102	107	98	147
Guyana	140	140	116	119	122	120	125
St. Kitts/Nevis	37	41	49	45	42	50	50
Barbados	39	40	34	44	37	32	34
Brit. Virgin Is.	31	12	41	35	17	34	26
St. Lucia	22	29	19	13	14	32	30
Antigua/Barbu.	3	4	4	13	5	4	6
Grenada	27	24	7	8	5	6	5
St. Vincent/the Grenadines	9	23	17	4	4	16	2
Dominica	7	5	5	5	3	3	3
Montserrat	0*	0*	0*	1	0*	1	1
Total	22,559	20,911	21,380	24,715	27,750	32,054	33,183

Data source: U.S. Department of Commerce.

Notes: *less than 0.5 million. # Preliminary estimates. Bold figures reflect imports no longer eligible for CBI benefits because country has implemented the CAFTA-DR agreement.

TRADE PREFERENCE PROGRAMS IN PERSPECTIVE

Since implemented in 1984, the various Caribbean tariff preference programs were intended to assist beneficiary countries with creating an export-led development strategy. The target countries have combined U.S. trade preferences with their own market niching strategies based on proximity to the U.S. market that has allowed them to maintain their market share. It is a strategy that may have led to some growth in exports and helped promote the development agenda in many countries.

The effects, however, may have run their course given the growth of large low-cost producers in China, India, Malaysia and other Asian countries. In addition, many economists have long been skeptical about the efficacy of trade preferences as a development strategy, pointing to two areas in particular: design and administration of the preference programs and weak trade effects.

Structural design flaws that limit the effectiveness of unilateral trade preferences is a common concern. Trade preferences are paternalistic in nature; designed by developed countries to give "generous" one-way benefits to developing countries, but as unilateral concessions, they are self-limiting often for political reasons. For example, critics argue that:[37]

- unilateral agreements are non-binding, often subject to renewal, and can be denied or suspended (and have been) on a product or country basis, which can hinder investors from committing more fully to developing economies;
- eligibility criteria are based on foreign policy and political goals of the developed country, often unrelated to enhancing trade performance, so they are not a costless proposition; and
- program details are subject to domestic economic pressures, typically excluding articles that are import sensitive, which can cause the developed country to apply higher than average tariffs on these goods for non-beneficiary countries.

The CBI programs are not immune to some of these criticisms. Beneficiary countries have no say in the design of the tariff preferences, must lobby the U.S. Congress and Executive Branch to make a case for their continuance, must comply with numerous foreign policy and political requirements to maintain eligibility, and have not always been able to export key products under preference programs. Results of the CBERA program disappointed some because of its many limitations. Even with CBI II making the program permanent and the CBTPA adding many new products to the list of eligible exports, including textile and apparel articles, success has not been overwhelming.

Critics also fault preferences for their limited trade effects and the distortions they can introduce into the economies of recipient countries and the global trading system. U.S. tariff preferences offered to the Caribbean countries often:[38]

- replaced tariff with nontariff barriers, usually quantitative restrictions, as is case for CBERA, CBTPA, and the HOPE Act;
- have complicated rules of origin that are costly, cumbersome to implement, and frequently inhibit use of preferences;
- required use of relatively higher-cost U.S. inputs, offsetting the cost competitiveness benefit of the tariff concessions;
- induce trade growth explicitly through trade diversion (Caribbean apparel instead of Asian);

- can bias a country's investment pattern toward particular industries, limiting incentives to diversify their economies, and also prolonging other market-based adjustments;[39]
- can induce recipients to limit export promotion and increase barriers to entry in industries facing CBI quantitative restrictions, and;
- can act as a disincentive to participate in multilateral trade negotiations, given they lead to an erosion of regional preference margins.

U.S.-Caribbean Basin Trade Relations: Policy Options

For over 40 years, the United States has provided some type of trade preference program to the countries of the Caribbean Basin. A central reason has been to promote an export-led development strategy with an eye on encouraging long-term political and social stability — on balance, all considered in the best commercial and strategic interests of the United States. The time for evaluating these programs is ripe because multilateral liberalization and Asian low-cost producers are eroding the effects of tariff preferences. In addition, U.S. trade policy in the region has been moving toward reciprocal free trade agreements, reducing the number of beneficiary countries and amount of trade eligible under these preferences.

With the largest of the CBI economies now part of CAFTA-DR, a remaining U.S. trade policy question is what to do with the smallest Caribbean nations. These, by definition, are the smallest and some of the most economically vulnerable countries that have banded together in their own regional arrangement known as the Caribbean Community and Common Market (CARICOM — see Appendix 1).

Options include: 1) allow trade preference programs to expire; 2) renew them as is or with more generous and flexible preferences; or 3) negotiate an FTA.

Allow Trade Preference Programs to Expire

One option is to allow the trade preference programs to expire. The CBTPA, perhaps the most effective of the programs, is set to expire on September 30, 2008. CBERA is permanent and would require an act of Congress to terminate. The CARICOM countries have expressed a preference to retain the trade preferences, even though they have not been big users of the program. Allowing the programs to expire would likely raise the stakes on consideration of a bilateral FTA with the United States. In any case, even if the preferences are not widely used, eliminating them is a step backwards in the CARICOM countries' strategy of seeking special and differential treatment.

Renew Trade Preference Programs

A second option is to consider redefining the trade preference programs in a way that might provide more benefit to the CARICOM countries.[40] This option recognizes that while the trade preference programs have not been perfect, they have evolved over time in an attempt to become more economically relevant to the countries they were designed to be helping. The evolution from CBERA through CBI II to CBTPA bears witness to this fact, even if the current preferences are being eroded by broader trade trends and policies.

The central problem is that except for the energy and chemical exports, which constitute 80% of CARICOM's merchandise exports to the United States, there is little for the CARICOM countries to take advantage of in the CBI preference programs. Apparel goods amount to slightly less than 5% of total exports to the United States and the complexities of U.S. rules of origin and Caribbean supply constraints raise doubts about the ability of CARICOM countries to expand this sector significantly. Unless apparel rules of origin are relaxed even further, those products would not be competitive with those receiving benefits under CAFTA-DR or with Asian goods.

It is conceivable that the CBI programs could be amended to target the specific export sectors of the CARICOM countries and perhaps deepen existing benefits for certain industries. The opportunities, however, may be limited. The CARICOM countries are largely service sector economies (tourism, financial services, professional services) and do not view U.S. market access for goods with the same sense of necessity that many other countries in the Western Hemisphere have, even if rules of origin and cumulation could be made more flexible. Trinidad and Tobago, the country that benefits the most from CBTPA given its large energy related exports, is also most likely to consider an FTA of benefit relative to the smaller island economies.

A Reciprocal FTA and CARICOM

A third option is to approach the CARICOM countries regarding a bilateral FTA similar to those in place for much of the region, which might provide some appeal if crafted in a way that would benefit the small Caribbean nations. It is far from clear, however, that such a transition could be easily achieved, given the different commitments involved between the two types of trade arrangements. FTAs operate much differently than unilateral trade preferences. Trade preferences are unilateral concessions of one country to another, offering little in the way of recourse to the recipient country if a dispute arises. FTAs, by contrast, are negotiated agreements, with mutual obligations and disputes subject to a resolution mechanism defined in the FTA. Preferences are also limited commitments, usually focusing on market access. FTAs are comprehensive, covering a vast array of rules, practices, and obligations from investment to labor and environment provisions. Preferences are often time limited and subject to unilateral suspensions, whereas FTAs are permanent arrangements, codified by each member in domestic law.

An FTA would be consistent with U.S. trade policy in the rest of the region. The United States vision for hemispheric integration has revolved around the comprehensive FTA model as implemented with Mexico, Canada, Central America, Chile, and possibly in the near future, Peru, Panama, and Colombia. If the integration path were to emanate from a harmonization of these agreements, having an FTA in place with CARICOM would appear to further the broader U.S. trade agenda.

The CARICOM countries, by contrast, are a diverse group of mostly island countries with vastly different economies, and therefore, varying perspectives on trade policy and an FTA with the United States.[41] The more developed economies (energy-rich Trinidad and

Tobago and tourism-driven Barbados) are far more open to the prospects of an FTA than the natural resource-based countries (Guyana and Jamaica) and the micro economies of the Eastern Caribbean, which have a fearful reluctance to begin negotiations. All of the CARICOM countries, however, have expressed some overriding concerns over the limitations of small economies to undertake the obligations of an FTA without some type of "compensatory mechanism" to replace trade preferences. Among the major concerns are:[42]

- questions over the United States' willingness to accommodate their need for special and differential treatment (SDT) such as long phase-in periods to meet FTA commitments, trade capacity building (TCB) assistance, trade adjustment assistance (TAA), and perhaps a financial component to implement these options;[43]
- the high transition costs of fiscal adjustment (from a high tariff dependency), discontinuing protection for manufacturing and agriculture sectors, implementing obligations like government procurement, intellectual property rights, labor, environment, sanitary and phytosantiary (SPS) regulations;
- supply-side constraints (dearth of arable land, small-scale production) that limit their ability to take advantage of market access;
- a perceived lack of support for their growing services trade, particularly movement of professionals, and concerns over U.S. agricultural subsidies, two issues the United States is reluctant to address, and
- asymmetrical negotiating capacity.

OUTLOOK

A number of issues and circumstances are converging during the 110th Congress that will be a challenge for U.S. trade policy in the Caribbean region. Among these circumstances is the expiring trade preference programs, the benefits of which, in any case, have been eroded over time by multilateral trade liberalization and new reciprocal bilateral FTAs. Further, these programs are little used by the remaining eligible beneficiary countries, which also have expressed a reluctance to move toward an FTA with the United States without some guarantee of a "development component" to the agreement, despite the promise of permanent market access and increased investment that an FTA holds out. The Caribbean countries, long accustomed to dependent economic relationships, appear content to take a cautious and leisurely path toward any new trade arrangement with the United States.

For U.S. trade policy, which is still committed to achieving regional integration, these circumstances present a special challenge. Broader integration may be difficult to achieve and still meet the needs of very small developing countries. Their economies are highly vulnerable to the vicissitudes of global economic trends and may require new and creative solutions to make the adjustment to reciprocal free trade. U.S. trade policy toward the region has also long had a historical focus on development and regional security issues in addition to trade liberalization, suggesting that trade liberalization will not be the only factor to determine policy specifics. In the context of continuing with trade preferences in similar or altered form, or opting for an FTA, the solution is not immediately obvious.

Appendix A: Country Groups

A. Beneficiary Countries Designated under the CBERA:[44]		
Antigua and Barbuda	Dominican Republic	Panama
Aruba	Grenada	St. Kitts and Nevis
Bahamas	Guyana	Saint Lucia
Barbados	Haiti	St. Vincent and the
Belize	Jamaica	Grenadines
Costa Rica	Montserrat	Trinidad and Tobago
Dominica	Netherlands Antilles	British Virgin Islands
B. Beneficiary Countries Designated under the CBTPA:[45]		
Barbados	Guyana	Panama
Belize	Haiti	Saint Lucia
Costa Rica	Jamaica	Trinidad and Tobago
Dominican Republic		
C. Caribbean Community (CARICOM) Countries:		
Antigua and Barbuda	Guyana	St. Lucia
Bahamas	Haiti (provisional)	St. Vincent and the
Barbados	Jamaica	Grenadines
Belize	Montserrat	Suriname
Dominica	St. Kitts and Nevis	Trinidad and Tobago
Grenada		

References

[1] NTR is the acronym for "normal trade relations," a phrase adopted by the United States in lieu of the often confusing "most-favored-nation" (MFN) term used internationally. Both refer to the application of tariffs on a non-discriminatory basis. Tariff preferences are by definition inconsistent with NTR/MFN treatment, requiring a waiver from the World Trade Organization (WTO). See CRS Report RS22183, *Trade Preferences for Developing Countries and the WTO*, by Jeanne J. Grimmett.

[2] Caribbean Basin countries include: Antigua and Barbuda, Aruba, Bahamas, Barbados, Belize, British Virgin Islands, Costa Rica, Dominica, Dominican Republic, El Salvador, Grenada, Guatemala, Guyana, Haiti, Honduras, Jamaica, Montserrat, Netherlands Antilles, Nicaragua, Panama, St. Kitts and Nevis, St. Lucia, St. Vincent and the Grenadines, and Trinidad and Tobago.

[3] Initially defined under Item 807 of the U.S. tariff schedule, and later in Chapter 98 of the U.S. Harmonized Tariff Schedule (HTS). United States International Trade Commission. *Production Sharing: Use of U.S. Components and Materials in Foreign Assembly Operations, 1995-1998.* Washington, D.C. USITC Publication 3265. December 1999. pp. 1-1 and 1-2.

[4] Production sharing is also done by European and Asian firms.

[5] See CRS Report RL33663, Generalized System of Preferences: Background and Renewal Debate, by Vivian C. Jones.

[6] Other geographically targeted trade preference programs would be created in the Andean Trade Preference Act (ATPA) and the African Growth and Opportunity Act (AGOA).

[7] See Pastor, Robert A. Exiting the Whirlpool: U.S. Foreign Policy Toward Latin America and the Caribbean, Second Edition. Boulder: Westview Press, 2001. pp. 19-20.

[8] 1982 CQ Almanac. *Caribbean Trade Plan.* pp. 54-55 and 129.

[9] The CBI was a comprehensive program, with the tariff preferences codified in the CBERA.

[10] 1983 CQ Almanac. *Caribbean Trade Plan.* pp. 252-53.

[11] Some of these conditions may be waived by the President for national security reasons. Other requirements were also in force. For a summary, see U.S. Congress. House. 109th Congress. 1st Session. Committee Print. Committee on Ways and Means. *Overview and Compilation of U.S. Trade Statutes.* Part I of II. June 2005. pp. 23-24.

[12] Recast in 1994 under GATT as the Agreement on Textiles and Clothing (ATC), it was the framework for the global bilateral textile quota agreements that were finally phased out on January 1, 2005.

[13] P.L. 98-67, section 213.

[14] Ibid, pp. 26-28 and CRS Report RS21930, *Ethanol Imports and the Caribbean Basin Initiative,* by Brent D. Yacobucci.

[15] USITC, Production Sharing: Use of U.S. Components and Materials in Foreign Assembly Operations, 1995-1998, pp. A-4 and A-5.

[16] USITC. Annual Report on the Impact of the Caribbean Basin Economic Recovery Act on U.S. Industries and Consumers. Sixth Report. Washington, DC, 1990. pp. 1-6 and 2-9.

[17] CRS Report RL31723, *Textile and Apparel Trade Issues,* by Bernard A. Gelb.

[18] For details on the legislative development of this act, see archived CRS Issue Brief IB95050, *Caribbean Basin Interim Trade Program: CBI/NAFTA Parity,* by Vladimir N. Pregelj, available from the author.

[19] The CBTPA is not an amended version of CBERA, but an additional piece of legislation defining a separate and temporary program of tariff preferences.

[20] The irony of formally requiring beneficiary countries to meet their WTO obligations in a preference program that runs contrary to the WTO-enshrined MFN principle was not lost on the Caribbean countries. See Caribbean Community and Common Market. *CARICOM Trade and Investment Report 2005.* Georgetown, Guyana. 2006. p. 69.

[21] For a summary, see U.S. Congress, *Overview and Compilation of U.S. Trade Statutes.* op.cit., pp. 32-33. Details of the parity issue may be found in archived CRS Issue Brief IB95050, *Caribbean Basin Interim Trade Program: CBI/NAFTA Parity,* by Vladimir N. Pregelj, available from the author.

[22] For details, see USITC. *The Impact of the Caribbean Asin Economic Recovery Act: Seventeenth Report, 2003-2004.* USITC Publication No. 332-227. September 2005. pp. 1-9 thru 1-12.

[23] To date, El Salvador, Honduras, Nicaragua, Guatemala, and the Dominican Republic have implemented the agreement. Costa Rica's legislature is still considering the FTA.

[24] USITC. U.S.-Central America-Dominican Republic Free Trade Agreement: *Potential Economywide and Selected Sectoral Effects.* USITC Publication 3717. August 2004. p. 27-28.

[25] Ibid., pp. 28-30.
[26] Latin American Newsletters. *Latin American Mexico and NAFTA Report.* February 2007. p. 14.
[27] For more on Haiti, see CRS Report RS21839, Haitian Textile Industry: Impact of Proposed Trade Assistance, by Bernard A. Gelb, and CRS Report RL32294, Haiti: Developments and U.S. Policy Since 1991 and Current Congressional Concerns, by Maureen Taft-Morales.
[28] CRS Report RS21839, Haitian Textile Industry: Impacts of Proposed Trade Assistance, by Bernard A. Gelb.
[29] This discussion draws on a more detailed analysis in: USITC, *The Impact of the Caribbean Basin Economic Recovery Act*, Seventeenth Report, September 2005.
[30] To simplify table 1, a small percentage (usually less than 1%) of imports that enter under reduced duties per various programs has been combined with "other dutiable" imports.
[31] USITC, The Impact of the Caribbean Basin Economic Recovery Act: Seventeenth Report, pp. 2-10 to 2-12.
[32] Ibid.
[33] For more detailed data, ibid., pp. 2-11 and 3-4.
[34] Ibid., p. 2-13.
[35] Ibid., p. 2-18.
[36] USITC, The Impact of the Caribbean Basin Economic Recovery Act: Seventeenth Report, pp. 2-12 to 2-18.
[37] Srinivasan, T. N. *The Costs of Hesitant and Reluctant Globalization: India.* p. 31. [http://www.econ.yale.edu/~srinivas/] and Özden, Caglar and Eric Reinhardt. Unilateral Preference Programs: The Evidence. In: Evenett, Simon J. And Bernard M. Hoekman, eds. *Economic Development and Multilateral Trade Cooperation.* World Bank. Washington, D.C. 2006. p. 190-192, 197-198 and 204-205, and CARICOM Secretariat. *Caribbean Trade and Investment Report 2005.* Caribbean Community Secretariat. Georgetown, Guyana. 2006. p. 61.
[38] Özden and Reinhardt, Unilateral Preference Programs: The Evidence, p. 191, and CARICOM Trade and Investment Report 2005, pp. 61-62.
[39] In fact, the two major industries affected show limited promise for growth. Energy-based exports are limited by available resources and manufacturing is done on such a small scale as to be increasingly less competitive with Asian producers.
[40] Rangaswami, Viji. *Nickel and Diming the Poor: U.S. Implementation of the LDC Initiative.* Carnegie Endowment for International Peace. Policy Outlook. July 2006. p. 7.
[41] For a recent historical survey of the different trade regimes, see McBain, Helen. Challenges to Caribbean Economies in the Era of Globalization. In: Knight, Franklin W. And Teresita Martínez-Verque. *Contemporary Caribbean Cultures and Societies in a Global Context.* University of North Carolina Press. Chapel Hill. 2005.
[42] Based in part on author interviews during a two-week trip through the Eastern Caribbean in 2006 and *CARICOM Trade and Investment Report*, p. 61.
[43] CARICOM Trade and Investment Report 2005, p. 61.
[44] The CAFTA-DR implementing Act (P.L. 109-53) modifies the CBERA legislation by adding the term "former beneficiary country," meaning a country that ceases to be

designated as a beneficiary country under CBERA because it has become a party to the CAFTA-DR. To date, El Salvador, Guatemala, Honduras, Nicaragua, and the Dominican Republic have implemented the CAFTA-DR, essentially trading their benefits under CBERA for equal or better treatment under the free trade agreement.

[45] P.L. 109-53, as with the CBERA, amends CBTPA status by including a new category of "former beneficiary country." In cases where a good is produced in both a former and current CBTPA country, it shall not receive any less treatment than as if it had been produced by a CBTPA country.

In: Trade Policies and Agreements in the Era of Globalization ISBN: 978-1-60021-836-1
Editor: Paul B. Lucus, pp. 115-134

Chapter 5

TRADE PROMOTION AUTHORITY (TPA)/FAST-TRACK RENEWAL: LABOR ISSUES*

Mary Jane Bolle

ABSTRACT

Trade promotion authority (TPA), formerly known as "fast-track" authority, is scheduled to expire July 1, 2007. With it will expire the authority: (a) that Congress grants the President to enter into certain trade agreements, and (b) for Congress to consider the agreements' implementing legislation under expedited procedures. Currently, the Administration is negotiating a number of trade agreements that may not be completed before the current TPA is set to expire. If these activities are to continue, TPA/fast-track renewal may be a central issue in the 110th Congress. Within the debate, a major issue is expected to be whether to include as a principal negotiating objective in trade agreements, "enforceable core labor standards."

Two TPA/fast-track authorities have incorporated labor provisions. The first, the *Omnibus Trade and Competitiveness Act of 1988* (OTCA), which expired in 1994, included the broad, general objective: "to promote worker rights." The *North American Free Trade Agreement*, with its labor side agreement, was negotiated under OTCA. The second and current TPA/fast-track authority with labor provisions, the *Trade Act of 2002*, includes protections for labor, modified by protections for country governments, businesses and investors. Seven free trade agreements (FTAs) — with Chile, Singapore, Australia, Morocco, Bahrain, Oman, and the Dominican Republic and Central America — were negotiated under this authority. All have only one enforceable labor requirement: that each country not fail to enforce its own labor laws in a manner affecting trade between the parties. (In contrast to this, the U.S.-Jordan FTA, negotiated in 2000 and approved in 2001 without TPA/fast track authority, includes enforceable labor provisions.)

Major options for labor provisions in renewed TPA focus on whether principal negotiating objectives should include "enforceable core labor standards." Supporters argue that including these could help: (1) slow the offshoring of certain U.S. jobs; (2) protect foreign workers against exploitative corporate behavior; (3) support the ability of workers to share in the gains from international trade; and (4) fend off an international

---
* Excerpted from CRS Report RL33864, dated February 2, 2007.

"race to the bottom" based on labor costs. Opponents argue that: (1) core labor standards should be promoted by the International Labor Organization, not by trade agreements; (2) as countries develop, they adopt higher labor standards on their own; (3) stronger worker protections could discourage international investment; and (4) labor standards are disguised protectionism. History shows that with or without FTAs, trade will likely continue to grow.

This report examines issues relating to TPA/fast-track labor provisions in the larger context of global labor issues. It: (1) identifies the players and their positions; (2) tracks the enforceable labor provisions in TPA/fast-track laws and the FTAs negotiated under them; (3) presents some legislative options for new TPA/fast-track labor provisions; and (4) sets out arguments for and against enforceable core labor standards. Finally, it looks at possible outcomes and implications of the various legislative options.

INTRODUCTION

Trade promotion authority (TPA), formerly known as "fast track" authority, is scheduled to expire July 1, 2007. With it will expire the authority that Congress grants the President to enter into certain trade agreements, and the authority for Congress to consider implementing legislation for them under expedited procedures. The Administration is still negotiating a number of trade agreements that may not be completed before the TPA/fast-track authority is set to expire. Thus, TPA/fast-track renewal may be a central issue in the 110th Congress if these activities are to continue.[1]

Within the TPA/fast-track renewal debate, a major issue is expected to be which labor provisions to set forth as as "principal negotiating objectives" — that is, which labor provisions to set forth as "a priority for negotiators to seek" in trade agreements.[2] Two sets of provisions are probable candidates.

One, supported by labor advocates, is expected to be: to ensure that a party does not fail to *enforce core labor standards* in a manner affecting trade. Related provisions could (1) identify a set of mutually agreed upon "core labor standards" (defined in the next section) and (2) provide that violation of these standards would be subject to enforcement under the single set of dispute settlement procedures that would be applicable to all disputes.

An alternative is expected to be the current principal negotiating objective: to ensure that a party does not fail to *enforce its own labor laws*, commonly referred to as the "enforce-your-own" standard. This provision would be enforceable under current dispute settlement procedures that call for treating principal negotiating objectives "equally."

The difference between the two approaches reflects criticism by labor advocates that, in general, labor provisions in FTAs negotiated so far: (1) lack the enforceability of commercial provisions; (2) "clearly fail to meet some congressional negotiating objectives [for trade agreements and] barely comply with others"; (3) "represent a big step back" from both the U.S.-Jordan FTA (negotiated and approved during a hiatus when TPA/fast-track authority had expired), and from U.S. unilateral trade preference programs such as the Generalized System of Preferences (GSP); and (4) "completely exclude obligations for governments to meet such international standards as worker rights."[3] The issue of including enforceable core labor standards as a principal negotiating objective also reflects a strategy to change the way labor interests are mirrored in trade agreements by tightening the blueprint for them.

Opponents argue that provisions in FTAs negotiated under the current TPA/fast-track authority: (1) are the strongest labor provisions attached to FTAs to date; (2) are the product of bilateral negotiation; and (3) both depend on and reflect mutual agreement by negotiating countries over which provisions to include. Opponents also argue: (4) that enforceable core labor standards would raise sovereignty issues.

This report examines the issues raised by labor advocates and responses by opponents. It does so in the larger context of how and where enforceable labor provisions in TPA/fast-track authority and the trade agreements negotiated under them intersect with global labor issues. Thus, it first identifies the stakeholders who care (positively or negatively) about enforceable labor provisions, and their positions on the issue. After that, it: (1) tracks the enforceable labor provisions in TPA/fast-track laws and the FTAs they have spawned; (2) presents some legislative options for new TPA/fast-track provisions relating to enforceable labor provisions; and (3) sets out arguments for and against enforceable core labor standards from the perspective of the parties that could be affected by the standards. Finally, it looks at possible outcomes and implications of the various legislative options.

Which Set of Core Labor Standards?

As mentioned, labor advocates are proposing that renewed TPA/fast-track authority include, as a principal negotiating objective for trade agreements, a handful of "enforceable" "core labor standards," or "internationally recognized worker rights." The terms "internationally recognized worker rights" or "core labor standards" are technically defined in separate ways, by U.S. Trade law (the *Trade Act of 1974, Sec. 507*), and the International Labor Organization (ILO, a United Nations organization).[4] Both definitions are almost identical, and share four standards or rights:

1. the right to organize,
2. the right to bargain collectively,
3. prohibition of forced labor, and
4. protections for child labor including the "worst forms of child labor"[5] They differ on the fifth standard. U.S. law identifies it as:
5. labor standards pertaining to minimum wages, maximum hours, and occupational safety and health. ILO conventions define it as:
6. freedom from employment discrimination.[6]

In recent years these terms have become somewhat confusing because the current TPA/fast-track law included in the *Trade Act of 2002* and trade agreements negotiated under it have adopted the U.S. list of "internationally recognized worker rights" as the definition of the term "core labor standards." Consequently, this report will use the term "core labor standards" to refer to either list, and will mention "ILO core labor standards," "U.S. internationally recognized worker rights," or "U.S. list" only when referring to standards defined by either specific source.

Who Cares about Enforceable Core Labor Standards, and Why?

Labor Advocates

Labor advocates appear to have two objectives in promoting some type of enforceable core labor standards — one international, and the other domestic.

Internationally, the objective of labor advocates seemingly is humanitarian: to promote the protection of workers around the world, particularly those in developing countries, where global investment converges to take advantage of cheap labor. In such countries adults or even children may have to work long hours, under unhealthy and unsafe conditions, with few personal or hygienic freedoms, for low pay. Moreover, they may not be permitted the basic right to form unions and bargain collectively with their employers to improve those conditions.[7]

Domestically, the objective of labor advocates is seemingly more economic: to help "level the playing field "between U.S. and foreign workers, so that U.S. workers can compete with those in developing countries on a more equitable basis. A more equitable playing field, they argue, would provide at least some incentive for businesses to find ways to remain and/or expand in the United States instead of looking for ways to "offshore" parts of their operations to countries where labor costs are cheaper. Estimates on U.S. jobs "lost" to international trade and offshore outsourcing are hard to come by. However, jobs at risk have expanded from blue collar to white collar and from the manufacturing to high end service sector and research and development jobs, and now include, in addition to call center and data entry jobs, higher skill professional jobs in fields such as engineering, computer chip design, nanotechnology, and medical test analysis, that have become important in the knowledge-based economy.

Business Groups

Opposite labor advocates are many business groups whose main objective is typically to support the passage of TPA/fast-track authority in order to facilitate the expansion of U.S. multinational corporations abroad — their most important avenue for continued growth. Both TPA/fast-track authority and trade agreements typically include many protections for investors.

For eight years between 1994 and 2002, however, the issue of whether or not to include any kind of enforceable labor provisions in trade agreements was a major point of contention in the debate over renewal of TPA/fast-track authority. During that time, some TPA/fast-track renewal bills would have prohibited some types of labor provisions in trade agreements negotiated under them.[8] Ultimately, a 2001 report prepared for the U.S. Trade Representative by the Business Roundtable, made up of chief executive officers from roughly 200 major companies, led the way toward TPA/fast-track renewal in 2002 when it said, "in pursuing labor (and environmental) objectives in trade and investment negotiations, the United States must grant our trade negotiators the flexibility to negotiate." It stressed that "International labor and environmental issues have emerged as the principal stumbling blocks. The Business Roundtable believes. . . that the issue is no longer whether they should be addressed in international trade and investment negotiations, but rather how to address them constructively."[9]

Developing Countries

Developing countries care about how enforceable core labor standards affect (either positively or negatively) their ability to attract investment. In 1996, at the World Trade Organization (WTO) Singapore Ministerial (a meeting of ministers of WTO members), developing countries, which formed a majority there, voted down the U.S. proposal for a committee to study the relationship between worker rights and trade. They did so because they were afraid formation of such a committee could lead to the imposition of enforceable labor standards that could undercut their comparative advantage in low-cost labor. As a result of these votes, the Singapore Declaration (the final document summarizing what they decided) named the ILO as the "competent body to set and deal with" international labor standards.[10] The ILO has as its main enforcement mechanism the tools of consensus and persuasion.

U.S. Executive Branch

The Administration's position on enforceable labor standards, although it reflects the principal negotiating objectives of the FTA/fast-track laws, has shifted with various presidents and various circumstances. It typically mirrors the interests of the party it represents. The Clinton Administration was supportive of enforceable labor standards in trade agreements. First, it negotiated the labor side agreement to the North American Free Trade Agreement (NAFTA). Then, it pushed for studying the link between worker rights and trade at the 1997 Singapore Ministerial as mentioned above. Next, it promoted worker rights protections at the subsequent 1999 Ministerial in Seattle, Washington. The conference there was cut short for a number of reasons including issues between developed and developing countries.[11] Finally, in 2000, it negotiated the U.S.-Jordan FTA that included enforceable U.S. and ILO core labor standards in the body of the agreement. More recently, the Bush Administration has negotiated bilateral and regional trade agreements with the first labor and the first enforceable labor provisions in the body of a trade agreement. At the same time, however, reportedly, an offer by Peru's President Alejandro Toledo to negotiate enforceable labor standards in the proposed U.S.-Peru FTA was not accepted by the Bush Administration.[12]

Key Labor Provisions in TPA/Fast-Track Laws and in Trade Agreements Negotiated under Them

Two of the three TPA/fast-track laws passed by Congress over the past 30 years have included labor provisions. These TPA/fast-track laws have facilitated the negotiation and approval of a total of eight FTAs so far, as follows:

Omnibus Trade and Competitiveness Act of 1988: NAFTA

The first TPA/fast-track law to include labor provisions as principal negotiating objectives was the *Omnibus Trade and Competitiveness Act of 1988* (OTCA, P.L. 100-418). Its full list of labor principal negotiating objectives is included in the Appendix table 1. Most importantly, these include the general but vague requirement: " to promote worker rights." This requirement led to the first labor provisions attached to a bilateral or regional trade agreement.[13] The agreement was NAFTA, and labor provisions were included in a labor side agreement, not in the body of the agreement itself. The labor side agreement included: (1) labor provisions with limited enforceability, detailed below; (2) its own dispute resolution procedures for labor issues; and (3) a dollar cap on penalties.

The labor provisions in the NAFTA labor side agreement required that each Party (the United States, Mexico, and Canada) enforce its own labor laws and standards. Only two of the five core labor standards, however, were to be enforceable, and one of these is only partially enforceable. The enforceable standards are for: (a) child labor protections; and (b) two components of labor standards: minimum wages and occupational safety and health. Among standards not enforceable under the NAFTA labor side agreement were a country's own laws protecting the rights of workers to organize and bargain collectively.

No TPA/Fast-Track Law: The Jordan Agreement

After the OTCA, there was an eight-year hiatus when there was no TPA/fast-track law, 1994-2002. During this time, the Administration negotiated and Congress approved the U.S.-Jordan FTA. This agreement included a number of labor provisions in the body of the agreement that were technically enforceable through the agreement's single dispute resolution procedure. Some of these provisions were later echoed in the *Bipartisan Trade Promotion Authority Act of 2002*, discussed below. The most important such labor provision specified that parties "shall not fail to effectively enforce" their own labor laws "through a sustained or recurring course of action or inaction in a manner affecting trade between the parties." Labor laws were defined as the U.S. list, recognizing the right of each party to exercise enforcement discretion. Parties also agreed to: (a) strive to ensure that both ILO and U.S. core labor standards are recognized and protected by domestic law; and (b) recognize the right of each party to establish, modify, and improve its labor standards. For more details on these provisions, see Appendix table 2.

Bipartisan Trade Promotion Authority Act of 2002: Seven Trade Agreements

The second TPA/fast-track law with principal negotiating objectives for labor was the *Bipartisan Trade Promotion Authority Act of 2002* (Title XXI of the *Trade Act of 2002*, P.L. 107-210), which is set to expire July 1, 2007. Its principal negotiating objectives for labor (repeated in Appendix table 1) include: (1) "to ensure that a party does not fail to effectively enforce its own labor laws"; and (2) "to strengthen the capacity of U.S. trading partners to promote respect for core labor standards." Modifying these provisions are others in the list of principal negotiating objectives for labor that offer protections for governments, businesses, and investors: (3) to recognize that parties to a trade agreement retain the right to exercise discretion in the allocation of enforcement resources; and (4) to ensure that labor practices of the parties do not arbitrarily or unjustifiably discriminate against U.S. exports or serve as disguised barriers to trade.

Under this TPA/fast-track authority seven trade agreements have been negotiated and approved.[14] These are with Chile, Singapore, Australia, Morocco, Bahrain, Oman, and a single agreement with five Central American Countries (Costa Rica, El Salvador, Guatemala, Honduras, and Nicaragua) and the Dominican Republic, known as CAFTA-DR. In addition, this TPA/fast-track authority has facilitated agreements with two other countries (Peru and Colombia) which are awaiting congressional action.[15] Labor provisions in the various agreements are detailed in Appendix table 2.

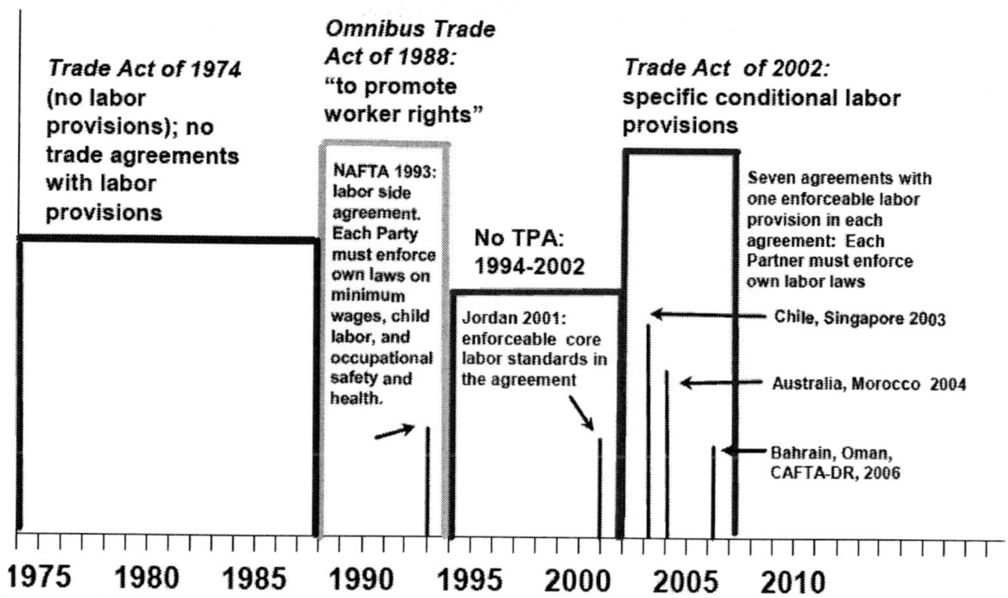

Source: of information: various TPA laws and FTA implementation laws. Dates reflect years that Congress approved the documents.

Figure 1. TPA/Fast-Track Laws and Their Labor Provisions, and FTAs and Their Enforceable Labor Provisions, 1974-2007.

For dispute resolution, the principal negotiating objective is (5) "to seek provisions that treat [all — i.e. including those for labor and those for commercial disputes] U.S. principal negotiating objectives equally with respect to the ability to resort to dispute settlement and the availability of equivalent dispute settlement procedures and remedies." In what is seen by labor advocates as a departure from this language, two characteristics stand out. First, each of the seven trade agreements has only one labor provision subject to the agreement's dispute settlement process — *that each country must enforce its own labor laws*. Second, procedures for labor disputes differ in several respects from those for commercial disputes and include a cap on monetary penalties. Opponents, argue, however, that the treatment of labor and commercial disputes is equal because the procedures and remedies are "equivalent."

Figure 1 summarizes, along a time line, the congressionally-passed sequence of TPA/fast-track authorities (in larger type) and the trade agreements negotiated under them (smaller type). Also listed are the key labor provisions in each.

LEGISLATIVE OPTIONS FOR TPA/FAST-TRACK RENEWAL

When discussing legislative options for renewal of the TPA/fast-track authority, it is important to keep in mind several things: First, TPA/fast-track authority represents statutory requirements for presidential *negotiation* of FTAs, rather than requirements for ultimate *provisions* in the FTAs. Second, a number of factors may converge to determine the ultimate labor provisions in FTAs, including: (1) the labor agenda of the negotiating Parties; (2) the ability of the United States to persuade potential partner countries to agree to various provisions; (3) the political makeup of the Congress which must vote the agreements up or down; and (4) the level of acceptance of labor provisions by the business community. While there may be any number of possible legislative options to address the issue of enforceable labor provisions in TPA/fast-track renewal, four are discussed below.

Option 1: No TPA/Fast-Track Renewal

Without the protection of TPA/fast-track authority, with its prohibition on amendments to FTAs and its requirement for limited debates, some argue, foreign countries may be less inclined to negotiate trade agreements with the United States. This is because foreign countries would know that anything they agreed upon could possibly be amended by Congress and sent back for further negotiation. On the other hand, Congress would be more involved in negotiating any agreements the Administration desired to pursue.

Option 2: TPA/Fast-Track Renewal with No Enforceable Labor Provisions

TPA/fast-track renewal that does not include enforceable labor provisions as a principal negotiating objective would likely be viewed by some as a step back from the expiring TPA/fast-track authority. On the other hand, this does not preclude the President from negotiating labor provisions.

Option 3: TPA/Fast-Track Labor Provisions Similar to Those under the Expiring Authority

Current TPA/fast-track principal negotiating objectives include three key elements plus their modifying qualifications, mentioned earlier: (1) to ensure that a party does not fail to enforce its own labor laws; 2) to strengthen the capacity of U.S. trading partners to promote respect for core labor standards; and (3) to seek provisions that treat [all] U.S. principal negotiating objectives equally with respect to the ability to resort to dispute settlement, the availability of equivalent dispute settlement procedures, and the availability of equivalent remedies.

Option 4: TPA/Fast-Track Labor Provisions Setting out Enforceable Core Labor Provisions as Principal Negotiating Objectives

Option four includes principal negotiating objectives that would go one step beyond those in option 3, and actually list "enforceable core labor standards" as a principal negotiating objective. They could also include language in principal negotiating objectives for dispute resolution procedures to ensure that all principal negotiating objectives (i.e. for both labor and commercial issues) are fully disputable and covered by a single dispute resolution process.

THE 2001 RANGEL BILL

One possible configuration of option 4 was reflected in a TPA/fast-track renewal bill introduced by Representative Charles Rangel in the 107th Congress in 2001 (H.R. 3019). H.R. 3019 would have included enforceable labor standards defined by a short list of ILO core labor standards as principal negotiating objectives for labor. It would also have included: (a) protections and assistance for governments; and (b) a single set of dispute resolution procedures relating to all principal negotiating objectives.

More specifically, in H.R. 3019, these concepts translated into the following provisions (further detailed in Appendix table 3): (1) to negotiate enforceable rules that provide for the adoption and enforcement of a handful of standards that read like ILO core labor standards; (2) to establish as a trigger for invoking the dispute settlement process either: (a) failure to effectively enforce one's own domestic labor standards; or (b) waiver or derogation from domestic labor standards in order to attract investment or gain a competitive advantage; and (3) a single dispute resolution procedure for all types of complaints. Its would also have contained the following types of provisions relating to enforcement assistance, flexibility, and monitoring: (a) the right of Parties to exercise enforcement discretion; (b) the right of parties to establish, adopt, or modify their own labor standards consistent with core labor standards; (c) phased-in compliance for least-developed countries; (d) a program of technical assistance; and (e) regular review of adherence to core labor standards.

Arguments for and Against Enforceable Core Labor Standards as a Principal Negotiating Objective

"Should enforceable core labor standards be included as a principal negotiating objective?" is likely to be the main labor issue for Congress to consider in TPA/fast-track renewal. If the answer to this question is "yes," the follow-up question would be, "Which definition or definitions of core labor standards should be included?" While the AFL-CIO and other labor advocates argue in favor of ILO core labor standards or their equivalents, the U.S. Council for International Business (USCIB) argues against this position, saying it could require that U.S. laws be changed to comply. The model of the U.S.-Jordan FTA offers a third option.

In the arguments below, those against enforceable labor standards as principal negotiating objectives are generally in favor of continuing the enforce-your-own labor standards in the current TPA/fast-track authority. The ILO is not represented in this debate. It typically does not take a position on specific legislation including TPA/fast-track renewal. This is because its official role is that of promoting worker rights through technical assistance and consensus building.[16]

General Arguments

For Enforceable Core Labor Standards as a Principal Negotiating Objective

Those in favor of a principal negotiating objective for FTA/fast-track legislation that calls for strong enforceable labor standards in the body of the agreement include the AFL-CIO,[17] Human Rights Watch,[18] and the International Labor Rights Fund.[19]

Human Rights Watch argues that "the debate over TPA/fast-track renewal presents a unique and important opportunity to think creatively on protecting worker rights in the context of trade, learning from the example of the U.S.-Cambodia Textile Agreement.[20] The U.S.-Cambodia Textile Agreement rewards compliance with local labor laws and international standards with an increase in export quotas to the United States.

Labor advocates traditionally argue that enforceable core labor standards in trade agreements can define the line between comparative advantage and "social dumping" — competing by denying worker rights. Such denial, they argue, ends up in a "race to the bottom," as workers all over the world compete against each other for scarce jobs. They also argue that labor standards do not interfere with natural comparative advantage in developing countries because labor standards are only one basis for comparative advantage. Others are: (a) abundance of available workforce; (b) skills and education level of the available labor force; (c) infrastructure; (d) level of technological development of the country; and (e) natural resource base.[21]

Against

The USCIB is the American affiliate of the International Chamber of Commerce, the International Organization of Employers, and the Business and Industry Advisory Committee to the OECD. Its membership includes some 300 leading U.S. companies, professional services firms, and associations. It argues for the continuation of the enforce-your-own standard and against enforceable core labor standards as a principal negotiating objective. This is because it supports and promotes an open system of global commerce in which businesses can flourish and contribute to economic growth, human welfare, and protection of the environment.[22]

Those against principal negotiating objectives that call for enforceable core labor standards in trade agreements also typically argue that the enforce-your-own standards model provides a more direct, less encumbered path to economic growth. In addition, most developing countries have few resources to devote to labor standards enforcement, given the many competing needs for use of scarce resources. Meanwhile, once a developing country is more economially developed and relatively near full employment, workers typically have the clout to begin to demand better protection from their governments on their own. Imposing core labor standards on developing countries too soon, some argue, could: (1) interfere with their comparative advantage in cheap labor; and (2) amount to protectionism — the imposition of an additional set of non-tariff barriers — when the purpose of trade agreements is to reduce trade barriers and stimulate trade and investment.

Arguments Related To U.S. Workers

For Enforceable Labor Standards as a Principal Negotiating Objective

Labor advocates argue that a principal negotiating objective calling for enforceable labor standards can help level the playing field for U.S. workers and make them more competitive internationally.

Against

Others argue that there are better ways to help U.S. workers than to try to level the playing field, which, at best, may only slow the offshore movement of some U.S. jobs. A better way, they argue, may be to expand trade adjustment assistance benefits, educational benefits, or other training and retraining programs to cover all job losers and help them transition into new careers. Still others might argue that the need or desire to earn a living is often incentive enough to encourage workers displaced by offshoring to find new employment.

Arguments Related to Foreign Workers

For Enforceable Labor Standards as a Principal Negotiating Objective

Labor advocates argue that in order for workers to become consumers, they must share in the gains of increasing productivity and economic expansion, and that enforceable core labor standards can help promote these gains.

Against

Opponents argue that real gains in standard of living come from rising productivity, not artificially imposed labor standards including minimum wages. In addition some workers do not want enforceable core labor standards because these, they argue, could limit their ability to maximize their earnings through overtime hours.

Opponents also argue that enforceable labor standards are not needed in principal negotiating objectives because other resources besides trade agreements are available to encourage countries to help raise labor standards to protect foreign workers. These include: (1) U.S. trade preference programs which require that beneficiary countries either currently afford or be taking steps to afford their workers internationally recognized worker rights;[23] (2) the ILO which offers technical support to countries to help them adopt and enforce core labor standards; (3) international labor groups which serve as "watchdogs" bringing abusive labor conditions to light in the radio, print, and film/video media; (4) evolutionary forces in countries characterized by workers themselves insisting on better labor conditions as their economies grow; (5) codes of conduct for multinational corporations which provide some level of accountability for corporations doing business in developing countries; and (6) U.S. government grants for improving labor standards and their enforcement through "trade capacity building."

Sovereignty Issues

For Enforceable Core Labor Standards as a Principal Negotiating Objective

Those in favor of enforceable core labor standards as a principal negotiating objective could argue that the ILO already requires that countries comply with ILO core labor standards as a condition of remaining members in good standing, even if they do not formally approve the ILO conventions.[24]

Against

Those against enforceable core labor standards as a principal negotiating objective might argue that including enforceable ILO core labor standards as principal negotiating objectives could come very close to interfering with national sovereignty. They might also point out that under the ILO, a country's failure to adhere to core labor standards is not punishable with sanctions. Such observers would be likely to support, as an alternative, the enforce-your-own standards in the current TPA/fast-track authority.

Arguments on the Definition of Core Labor Standards

One option for the definition of core labor standards is the ILO definition. Those against this option could be in favor of the U.S. definition of "internationally recognized worker rights." Still others could be in favor of a more flexible definition that could accommodate a country's compliance with the spirit and/or details of either the ILO or the U.S. definition, or both.

For Using the ILO Definition of Core Labor Standards

The AFL-CIO is strongly in favor of enforceable ILO core labor standards as a principal negotiating objective, arguing that the ILO conventions are more current than U.S. internationally recognized worker rights.[25] Human Rights Watch, while not arguing for either ILO core labor standards or U.S. internationally recognized worker rights by name, argues that the definition of core labor standard must include employment discrimination (which is in the ILO but not the U.S. definition.)

Against

If the ILO definition is adopted, foreign governments could hold existing U.S. labor laws up to scrutiny, arguing that they don't totally comply with ILO Core Labor Standards. In fact, the United States has ratified only two conventions (one on forced labor and one on the worst forms of child labor).[26] Accordingly, the USCIB argues that many U.S. labor laws would need to be changed to come into compliance with the ILO definition of core labor standards. U.S. law would particularly need to be amended, the USCIB argues, in such areas as forced labor, minimum age for employment, and employment discrimination. This conclusion was reached through a number of studies by the presidentially appointed Tripartite Advisory Panel on International Labor Standards (TAPILS) — a research group made up of USCIB as a representative of business, the AFL-CIO representing labor, and the U.S. government.[27]

Another Option: The U.S.-Jordan FTA Approach

The enforceable labor provisions in the Jordan FTA (included in Appendix table 2), negotiated and approved when there was no TPA/fast-track coverage, represent a third option for the definition of core labor standards. The Jordan FTA carries what many observers consider the strongest labor provisions yet. All labor provisions are located in the body of the agreement and all are fully enforceable.[28] Under the U.S.-Jordan FTA, Parties agree to: (1) Reaffirm obligations under the ILO and strive to ensure that both these labor principles and "internationally recognized worker rights" are recognized and protected by domestic law. Parties also: (2) agree to not fail to effectively enforce their own labor laws in a manner that affects trade between the Parties; (3) agree to strive to ensure that they do not waiver or derogate from their own labor laws in order to encourage trade with the other party; (4) recognize the right of each party to establish, adopt, or modify its labor laws and regulations, and strive to ensure that its laws provide for labor standards consistent with [U.S. defined] internationally recognized worker rights; and (5) recognize that each party retains enforcement discretion with respect to other matters deemed to have higher priority.

Others argue that while the dispute resolution procedures for the Jordan agreement do not preclude a broad array of sanctions for non-compliance, most of the obligations in the Jordan agreement are "hortatory" or strongly urged rather than mandates. Thus, there is only one obligation that may be enforced, and a party wishing to complain over the existence and administration of labor laws would need to make the more difficult case that government conduct "severely distort[s] the balance of trade benefits" or "substantially undermine[s] fundamental objectives of [the] Agreement."[29]

POSSIBLE OUTCOMES AND IMPLICATIONS

Whether TPA/fast-track is renewed, and whether the negotiation of enforceable core labor standards is included in any such renewal, international trade is likely to continue to expand in both volume and complexity. If TPA/fast-track renewal is proposed and debated, the issue of enforceable core labor standards is likely to remain important to labor advocates, business groups, the U.S. government, and foreign governments, for various reasons, as efforts are made to find a compromise position.

If enforceable core labor standards were to be adopted as a principal negotiating objective in TPA/fast-track authority, and if enforceable core labor standards were then to be negotiated into trade agreements approved by Congress, the inclusion of the enforceable standards could move TPA/fast-track authority along its evolutionary path to a new level of protection for U.S. and foreign workers. Business advocates, however, could continue to hold concerns that such standards could interfere with their economic efficiency.

The economic effects of any enforceable core labor standards in any TPA/fast-track renewal on U.S. workers, foreign workers, and businesses, however, would likely be small, and would depend on a number of factors including: 1) the extent to which enforceable core labor standards were adopted and implemented in trade agreements; 2) the number of trade agreements affected; 3) the magnitude of U.S. trade with countries affected by any such agreements; and 4) the extent of actual enforcement of any such standards in trade agreements. In addition, the effects from any of these four factors could be dwarfed by any shifts in the value of the dollar that might occur relative to other currencies.

If enforceable core labor standards were to be included in any renewed TPA/fast-track authority and were then to be included in trade agreements negotiated thereunder, many challenges would remain with regard to enforcement. Foreign governments typically have many competing needs for scarce resources besides protecting the health and safety of their workers. In addition, the Office of the U.S. Trade Representative and the Commerce Department, working together to process trade disputes, would have to choose which disputes to pursue in order to make the best use of scarce agency resources. If core labor standards were to be enforced, businesses would then have to face a decision as to what impact, if any, this would have on their investment decisions.

If enforceable core labor standards should be adopted as a principal negotiating objective in TPA/fast-track legislation, whether or not the United States would need to make any changes to its labor laws could depend on which definition of core labor standards were to be adopted. It is likely that if "enforceable core labor standards" were to be identified as a principal negotiating objective, they would be defined in such a way that no changes in U.S. law might be required.

If TPA/fast-track authority is not renewed, or if it should be renewed without enforceable core labor standards, a number of ways remain to promote labor standards and protect worker rights. These include standards currently incorporated into U.S. trade preference programs; continuing efforts of the ILO to promote core labor standards; the efforts of various labor advocates and international labor "watchdog" groups; economic development forces in various countries which eventually lead to protections of the rights of workers; codes of conduct guiding the actions of corporations in protecting the rights of international workers; and U.S. government "trade capacity building" grants which help to improve labor standards in developing countries.

APPENDIX

Table 1. Worker Rights Provisions in TPA/Fast-Track Authority, 1974-2007

Year	TPA/Fast-Track Authority	Worker Rights Provisions in Principal Negotiating Objectives	Agreements Approved Under this TPA/Fast- Track Authority and Approval Year
1974-1988	Trade Act of 1974 (P.L. 93-68) as amended ultimately expiring January 3, 1988	No worker rights provisions.	U.S.-Israel Free Trade Agreement (FTA), 1985 U.S.-Canada FTA,1988
1988-1993	Omnibus Trade Act of 1988 (P.L. 100-418) as amended, ultimately expiring December 31, 1993	Sec. 1101, PRINCIPAL NEGOTIATING OBJECTIVES, specifies worker rights in principal negotiating objectives: (a) to promote worker rights; (b) to secure a review of the relationship of worker rights to General Agreement on Tariff and Trade (GATT, the predecessor to the World Trade Organization -WTO) articles; (c) to ensure that the benefits of the trading system are available to all workers; and (d) to adopt as a principle of the GATT that the denial of worker rights should not be a means for a country of its industries to gain competitive advantage in international trade.	North American Free Trade Agreement (NAFTA), 1993
1994-2002	None	None	Jordan, 2001
2002-2007	Trade Act of 2002 (P.L. 107-210, set to expire July 1, 2007)	Sec. 2102(a) OVERALL NEGOTIATING OBJECTIVES for Labor: (6) to promote respect for worker rights consistent with core labor standards of the ILO.	Free Trade Agreements with:
		Sec. 2102 (b) (11) PRINCIPAL NEGOTIATING OBJECTIVES for Labor: (A) To ensure a party does not fail to effectively enforce its own labor laws; [BUT] (B) To recognize that parties to a trade agreement retain the right to exercise discretion and make decisions regarding the allocation of enforcement resources; (C) To strengthen the capacity of U.S. trading partners to promote respect for core labor standards; [BUT] (G) To ensure that labor practices of the parties do not arbitrarily or unjustifiably discriminate against U.S. exports or serve as disguised barriers to trade.	Chile, 2003 Singapore, 2003 Australia, 2004 Morocco, 2004 Bahrain, 2006 Oman, 2006 Central America and the Dominican Republic (known as CAFTA-DR), 2006

Table 1. Continued

Year	TPA/Fast-Track Authority	Worker Rights Provisions in Principal Negotiating Objectives	Agreements Approved Under this TPA/Fast- Track Authority and Approval Year
		Sec. 2102(b)(12) DISPUTE SETTLEMENT AND ENFORCEMENT: (G) To seek provisions that treat U.S. principal negotiating objectives equally with respect to — (i) The ability to resort to dispute settlement; (ii) The availability of equivalent dispute settlement procedures; and (iii) The availability of equivalent remedies.	
		Sec. 2102(b)(17) WORST FORMS OF CHILD LABOR: to seek commitments by parties to trade agreements to vigorously enforce their own laws prohibiting the "worst forms of child labor" [pertaining to use in such things as war, drug trade, trafficking, or pornography].	

APPENDIX

Table 2. Key Labor Provisions in FTAs Negotiated under Various TPA/Fast-Track Laws

TPA/Fast-Track Authority	Free Trade Agreement or Partner Country	Enforceable Labor Provisions and Their Location
Omnibus Trade Act of 1988	North American Free Trade Agreement (NAFTA)	In LABOR SIDE AGREEMENT: The only enforceable labor provision is for a party's failure to enforce its own laws relating to child labor, minimum wage, or occupational safety and health where the violation is trade-related and covered by mutually-recognized labor laws. DISPUTE SETTLEMENT PROCEDURES: The labor side agreement has its own dispute settlement procedures with lower maximum penalties than are in the agreement itself.

Table 2. (Continued).

TPA/Fast-Track Authority	Free Trade Agreement or Partner Country	Enforceable Labor Provisions and Their Location
No TPAS Authority	Jordan	In the BODY OF THE AGREEMENT : (Technically all provisions are enforceable; although an exchange of letters between the U.S. and Jordanian governments agreed to resolve any potential disputes without resorting to sanctions.) LABOR PROVISIONS: Parties: 1. Agree to not to fail to enforce their own laws, through a sustained or recurring course of action or inaction, in a manner affecting trade between the Parties; but retain the right to exercise discretion in that enforcement; 2. Reaffirm obligations under the International Labor Organization (ILO) and strive to ensure that these labor principles and "internationally recognized worker rights" are recognized and protected by domestic law; 3. Recognize that it is inappropriate to encourage trade by relaxing domestic labor laws. Therefore, the parties strive to ensure they do not waive or derogate from such laws in order to encourage trade with the other party; 4. Recognize the right of the other party to establish its own labor standards and adopt or modify its labor laws and regulations accordingly; and to strive to ensure that those laws are consistent with the U.S. definition of core labor standards. 5. Recognize that cooperation between them provides enhanced opportunities to improve labor standards. DISPUTE SETTLEMENT PROCEDURES: The same procedures apply to all agreement provisions equally.
Trade Act of 2002	Free Trade Agreements with: Chile Singapore Australia Morocco Bahrain Oman Central America and the Dominican Republic (known as CAFTA-DR)	In the BODY OF THE AGREEMENT: THE ONLY LABOR PROVISION THAT IS ENFORCEABLE UNDER DISPUTE SETTLEMENT PROCEDURES IS: All parties: 1. Agree to not to fail to enforce their own laws, through a sustained or recurring course of action or inaction, in a manner affecting trade between the Parties; but retain the right to exercise discretion in that enforcement. DISPUTE SETTLEMENT PROCEDURES: Labor (and environment) provisions have some different dispute settlement procedures with a lower maximum fines and/or sanctions.

Appendix

Table 3. Enforceable Labor Provisions Included in H.R. 3019 (Rangel, 107th Congress)

TPA/Fast-Track Authority	Enforceable Labor Provisions
H.R. 3019	Sec. 2(d)(1). PRINCIPAL NEGOTIATING OBJECTIVES FOR BILATERAL TRADE AGREEMENTS:
(Comprehensive Trade Negotiating Authority Act of 2001)	(1) To include enforceable rules that provide for the adoption and enforcement of the following core labor standards: the right of association, the right to bargain collectively, and prohibitions on employment discrimination, child labor, and slave labor;
	(2) To establish as the trigger for invoking the dispute settlement process with respect to the obligations above: (a) failure to effectively enforce one's own domestic labor standards through a sustained or recurring course of action or inaction, in a manner affecting trade or investment; or (b) waiver or derogation from domestic labor standards in order to attract investment, inhibit exports, or otherwise gain a competitive advantage; Recognizing that: (A) Parties retain the right to exercise discretion regarding investigatory, prosecutorial, regulatory, and compliance matters and to make decisions regarding the allocation of resources to enforcement with respect to other labor matters determined to have higher priorities [same as in *Trade Act of 2002*]; and (B) Parties retain the right to establish their own domestic labor standards, and to adopt or modify accordingly labor policies, laws, and regulations, in a manner consistent with the core labor standards identified in (1) above.
	(3) To provide for phased-in compliance for least-developed countries comparable to mechanisms used in other agreements;
	(4) To create a work program to provide guidance and technical assistance to [Parties] in strengthening their labor laws and regulations and commitments for market access incentives for least developed [Parties] to improve adherence and enforcement of core labor standards;
	(5) To provide for regular review of adherence to core labor standards; and
	(6) To create exceptions from obligations under the ... agreements for products produced by prison or slave labor and products produced by child labor; and for actions taken consistent with and in furtherance of recommendations made by the ILO.
	DISPUTE SETTLEMENT PROCEDURE
	(7) To provide for a single effective and expeditious dispute settlement mechanism and set of procedures that applies to all ... agreements.

References

[1] For a general discussion on TPA renewal, see CRS Report RL33743, *Trade Promotion Authority (TPA): Issues, Options, and Prospects for Renewal*, by J.F. Hornbeck and William H. Cooper.

[2] The *Trade Act of 2002* does not specifically define "principal negotiating objective." However, the Conference Report, H.Rept. 107-624, p. 229, defines it using the words quoted above.

[3] See, for example, U.S. Chile Free Trade Agreement, Report of the Labor Advisory Committee for Trade Negotiations and Trade Policy (LAC), February 28, 2003, p. 3. (The LAC consisted of 58 members of various unions.)

[4] For the ILO definition of "core labor standards" and a table of countries that have signed onto each, see the ILO table of "Ratifications of the Fundamental human rights Conventions by country" at [http://www.ilo.org/ilolex/english/docs/declworld.htm] which includes direct links to the texts of each core labor standard.

[5] The "worst forms of child labor" include the employment of children for purposes including prostitution, pornography, drug trafficking, armed conflict, and forced labor.

[6] The *Trade Act of 1974* refers to the U.S. list as "internationally recognized worker rights." The ILO refers to its list as "core labor standards." The current TPA authority in the *Bipartisan Trade Promotion Authority Act of 2002*, Title XXI of the *Trade Act of 2002*, combines the ILO name and the U.S. list, defining the U.S. list as "core labor standards."

[7] For a summary on working conditions in various countries, see the State Department's *Country Reports on Human Rights Practices*, updated yearly. Each year the volume updates reports on worker rights conditions in many countries around the world.

[8] See CRS Report RL31178, Trade Promotion Authority (Fast-Track): Labor Issues (Including H.R. 3005 and H.R. 3009), by Mary Jane Bolle.

[9] Business Round Table. The Case for U.S. Trade Leadership: the United States is Falling Behind, February 9, 2001, p. 4, 20.

[10] From the Singapore Declaration, signed by representatives of WTO countries present at the first meeting of Ministers of WTO countries in Singapore, December, 1996, contained in the *WTO Annual Report*, 1997.

[11] See WTO Protests in Seattle, 1999. *Free Trade and Globalization*, February 18, 2001.

[12] See Senate, House Floor Action on Peru seen as Doubtful Before Break. *Inside U.S. Trade*, July 21, 2006.

[13] Article XX(e) of the General Agreement on Tariffs and Trade (GATT), 1969, establishing the predecessor to the World Trade Organization (WTO), permits discrimination against products produced by prison labor.

[14] CRS reports addressing these FTAs include the following: CRS Report RL31356, *Free Trade Agreements: Impact on U.S. Trade and Implications for U.S. Trade Policy*, by William H. Cooper; CRS Report RS21846, *U.S. Bahrain Free Trade Agreement*, by Martin A. Weiss; CRS Report RL31870, *The Dominican Republic-Central America-United States Free Trade Agreement (CAFTA-DR)*, by J.F. Hornbeck; CRS Report RS21560, *Free Trade Agreements with Singapore and Chile: Labor Issues*, by Mary Jane Bolle; CRS Report RL32375, *The U.S.-Australia Free Trade Agreement: Provisions and Implications*, by William H. Cooper; CRS Report RL33328, *U.S.-Oman Free Trade Agreement*, by Mary Jane Bolle; CRS Report RS20968, *Jordan-U.S. Free Trade Agreement: Labor Issues*, by Mary Jane Bolle; CRS Report RS21464, *Morocco-U.S. Free Trade Agreement*, by Raymond J. Ahearn; CRS Report RS22159, *DR-CAFTA Labor Rights Issues*, by Mary Jane Bolle; and CRS Report 97-861, *NAFTA*

Labor Side Agreement: Lessons for the Worker Rights and FAST-Track Debate, by Mary Jane Bolle.

[15] See CRS Report RS22521, *Peru Trade Promotion Agreement: Labor Issues*, by M. Angeles Villarreal and Mary Jane Bolle; and CRS Report RS22419, *U.S.- Colombia Trade Promotion Agreement*, by M. Angeles Villarreal.

[16] CRS conversation with ILO Washington staff in the Spring of 2006.

[17] CRS conversation with Thea Lee, Policy Director of the AFL-CIO, January 16, 2007.

[18] CRS conversation with Carol Pier, Labor Rights and Trade Senior Researcher, Human Rights Watch, January 16, 2007.

[19] CRS conversation with Bama Althreya, Executive Director of the International Labor Rights Fund, January 16, 2007.

[20] CRS conversation with Carol Pier, op. cit. *The U.S.-Cambodia Textile Agreement* provides for a 6% minimum annual quota increase for Cambodia textile imports, but allows the United States to raise quota limits up to an additional 18% if working conditions in that sector substantially comply with local labor laws and international standards. Source: *Labor Rights Protections in CAFTA*, A Human Rights Watch briefing paper, October, 2003.

[21] See CRS Report 96-661, Worker Rights Provisions and Trade Policy: Should They Be Linked? by Mary Jane Bolle.

[22] CRS communication from Adam B. Greene, Vice President, Labor Affairs and Corporate Responsibility, USCIB, January 18, 2007.

[23] U.S. trade preference programs include the Generalized System of Preferences (GSP), the Caribbean Basin Economic Recovery Act (CBERA), the Caribbean Basin Trade Partnership Act (CBTPA), the Andean Trade Preference Act (ATPA), and the African Growth and Opportunity Act (AGOA.) In some cases, the U.S. government has withdrawn or is anticipating withdrawal of preferential trade status from countries after an FTA with them has gone into effect.

[24] *About the Declaration* (on Fundamental Principals and Rights at Work). ILO website at [http://www.ilo.org].

[25] CRS conversation with Thea Lee, op. cit.

[26] See ILO table of ratifications at [http://www.ilo.org/ilolex/english/docs/declworld.htm].

[27] CRS communication from Adam B. Greene, op. cit.

[28] However, in anticipation of and just prior to congressional floor consideration of the Jordan agreement, the U.S. Ambassador from Jordan Marwan Muasher and the U.S. Trade Representative Robert Zoellick, exchanged letters agreeing to resolve any disputes that might arise without resort to sanctions.

[29] See Article 17(1)(a)(iii) of the U.S.- Jordan FTA. This is often referred to as a "nonviolation" case.

In: Trade Policies and Agreements in the Era of Globalization ISBN: 978-1-60021-836-1
Editor: Paul B. Lucus, pp. 135-148

Chapter 6

MERCOSUR: EVOLUTION AND IMPLICATIONS FOR U.S. TRADE POLICY*

J. F. Hornbeck

ABSTRACT

Mercosur is the Common Market of the South established by Brazil, Argentina, Uruguay, and Paraguay in 1991 to improve political and economic cooperation in the region following a lengthy period of military rule and mutual distrust. On July 2, 2006, Venezuela acceded to the pact as its first new full member, making Mercosur the undisputed economic counterweight to U.S. trade policy in the region, but raising questions about how it may shift regional political and trade dynamics. Collectively, the Mercosur countries have a diversified trade relationship with the world. The United States is the largest trade partner, the European Union (EU) a close second, with each claiming about 25% of total Mercosur trade. By contrast, the four Mercosur countries together account for only 2% of total U.S. trade. Including U.S. imports of Venezuelan oil, the "Mercosur 5" constitute 3.5% of total U.S. trade.

The Mercosur pact calls for an incremental path to a common market, but after 15 years only a limited customs union has been achieved. From the outset, Mercosur struggled to reconcile a basic inconsistency in its goals for partial economic union: how to achieve trade integration, while also ensuring that the benefits would be balanced among members and that each country would retain some control over its trade, production, and consumption structure. This delicate balance faced serious structural and policy asymmetries that became clear when Brazil and Argentina experienced financial crises and deep recessions. These economic setbacks disrupted trade flows among members, causing friction, the adoption of new bilateral safeguards, and a retreat from the commitment to deeper integration.

For now, Mercosur has turned to expanding rather than deepening the agreement. Many South American countries have been added as "associate members" and Mercosur has reached out for other South-South arrangements in Africa and Asia. These are limited agreements and unlikely paths to continental economic integration. Internal conflicts have highlighted Mercosur's institutional weaknesses and slowed the integration process. Uruguay has diversified its trade more toward the United States, and is showing signs of

---

* Excerpted from CRS Report RL33620, dated January 5, 2007.

reconsidering the benefits of an "exclusive" Mercosur trade arrangement. Venezuela's accession to the pact adds a decidedly anti-American factor and may complicate both Mercosur's internal balance and regional trade relationships.

It appears Mercosur has opted for political cohesion over deeper economic integration. Mercosur, especially with Venezuela, will likely continue to resist movement toward a Free Trade Area of the Americas (FTAA), with Brazil in particular viewing the World Trade Organization (WTO) as the preferred alternative for achieving its trade policy goals. Given this impasse, it seems that the United States and Mercosur may continue to expand their influence through smaller trade agreements, presenting the possibility of two very different overlapping trading systems emerging in the Western Hemisphere centered around the U.S. and Brazilian economies. Few, if any, view this as an economically and administratively optimal alternative, presenting a formidable challenge to the future direction of U.S. trade policy in Latin America.

On March 26, 1991, Brazil, Argentina, Uruguay, and Paraguay signed the Treaty of Asunción, establishing the Common Market of the South (Mercado Común del Sur — Mercosur) with the intention of strengthening sub-regional economic and political cooperation. Since then, Mercosur has struggled to achieve deep economic integration, but has made strides toward political cohesion and emerged as an influential voice in regional trade negotiations. In particular, Mercosur has advocated its own expansion as an alternative to completing the proposed Free Trade Area of the Americas (FTAA).[1] On July 2, 2006, Venezuela acceded to the pact as its first new full member, making Mercosur the undisputed economic counterweight to U.S. trade policy in the region, and perhaps diminishing further expectations for a hemispheric-wide trade agreement. In December 2006, Bolivia also requested to become a full member. This report examines the evolution of Mercosur's policy decisions and performance as important elements for understanding the challenges to U.S. trade policy in Latin America.

U.S.-Mercosur Trade Prospects

The Mercosur countries are experiencing a period of strong economic growth in the aftermath of a deep recession caused by financial crises in Brazil (1999) and Argentina (2001). They currently have competitive exchange rates, stable macroeconomic conditions, and improved terms of trade, which have opened the door for significant export growth, spurred also by rising prices and demand for many of their products, particularly primary goods. Strong economic growth at home has also increased demand for imports. Brazil and Argentina are running sizable intra-Mercosur trade surpluses, with the smaller economies, Uruguay and Paraguay, maintaining small trade deficits.[2]

The Mercosur countries have a well-diversified trade relationship with the world, although the United States still accounts for much of Mercosur's rebound in trade. It is Mercosur's largest trade partner, with the European Union a close second, each claiming about 25% of total Mercosur trade, followed by Asia with 10%. It is the largest market for Mercosur exports and a major source of its capital and technology imports. By contrast, in 2005, the four Mercosur countries together contributed to only 2.0% of total U.S. trade. With the recent addition of Venezuela, the "Mercosur 5" make up 3.5% of total U.S. trade, the increase accounted for almost entirely by U.S. imports of Venezuelan oil. Collectively, the "Mercosur 4" would rank 10th for U.S. exports and 15th for U.S. imports, just ahead of Brazil by itself, the largest economy in South America, representing over three-quarters of total Mercosur trade with the United States.[3]

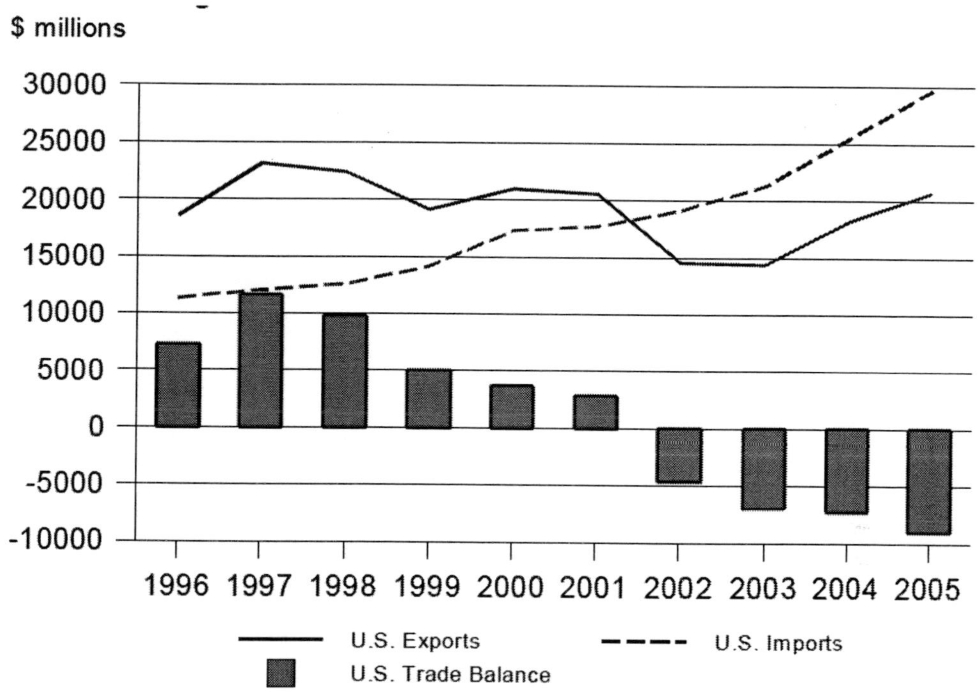

Data Source: U.S. Department of Commerce.

Figure 1. U.S.-"Mercosur-4" Balance of Trade.

Trends in U.S. trade with the original "Mercosur-4" appear in figure 1 (individual country data for all five appear in Appendix 1). It is important to remember that these trends are highly skewed by Brazil. As may be seen, U.S. imports from Mercosur grew steadily over the past decade, paralleling U.S. economic growth and the concomitant rise in U.S. demand for imports worldwide. Growth in U.S. exports was flat from 1996 to 2001, and then fell precipitously because of deep recessions in Brazil and Argentina. U.S. exports began to rebound in 2003 with Mercosur's economic recovery, but have just returned to levels attained ten years ago. During Mercosur's economic downturn, the U.S. trade balance shifted from a net surplus to deficit. Although macroeconomic trends explain most of these trade patterns, policies deterring trade liberalization remain an important issue for U.S.-Mercosur trade relations given their mutual interest in reducing barriers to trade and resolving, eventually, negotiations for a Free Trade Area of the Americas (FTAA).

The major U.S. exports to Mercosur include mostly capital and high technology goods such as mechanical and electrical machinery (computers), vehicles, aircraft, medical equipment, and pharmaceuticals. The primary U.S. imports are components for machinery and vehicles, agricultural products, and oil if Venezuela is included. Despite being a relatively small U.S. trading partner, Mercosur contains the largest South American economies, and so prospects for significant trade and investment growth may be driving the ongoing interest in maintaining cordial and cooperative relations, while also exploring avenues toward deeper Western Hemisphere integration, including the FTAA.

Formation and Institutional Development

Mercosur evolved from a series of mid-1980s bilateral agreements between Argentina and Brazil devised to foster new levels of political and economic openness and cooperation following a lengthy period of military rule and mutual distrust. As much as it may be considered a "political project," regional integration was also a response to economic stagnation, the 1980s debt crisis, and expanding regional trade agreements in the European Union (EU) and North America. The Treaty of Asunción called for the creation of a common market between Brazil, Argentina, Uruguay, and Paraguay for the stated purpose of accelerating economic development and social justice. It aims to improve living conditions in all member countries through "balanced and managed growth in trade flows."[4]

The treaty was made under guidelines of the Latin American Integration Association (Asociación Latinoamericana de Integración — ALADI). ALADI is a regional trade organization that provides a common, yet flexible framework for establishing sub-regional trade pacts that encourages inclusiveness and minimizing harm to non-members. This "umbrella" organization oversees integration pacts that are both "regional and partial in scope," in contrast to the U.S. free trade agreement (FTA) model that tends to be more comprehensive. As emphasized by ALADI, Mercosur adopted an approach based on "gradualism, flexibility, and balance," and allows for the negotiated accession of other ALADI member countries.[5]

Mercosur envisioned an incremental path to a common market, beginning with a transition period (1991-95) in which it operated as an increasingly comprehensive free trade agreement (FTA) based on a schedule of automatic tariff reductions. The formal jump to a common market was made on January 1, 1995, but in reality, Mercosur became (and remains) only a partial customs union.[6] It adopted a common trade policy and a schedule of common external tariffs (CETs) that applied to 85% of tariff line items, but with some very important exceptions for sensitive sectors such as automobiles, capital goods, computers, and other technology products. The exceptions were to be phased out by 2006, but many have been extended to 2011.[7] The achievement of a full common market remains a distant, if not illusory goal.

The Treaty of Asunción also provided for macroeconomic policy coordination and harmonization of policy legislation at the sectoral level (e.g. energy, agriculture, industry, technology). Some macroeconomic policies, such as exchange rates, have been forced toward complementarity by economic events, but differences remain significant and a designed coordination of policy is not currently feasible. The rationale for sectoral cooperation rests on inter-country factor mobility being pursued gradually, allowing comparative advantage to work, while easing the integration adjustment process. Nonetheless, sectoral issues remain a continuing challenge, especially between Brazil and Argentina.

All parties were required to accept a common set of rights and obligations (Article 2), with little allowance for special and differentiated treatment for smaller economies. There were many follow-on protocols. Among the most important was the December 17, 1994 Protocol of Ouro Preto, which formally established the common market and extended the institutional framework accordingly. Mercosur adopted a democratic commitment clause in 1996, and there were two protocols that clarified and expanded the dispute settlement process, the last being the Olivos Protocol signed on February 18, 2002, and implemented two years later.[8]

Two developments more recently may affect the institutional nature of Mercosur. First is the expansion of its membership. Venezuela was accepted as the first new full member on July 4, 2006 (discussed in detail below). In December 2006, Bolivia also requested to upgrade its status from associate to full member. Second is the announcement on December 14, 2006, of a new Mercosur Parliament to be formed and headquartered in Montevideo. It is to consist of 18 representatives from each full member country and has as its primary goal to work toward harmonization of national laws and policies.[9]

INTRA-MERCOSUR TRADE AND INTERNAL DYNAMICS

As Mercosur lowered tariffs, intra-Mercosur trade was expected to grow relative to trade with third-party countries. As seen in figure 2, this was the initial response from 1991 to 1998, with the jump in intra-Mercosur exports also due to its growth from an initially small base, the decade's lengthy global economic expansion, and other economic reforms. There is, however, an equally evident and sudden collapse of this trend, with intra-Mercosur exports falling from 25% of total trade in 1998 to 13% in 2005.[10] This setback reflects intra-Mercosur tariff increases in response to internal Mercosur problems and Argentina's pressure to lower the CET on capital goods, demonstrating a still strong dependence on trade with developed countries.[11]

From the outset, Mercosur struggled to reconcile a basic inconsistency of partial economic union: how to achieve trade integration, while also ensuring that the benefits would be balanced among members and that each country would retain some control over its trade, production, and consumption structure. At the heart of the problem are "natural asymmetries" that exist among four economies with large discrepancies in size, structure, resource endowment, and level of development. In addition to the absolute differences in size, relative differences fluctuate widely over time. For example, the size of Argentina's economy (GDP) tends to be half that of Brazil's, yet this metric has ranged from a high 60% in 1992 to a low of 22% in 2002 because of dramatic shifts in relative economic performance, in this case punctuated by the financial crisis and deep recession in Argentina.[12]

These structural differences can be compounded by "policy asymmetries" that arise from incongruities in fiscal, monetary, industrial, exchange rate, and other policies. Either type of asymmetry can dramatically alter commercial flows, as seen in figure 2, causing large trade imbalances that can threaten the stability of intra-Mercosur relations.[13] When they operate in tandem, the Mercosur policy adjustment framework has proven to be vulnerable, particularly at times when the countries face external economic shocks.

Such a confluence of events occurred in the late 1990s following a series of external shocks, beginning with the Asian financial crisis in July 1997. It was followed by the Russian default in summer 1998, which directly affected concerns over sovereign financial vulnerability in Brazil, causing prolonged capital flight in the fall of 1998, Brazil's steep currency devaluation in January 1999, and resulting loss of its fixed exchange rate program. With Argentina's strict dollar convertibility regime still in place at the time, the two countries faced a significant "exchange rate policy asymmetry" that altered trade patterns. This was compounded by Argentina's lengthy recession that also began in 1998, leading to its own, far more serious, financial crisis. The Brazilian devaluation further exacerbated Argentina's crisis, which ended with the loss of its fixed exchange rate in December 2001.

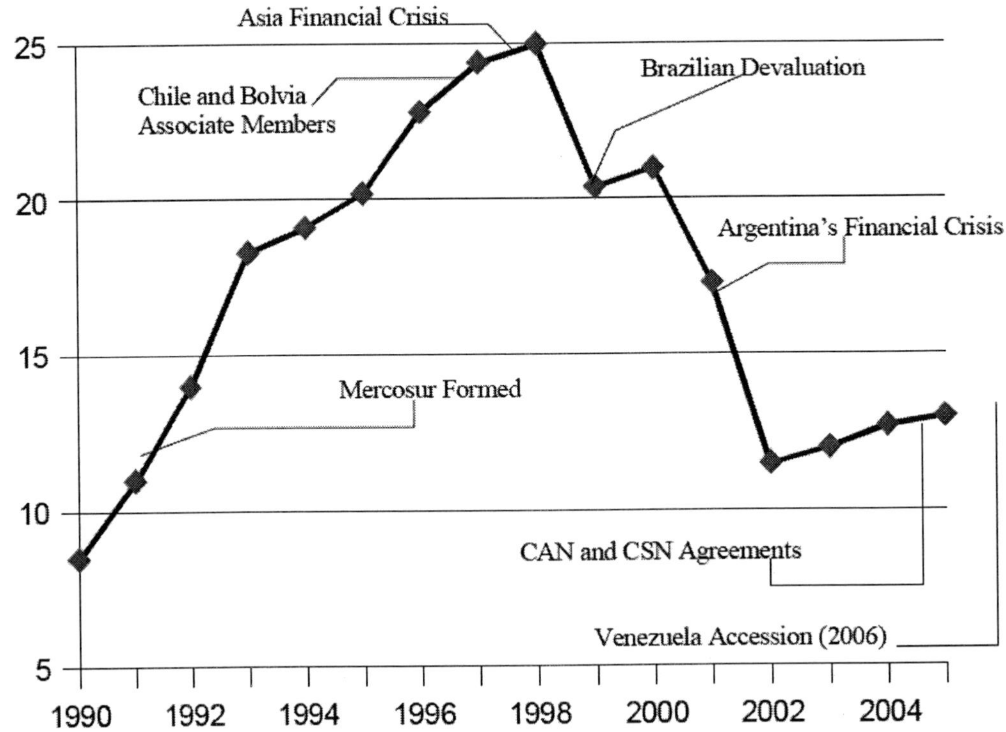

Data Source: Inter-American Development Bank, *MERCOSUR Report,* February 2006, p. 21.

Figure 2. Intra-Mercosur Exports as Percent of Total, 1990-2005.

Mercosur's leaders, aware of macroeconomic weaknesses exposed by these crises, proposed a Mercosur Relaunch program in May 2000. It formally reaffirmed a commitment to deeper integration and those policies that had so far proved elusive, but were still necessary to reach the common market goal. The countries agreed to take the first steps toward macroeconomic coordination by harmonizing their statistics and establishing "convergence criteria" on fiscal policies, prices, and public debt. They formally discouraged adoption of measures that would restrict reciprocal trade and reinforced those that would limit recourse to antidumping investigation and would improve dispute settlement. This renewed enthusiasm soon faded, however, as it proved unable to overcome the effects of financial crises, in particular, the fall in trade between Argentina and Brazil, which accounts for 90% of intra-Mercosur commercial exchange.[14] Relations became increasingly strained, with Argentina applying temporary restrictions on Brazilian imports, further reducing trade and diminishing incentives for deeper economic integration.

Since 2002, intra-Mercosur trade has rebounded slightly with economic growth and stability, but this did not alleviate problems with intra-Mercosur trade imbalances. Argentina's prolonged recession reduced demand for imports, and so it was able to maintain a small trade surplus with Brazil even after the Brazilian devaluation. With Argentina's economic recovery in 2003, however, it began to run large trade deficits with Brazil, mostly in industrial goods. Argentine exports fell from 13% of Brazilian imports in 1998 to 8% in 2004. Brazilian exports, in contrast, rose from 22% to 34% of Argentine imports. The growing imbalance resulted from numerous factors: 1) new exchange rate equilibriums that favored Brazilian goods in the Argentine market over U.S. and European products; 2) a post-recession jump in Argentine aggregate demand; and 3) Brazil's export promotion policy emphasizing greater use of domestic inputs.[15]

Mercosur was meant to achieve balanced gains for its members, but there was no enforceable mechanism to guard against sudden large trade imbalances. In 2003, Argentina once again called for a managed solution to the growing and, what some feared may be a structural bilateral trade imbalance with Brazil. By June 2004, Argentina had raised trade barriers on Brazilian appliances to protect its domestic production against what it considered to be its neighbor's unfair industrial development strategy. This was done in the context of Argentina's decision to "re-industrialize" its own economy, a policy that was threatened by the sharp rise in Brazilian exports.[16]

By February 2006, over the objections of Brazilian industry, Brazil and Argentina agreed to a Competitive Adaptation Mechanism (CAM). It allows for the application of tariffs and quotas in cases where sudden increases in imports of one country are deemed to hurt an industry of the other (safeguards). The CAM is a major policy shift for Mercosur and raises multiple issues. First, it is a bilateral arrangement between Brazil and Argentina established under the ALADI system and not governed by Mercosur. Second, import restrictions represent a retreat from the stated free trade philosophy of Mercosur, increasing doubts about its ability to proceed toward a common market. Third, the CAM has no enforcement mechanism under ALADI. In short, it presents serious institutional problems and may eventually undermine the Mercosur agreement even as it attempts to restore balance to the largest bilateral relationship within it.[17]

Expanding Mercosur

As Mercosur's relaunch effort dwindled, it shifted emphasis to expanding membership. To date, Mercosur has entered into "economic complementarity agreements" with most of South America, under ALADI guidelines. Also referred to as "associate membership," this arrangement is limited largely to the long-term pursuit of a free trade agreement, supported by sectoral cooperation. It does not convey membership status per se, and while members may attend meetings, they have no voting rights, do not participate in the internal functions of Mercosur, and are not required to adopt the CET. In 1996, Chile and Bolivia, following lengthy negotiations, became the first additions as associate members.[18] Peru followed in 2003 (not implemented) and Venezuela in 2004. Mexico has observer status.

In October 2004, after years of talks, Mercosur and the Andean Community of Nations (Comunidad Andina de Naciones — CAN) signed a trade pact, giving all Andean countries the equivalent of associate membership. This breakthrough led directly to creation of the South American Community of Nations (Comunidad Sudamericana de Naciones — CSN) two months later in a pact that included 12 countries (those in Mercosur, CAN, along with Chile, Guyana, and Suriname). The CAN and CSN are limited trade arrangements and in many ways not true regional agreements. Although they have common rules adopted by Mercosur and the CAN, details on market access and other specific provisions are bilateral arrangements between each Mercosur country and the CAN. Brazil also granted numerous unilateral concessions to ensure the agreement would be completed.[19] These constraints limit prospects for deep continental integration. Nonetheless, sectoral initiatives, such as the proposed South American gas pipeline, already reflect a growing attitude of cooperation and collective self-determination that is taking hold in the region, and which now has an institutional presence in the CSN.

Mercosur's other negotiations have had mixed success. Trade talks with the European Union and the Western Hemisphere countries for a proposed Free Trade Area of the Americas (FTAA) have both come to an impasse over the inability to reach an agricultural agreement acceptable to Brazil. Brazil has also declined U.S. and EU overtures on market access for industrial goods, services trade, enforceable intellectual property rights, and investment provisions. Speculation has also turned to dwindling interest by the EU given the stalemated FTAA, the growing EU perception of Mercosur as less than a credible collective negotiating authority, and the desire by all parties for a "successful" conclusion to the Doha Round, although this appears to be increasingly in doubt. South-South trade talks have advanced only in limited form. Mercosur has begun preliminary discussions with a host of countries that include China, India, SACU, Canada, the Russian Federation, Korea, Egypt, Morocco, and Pakistan. None has moved beyond a simple framework agreement.[20]

Venezuelan Accession

On July 4, 2006, Mercosur agreed to accept Venezuela as the first additional full member of the pact, although the accession has not been ratified by all member legislatures. The accession protocol was accelerated in mid-2006 at the behest of President Hugo Chávez, who saw it as being consistent with his effort to unify South America and advance his "Bolivarian agenda" that generally stands in opposition to U.S. influence in the region.

The expedited accession approval process was unhindered by any need for consultation with legislative or businesses interests, but was initially expected to be longer and more involved because of two significant hurdles: Venezuela's membership in the CAN, which would not have been allowed under Mercosur protocols; and the requirement to adopt the Mercosur CET. Venezuela dealt with the first issue by defiantly withdrawing from the Andean trade pact in April 2006. Citing Peru and Colombia's negotiations for FTAs with the United States as contrary to CAN's and Latin America's best interests, Chávez left the pact specifically to join Mercosur. To address the second issue, Mercosur, under Brazil's leadership, negotiated to give Venezuela four years to comply with the CET, with other obligations of the pact not completely phased in until 2014.[21]

Mercosur may have many incentives to bring Venezuela into the fold. The addition of a fifth member adds to the economic strength of the bloc, which now represents three-quarters of South American GDP. Venezuela also promised immediate selective duty-free treatment to Paraguay and Uruguay, with no requirement for reciprocal treatment until 2013. Venezuela may increase the potential for intra-Mercosur trade as a relatively large Latin American market that also offers sectoral complementarity and energy security with its vast oil reserves and plans for a regional pipeline. Interestingly, this anticipated trade growth would likely result in part from trade diversion, or an expected offsetting decline in trade from non-

Mercosur members who will face higher Venezuelan tariffs if and when the Mercosur CET is adopted.[22]

The political motivations for Venezuela's accession may be even more compelling. Until the accession is ratified by all Mercosur members, Venezuela remains a non-voting member. Venezuela does, however, have a voice in Mercosur affairs, increasing its influence on intra-pact and external trade negotiations, likely to the detriment of U.S. interests. The marginal effect may be to strengthen resolve in some countries to challenge U.S. influence in South America, although Brazil and others may prove to be moderating influences. Uruguay and Paraguay may also view Venezuela as having a diluting force on Brazil's political dominance in the pact.

Venezuela's accession, however, may have unintended regional consequences should countries outside Mercosur be put in a position of having to choose between a U.S. or Mercosur trade agreement. Peru has even suggested forming a new trade bloc, the Community of the Pacific, which would include countries with complementary trade arrangements: the United States, Canada, Mexico, the Central American countries, Panama, Colombia, Peru, and Chile.[23] This prospect may be further reinforced by Bolivia's recent request to become a full member of Mercosur.

Mercosur Internal Challenges

Two important internal disagreements currently challenge Mercosur's organizational cohesiveness. The first is Argentina's ongoing dispute with Uruguay over the planned construction of a pulp plant on the Uruguay River by a Finnish firm.[24] Argentina alleges that it is in violation of a bilateral environmental protocol the two countries signed in 1975. Although a World Bank review concluded that the plant poses no serious environmental problems and has provided $100 million in financing for the project, the issue continues to spawn protests and diplomatic flare-ups. In particular, Argentine protesters have blocked bridges over the Uruguay River, disrupting trade and tourist traffic between the two countries. Uruguay turned to the Mercosur system for dispute settlement, and a ruling by the Mercosur Ad-Hoc Arbitration Tribunal on September 6, 2006, found that Argentina had failed to live up to its commitment to ensure the free movement of people, goods, and services under the pact. The tribunal, however, did not make any awards in the case.[25]

Argentina has also filed a petition with the International Court of Justice (ICJ) at The Hague for arbitration. The ICJ denied Argentina's request for an injunction to terminate construction and set January 15, 2007, as the final date for Argentina to submit its case. Uruguay subsequently filed a counter claim, arguing that Argentina has failed to take action against the protesters. In the meantime, both Brazil and Venezuela have declined to help mediate a solution and the dispute remains a serious point of contention, raising a question regarding the institutional capacity of Mercosur to arbitrate disputes within the bloc.[26]

A second recurring challenge to Mercosur concerns perceived asymmetries in trade benefits and in the exercise of power. Both Paraguay and Uruguay have complained that Mercosur disproportionally benefits the larger countries, to the detriment of export growth in the smaller countries. In part, this is a structural element of the Mercosur agreement that promises "balanced" benefits, but which gives little in the way of special and differential treatment to the smaller economies and allows Mercosur diplomacy to occur bilaterally through presidential summitry rather than the formal Mercosur system.[27] The safeguards mechanism adopted by Brazil and Argentina is another example, pointing to asymmetrical arrangements despite the Mercosur principle of reciprocity in rights and obligations. The "asymmetries" issue became even more inflammatory when Argentina and Brazil decided to exclude it from the January 18-19, 2007 Mercosur summit. This decision rankled Uruguay's President Vázquez, who has decided not to attend the summit.

Uruguay has further expressed its dissatisfaction with Mercosur by threatening to expand its trade affiliations outside the pact. On November 4, 2006, following U.S. Senate approval, a Bilateral Investment Treaty (BIT) between the United States and Uruguay went into force. Uruguay also sought and received permission from Brazil to explore an FTA with the United States. It subsequently decided to pursue a Trade and Investment Framework Agreement (TIFA) with the United States when faced with serious domestic political division over the FTA option. A Joint Commission on Trade and Investment will provide the means for ongoing U.S.-Uruguay discussions regarding opportunities for specific trade deals.

The TIFA approach provides a way for Uruguay to explore expanding its exports to the United States, without diminishing its commitment to Mercosur. In the past TIFAs have also served as precursors to FTA negotiations (e.g. Chile). Uruguay has directly linked its desire to develop closer U.S. trade ties with its concern over increasing "bilateralism" that it sees developing between Argentina and Brazil. In December 2006, Argentina again criticized Uruguay for attempting to circumvent Mercosur in its quest to diversify its trade relations, likely reflecting deepening tensions between the two countries.[28]

In January 2007, Argentina also filed a complaint in the WTO against Brazilian antidumping practices related to Argentine PET resin imports, without notifying Brazil or appealing to the Mercosur consultation or dispute resolution process. This tactic again points to a lack of confidence in the institutional capacity of Mercosur to adjudicate its own internal disagreements.[29]

Implications for U.S. Trade Policy

Historically, the United States has supported Mercosur as a potential complementary path to meeting its own goal of Western Hemisphere economic integration. By reemphasizing its political goals rooted in sub-regional stability and cooperation, Mercosur, however, is evolving in ways that do not bode well for the U.S.-driven FTAA. In fact, Mercosur has taken a step backward in the commitment to its own common market by adopting a bilateral safeguards agreement between Brazil and Argentina, failing to resolve its internal bilateral economic disputes, and ceasing any pretense that deeper integration is feasible in the near future.

Mercosur's recent addition of Venezuela reinforces the political focus of the pact, particularly in light of the small amount of trade between Venezuela and the Mercosur-4. Venezuela has also been allowed four years to adopt the CET, which further weakens Mercosur's claim to being a functioning customs union with all members adhering to a common set of rights and obligations. The Venezuelan accession may also rebalance the internal Mercosur power structure in unpredictable ways, raising questions over the possible effect on trade relations in the region given Chávez's open anti-Americanism and determination to create a united South America in opposition to what he terms U.S. economic and political "imperialism."[30]

Internal challenges may further continue to hinder Mercosur's ability to advance economic complementarity. Mercosur faces ongoing complaints from the smaller partners, whose rising expectations for export growth may not be easily satisfied, and who may be exhibiting lingering doubts about deeper economic integration in the aftermath of their own deep recessions caused by financial crises in the two larger countries. Uruguay's dispute with Argentina and export diversification away from Mercosur toward the U.S. market, not to mention its interest in developing closer economic ties with the United States, presents another challenge to Mercosur cohesiveness. Mercosur's new alignment with Venezuela may also point to a not-so-subtle shift in regional trade dynamics. Although Mercosur has resisted the FTAA as envisioned by the United States, Venezuela is the only country in Latin America to reject the idea unequivocally. With Venezuela's new-found status as a negotiating member of Mercosur, the United States may find it more difficult to isolate Chávez's unabashedly negative influence on the FTAA negotiations.

Both the United States and Mercosur have reacted to the impasse in the FTAA talks by expanding their influence through smaller trade arrangements. This development points to the possibility of two overlapping, if not competing trading systems emerging in the Western Hemisphere centered on the U.S. and Brazilian economies. In fact, Peru's proposed Community of the Pacific points to just such a bifurcated trading system, with one group linked by U.S.-style FTAs (Canada, Mexico, Chile, Central America, the Caribbean, Panama, Peru, and Colombia), juxtaposed with a Mercosur customs union-based pact (Brazil, Argentina, Paraguay, Uruguay, Venezuela, and possibly Bolivia and Ecuador).

Any type of dual or competing regional trading system would have awkward implications for businesses trying to operate under decidedly different commercial rules and for countries with multiple political and economic affiliations. For example, Chile has an open trade policy and announced in August 2006 that it would accept formal associate membership in the CAN, while also continuing to encourage commercial relations with both Mercosur and the United States. Talk of an Uruguay-U.S. FTA (currently focused on a TIFA) may suggest that allegiances could shift. Ecuador and Bolivia have resisted an FTA with the United States, and trade legislation passed at the close of the 109th Congress made clear that preferential treatment given to their imports under the Andean Trade Preference Act, as amended, would not be extended beyond June 30, 2007, unless they enter into an FTA with the United States.[31] This congressional response could either convince them to rethink their position on an FTA with the United States, or push them closer to the Mercosur camp, as appears to be the case with Bolivia. Given President Lula's preference for enlarging Mercosur over pursuit of the FTAA, he would likely welcome such an opportunity.

Finally, an important question for Mercosur's future is whether Venezuela will come to be a reliable and cooperative partner within the Mercosur system, or a destabilizing influence on the intricate, yet enduring, political and economic balances that have been the main reason for Mercosur's existence. The problem with over-politicizing a trade agreement is that political issues can be narrowly focused and eventually run head on into economic realities. For U.S.-Mercosur trade relations, the issue may have to be recast from basic premises. Perhaps the decision to continue pursuing a hemispheric trade agreement may not come down to whether Mercosur or the United States need each other, but whether the two can agree anew that closer commercial and economic ties are happening with or without a formal agreement and that an FTAA might still be pursued as matter of policy for its promise of long-term mutual benefit.

Appendix 1. U.S. Merchandise Trade with Mercosur ($ millions)

Country	2001	2002	2003	2004	2005	% Change 2004-05	% Change 2001-05
U.S. Exports							
Brazil	15,879	12,376	11,211	13,897	15,372	10.6%	-3.2%
Argentina	3,920	1,586	2,437	3,388	4,122	21.7%	5.2%
Uruguay	406	209	327	326	357	9.5%	-12.1%
Paraguay	389	433	484	623	896	43.8%	130.3%
Mercosur 4	20,594	14,604	14,459	18,234	20,747	13.8%	0.7%
Venezuela	5,642	4,430	2,831	4,767	6,421	34.7%	13.8%
Mercosur 5	26,236	19,034	17,290	23,001	27,168	18.1%	3.6%
Mexico	101,296	97,470	97,412	110,834	120,365	8.6%	18.8%
LAC*	58,157	51,551	51,946	61,465	72,407	17.8%	24.5%
Latin America	159,453	149,021	149,358	172,299	192,772	11.9%	20.9%
World	729,100	693,103	724,771	818,775	905,978	10.7%	24.3%
U.S. Imports							
Brazil	14,466	14,781	17,910	21,160	24,436	15.5%	68.9%
Argentina	3,013	3,187	3,170	3,745	4,584	22.4%	52.1%
Uruguay	228	193	256	580	732	26.2%	221.1%
Paraguay	33	44	53	59	52	-11.9%	57.6%
Mercosur 4	17,740	18,205	21,389	25,544	29,804	16.7%	68.0%
Venezuela	15,250	15,094	17,136	24,921	33,978	36.3%	122.8%
Mercosur 5	32,990	33,299	38,525	50,465	63,782	26.4%	93.3%
Mexico	131,338	134,616	138,060	155,902	170,109	9.1%	29.5%
LAC*	67,370	69,503	78,829	98,647	122,873	24.6%	82.4%
Latin America	198,708	204,119	216,889	254,549	292,982	15.1%	47.4%
World	1,140,999	1,161,366	1,257,121	1,469,704	1,673,455	13.9%	46.7%
U.S. Balance of Trade							
Brazil	1,413	-2,405	-6,699	-7,263	-9,064		
Argentina	907	-1,601	-733	-357	-462		
Uruguay	178	16	71	-254	-375		
Paraguay	356	389	431	564	844		
Mercosur 4	2,854	-3,601	-6,930	-7,310	-9,057		
Venezuela	-9,608	-10,664	-14,305	-20,154	-27,557		
Mercosur 5	-6,754	-14,265	-21,235	-27,464	-36,614		
Mexico	-30,042	-37,146	-40,648	-45,068	-49,744		
LAC*	-9,213	-17,952	-26,883	-37,182	-50,466		
Latin America	-39,256	-55,098	-67,531	-82,250	-100,210		
World	-411,899	-468,263	-532,350	-650,929	-767,477		

Source: Table created by CRS from U.S. Department of Commerce data.

* Latin America and the Caribbean, except Mexico.

References

[1] For more on the FTAA, see CRS Report RS20864, A Free Trade Area of the Americas: Status of Negotiations and Major Issues, by J. F. Hornbeck.

[2] Inter-American Development Bank. Integration and Regional Programs Department. MERCOSUR Report: 2004-2005. No. 10, February 2006. pp. 21-24.

[3] For details on U.S.-Brazil trade relations, see CRS Report RL33258, Brazilian Trade Policy and the United States, by J. F. Hornbeck.

[4] Costa Vaz, Alcides. Trade Strategies in the Context of Economic Regionalism: The Case of MERCOSUR. In: Aggarwal, Vinod K., Ralph Espach, and Joseph S. Tulchin, eds. The Strategic Dynamics of Latin American Trade. Washington, DC. Woodrow Wilson Center Press. 2004. pp. 234-35.

[5] Porrata-Doria, Jr., Rafael A. MERCOSUR: The Common Market of the Southern Cone. Durham: Carolina Academic Press. 2005. pp. 14-16.

[6] A free trade agreement (FTA) eliminates tariffs on goods exchanged among participating countries. In a customs union, the members also adopt a common external tariff (CET) and common trade policy toward third-party countries. A common market takes the next step of allowing for the free flow of all factors of production (capital and labor) among members.

[7] IDB, MERCOSUR Report: 2004-2005, p. 70.

[8] For details on the legal documents, see Porrata-Doria, MERCOSUR: The Common Market of the Southern Cone.

[9] Latin American Weekly Report. Mercosur Meeting Ends on Sour Note. December 19, 2006. p. 7.

[10] By comparison exports are 60% of intra-EU trade. Intra-Mercosur trade dependence varies by country. In 2005, Mercosur captured 9.8% of Brazil's total trade (exports plus imports) compared to 26.7% for Argentina, 38.8% for Uruguay, and 50.8% for Paraguay.

[11] Phillips, Nicola. The Southern Cone Model: The Political Economy of Regional Capitalist Development in Latin America. London: Routledge, Taylor and Francis Group. 2004. p. 94-95.

[12] Heymann, Daniel and Adrián Ramos. MERCOSUR in Transition: Macroeconomic Perspectives. United Nations. Economic Commission for Latin America and the Caribbean (ECLAC). Santiago, Chile. December 2005. p. 17.

[13] For details, see IDB, MERCOSUR Report: 2004-2005, pp. 39-41.

[14] Bouzas, Roberto. Mercosur After Ten Years. In: Tulchin, Joseph S. And Ralph H. Espach, eds. Paths to Regional Integration: The Case of Mercosur. Woodrow Wilson International Center for Scholars. Washington, DC. 2002. p. 120.

[15] Inter-American Development Bank, MERCOSUR Report: 2004-2005, pp. 30-32. Heymann and Ramos, MERCOSUR in Transition, p. 20.

[16] IDB, MERCOSUR Report: 2004-05, p. 47.

[17] Haskel, David. Bilateral Agreements: Argentina, Brazil Start Safeguard System To Shield Industries from Mutual Imports. International Trade Reporter. February 7, 2006. p. 247, and Inter-American Development Bank. Southern Common Market: New Integration and Co-operation Agreements Between Argentina and Brazil. [http://www.iadb.org/intal]

[18] Porrata-Doria, MERCOSUR: The Common Market of the Southern Cone, pp. 123-124.

[19] Inter-American Development Bank, MERCOSUR Report No. 10, 2004-2005, p. 93.

[20] Ibid., pp. 90 and 96-100.

[21] Mercosur. Protocolo de Adhesión de la República Bolivariana de Venezuela al Mercosur. Articulo 4. July 4, 2006. Haskel, David. Mercosur, Venezuela Agree on

Protocol for Caracas Accession to Trading Bloc. International Trade Reporter. BNA, Inc. June 1, 2006. p. 837.

[22] Ibid and Haskel, David. Venezuela's Full Membership in Mercosur Seen as Boon to Exports by Other Members. International Trade Reporter. BNA, Inc. August 24, 2006. p. 1262. Higher tariffs in Venezuela could also have an inflationary impact.

[23] Chauvin, Lucien O. Peru Proposes New Trade Bloc of Hemisphere Nations on Pacific Coast. International Trade Reporter. BNA, Inc. August 3, 2006. p. 1172.

[24] Originally, the dispute involved a second plant to be built by a Spanish firm. This plant has been relocated, defusing it as an issue.

[25] Inter-American Development Bank. Institute for the Integration of Latin America and the Caribbean. Dispute Between Argentina and Uruguay: Arbitration Tribunal Award. INTAL Monthly Letter. September 2006. This episode points to Mercosur's observed highly politicized dispute settlement and decision-making processes, which can allow for resolutions based on "political whim, unilateral action, and non-observance of agreed policy commitments." Phillips, op. cit., p. 99.

[26] One Year On, Small Dispute Threatens to Fracture Mercosur. Latin American Regional Report. Brazil and Southern Cone. April 2006. p. 1, Puentes, Alberto. Uruguay. Emerging Markets Economics Daily. July 14, 2006. p. 4, and Haskel, David. Uruguayan, Paraguayan Auto Parts Makers Ask for Bigger Share of Mercosur's Market. International Trade Reporter. BNA., Inc. August 24, 2006. p. 1261.

[27] Phillips, op. cit., p. 99.

[28] Haskel, David. Uruguayan President Turns Down Offer to Negotiate Free Trade Agreement with U.S. International Trade Reporter. BNA, Inc. October 5, 2006. p. 1440 and Argentina Blasts Uruguay's Pursuit of Free Trade with Non-Mercosur Nations. International Trade Reporter. BNA. Inc. January 4, 2007. p. 22.

[29] Marin. Denise Chrispim. Argentina Denuncia Brasil e Ameaca Cúpula do Mercosul. O Estado de Sao Paulo. Brasil. January 5, 2007.

[30] Obiko Pearson, Natalie. Chávez Hosts 6-Nation Trade Summit. Associated Press. July 5, 2006.

[31] P.L. 109-432.

In: Trade Policies and Agreements in the Era of Globalization ISBN: 978-1-60021-836-1
Editor: Paul B. Lucus, pp. 149-162

Chapter 7

U.S.-CANADA WTO CORN TRADE DISPUTE*

Randy Schnepf

ABSTRACT

On January 8, 2007, Canada initiated a World Trade Organization (WTO) dispute settlement case (DS357) against certain aspects of U.S. commodity programs in general, and the U.S. corn program in particular, by requesting consultations with the United States under the auspices of the WTO dispute settlement process. Canada's WTO case represents the present manifestation of long-simmering concerns that previously surfaced in 2005 in the form of an anti-dumping (AD) and countervailing (CV) duty case brought by Canadian corn producers who sought legal action for alleged unfair subsidization and dumping of U.S. corn in Canadian markets. Canada's International Trade Tribunal (CITT) ultimately ruled in favor of the United States on the 2005 AD/CV duty case. However, Canadian corn producers continued to press their concerns with the Canadian government about perceived unfair subsidization of U.S. corn. This pressure, and other supporting factors, likely contributed to the Canadian government's decision to request WTO consultations with the United States, thereby setting in motion the WTO dispute settlement process with its explicit rules and timetables for resolving a trade dispute.

In making its charges, Canada clearly seeks to build on Brazil's successful challenge of various provisions of the U.S. cotton program (WTO dispute settlement case DS267). Canada raises three explicit charges against U.S. farm programs. First, Canada contends that U.S. corn subsidies have caused serious prejudice to Canadian corn producers in the form of market price suppression in Canadian corn markets during the 1996 to 2006 period. Second, Canada argues that the U.S. export credit guarantee program operates as a WTO-illegal export subsidy. Third, Canada claims that U.S. fixed direct payments are not green-box compliant and should therefore be included with U.S. amber box payments, in which case the United States would be in violation of its $19.1 billion amber box spending limit for 1999, 2000, 2001, 2004, and 2005.

Since Canada's initial request for WTO consultations, several other WTO members — including Argentina, Australia, Brazil, the European Communities (EC), Guatemala, Nicaragua, Thailand, and Uruguay — have requested to join the consultations as interested third parties.

---

* Excerpted from CRS Report RL33853, dated January 31, 2007.

If successfully litigated, this case could affect all U.S. agricultural policy since the charges against the U.S. export credit guarantee and direct payment programs extend beyond corn to all major program crops. Should any eventual changes in U.S. farm policy be needed to comply with a WTO ruling in Canada's favor, such changes would likely involve action by Congress to produce new legislation. Congress will be revisiting U.S. farm legislation this year and could potentially address some of the issues raised by Canada's WTO challenge. U.S. Secretary of Agriculture, Mike Johanns, who has been advocating that a new Farm Act should be designed to make U.S. farm policy be "beyond challenge," has recently proposed changes to U.S. commodity programs that, if accepted in a new Farm Act, potentially could alleviate many of Canada's concerns while minimizing the likelihood of future WTO challenges.

Introduction

The United States and Canada conduct the world's largest bilateral trade relationship, with total merchandise trade (exports and imports) reaching almost $500 billion in 2005.[1] However, this economic trade success story is not without its disagreements.[2] For example, the two countries engaged in a dispute over wheat trade for several decades that included both an anti-dumping (AD) and countervailing (CV) duty case and a World Trade Organization (WTO) case brought against various aspects of Canada's wheat trading practices by U.S. wheat interests.[3]

In 2005, the two countries extended their agricultural disagreement to the corn sector when Canadian corn producers sought legal action for alleged unfair subsidization and dumping of U.S. corn in Canadian markets. Canada's International Trade Tribunal (CITT) ultimately ruled on the 2005 AD/CV duty case in favor of the United States. However, Canadian corn producers continued to press their concerns upon the Canadian government about perceived unfair subsidization of U.S. corn. On January 8, 2007, the Canadian government requested consultations under the official WTO dispute settlement process with the United States concerning U.S. corn subsidies and their alleged affect upon Canadian corn markets. Canada's request initiated an official WTO dispute settlement case (number DS357) and set in motion the explicit rules and timetables of the WTO dispute settlement process. This report provides background on both the U.S. and Canadian corn sectors and the historical development of their corn trade dispute. In addition, it provides a discussion of the potential implications of the case for U.S. farm policy.

Background on the U.S. and Canadian Corn Sectors

The United States is the world's leading producer and exporter of corn. Since 1980 U.S. corn production has accounted for over 40% of world production, while U.S. corn exports have represented over two-thirds of world corn trade. Canada is also an important producer and consumer of corn. However, Canada's average annual production of 8.7 million metric tons (MMT) since 2000 is markedly smaller than U.S. average annual production of nearly 262 MMT.[4]

Although it is grown widely throughout the world, corn grows best in temperate conditions with deep, fertile soils such as exist in the U.S. Corn Belt. Corn's agroclimatic requirements, coupled with Canada's northerly latitudes, limit the extent of Canadian corn planting to the more southerly regions of Ontario and Quebec. As a result, growth in Canada's corn production has been limited almost entirely to yield (i.e., bushels per acre) enhancement. In contrast, strong and steady domestic demand for corn — driven by the livestock (dairy, swine, and poultry) and ethanol sectors —has outpaced domestic production and made Canada a net importer of corn, primarily from the United States, since the early 1990s (figure 1).

The elimination of tariffs on corn trade between the United States and Canada, first under the U.S.-Canada Free Trade Agreement (FTA) and later under the North American Free Trade Agreement (NAFTA), have facilitated corn imports into Canada from the United States and strengthened the integration of the North American livestock feeding industry. Since 1989, over 99% of Canada's corn imports have come from the United States. During the 1990s, U.S. corn exports to Canada averaged less than 1 MMT per year; since 2000, they have averaged almost 2.8 MMT per year.[5]

The surge in imports of U.S. corn occurred at a time when U.S. government program payments to the corn sector were also growing (figure 2). During the 1990s, U.S. corn program payments averaged $2.8 billion per year; since 2000 they have essentially doubled in size to an average of $5.5 billion per year. The increases in both U.S. corn program payments and imports of U.S. corn drew the attention and ire of Canada's corn-producing sector, which claimed that U.S. corn exports were being facilitated by large U.S. government payments and being sold into Canada at less than the cost of production.

PREVIOUS ACTION BY CANADIAN CORN GROWERS

In August 2005, the Canadian Corn Producers — a coalition composed of the Ontario Corn Producer's Association, the Fédération des producteurs de cultures commerciales du Québec, and the Manitoba Corn Growers Association —announced that they would pursue action on three separate fronts against what they perceived as "unfairly traded U.S. grain corn imports."[6]

First, they asked the Canadian government to include U.S. grain corn imports on the list of products targeted for retaliation by Canada against the United States for the U.S. refusal to repeal the Byrd Amendment.[7] The Byrd Amendment had been ruled to violate WTO obligations in a dispute proceeding filed by Canada and other WTO members. Congress eventually repealed the Byrd Amendment in February 2006 with a several-month transition period, and a U.S. federal court ruled in July 2006 that the Byrd Amendment did not apply to imports from Canada. However, in mid-2005, Canada was particularly concerned about the economic effects of the Byrd Amendment because, at that time, it appeared that as much as $4 billion in anti-dumping (AD) and countervailing (CV) duty deposits on Canadian softwood lumber could eventually become available for distribution to U.S. lumber producers under this law.[8]

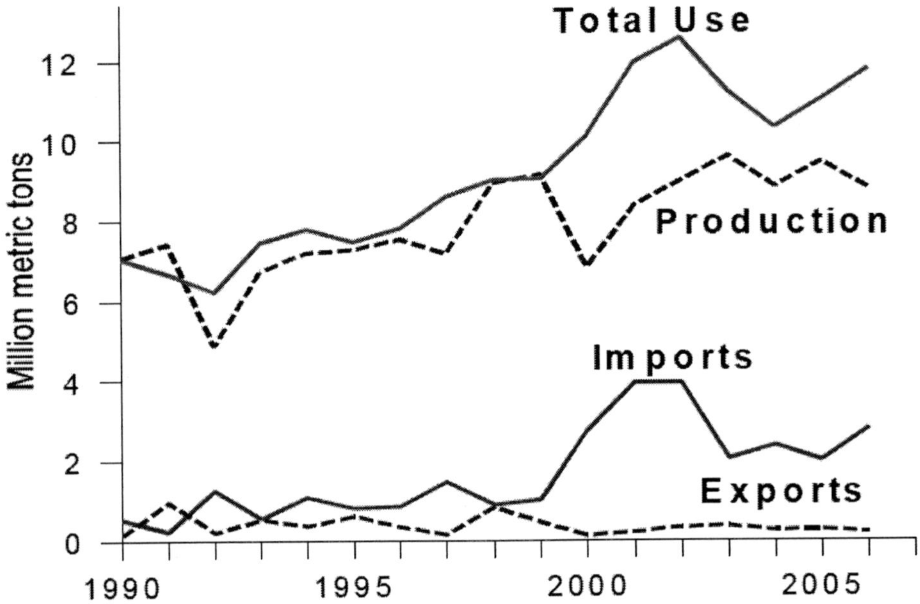

Note: data are on a corn marketing year (Sep-Aug) basis.
Source: USDA, PSD database, January 12, 2007.

Figure 1. Canada's Corn Supply and Use, 1990 to 2006.

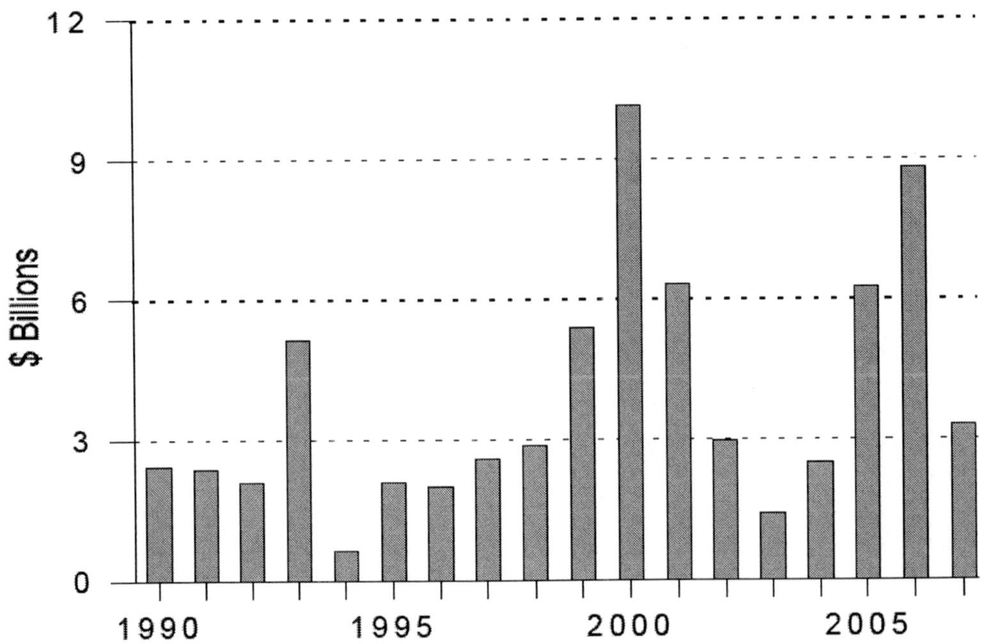

Data include fixed direct payments, counter-cyclical payments, loan deficiency payments, marketing loan gains, market loss payments, and payments under other provisions.
Source: USDA, Farm Service Agency, Table 35 – Net Outlays by Commodity and Function, Jan. 19, 2007; FY2007 is projected.

Figure 2. U.S. Government Payments in Support of Corn Production, FY1990 to FY2006.

Second, the Canadian Corn Producers asked the Canadian government to commence WTO dispute settlement proceedings by requesting consultations with the United States regarding the alleged "illegality of U.S. grain corn subsidies." Third, Canadian corn producers filed a domestic trade remedy complaint under Canada's Special Import Measures Act (SIMA) for the alleged "injurious subsidization and dumping of imports of U.S. corn."

Dumping occurs when goods are sold to importers at prices that are less than their selling prices in the exporter's domestic market or at unprofitable prices. If proven, dumping is addressed by the imposition of AD duties. Subsidizing occurs when imported goods benefit from government financial assistance in the exporting country. If proven, subsidizing is addressed by the imposition of CV duties. Canada's SIMA protects Canadian producers from the damaging effects of both of these unfair trade practices.

Canadian AD/CV Duty Investigation of U.S. Corn

On September 16, 2005, the Canadian Border Services Agency (CBSA) announced that, in response to the trade remedy complaint filed by the Canadian Corn Producers, it was beginning an investigation into the alleged dumping and subsidizing of grain corn from the United States. (Unprocessed grain corn includes whole-kernel grain corn and grain corn that has been milled to a limited degree, i.e., milled grain corn, regardless of its physical form, that preserves all the constituent parts of whole kernel grain corn and is chemically identical to whole kernel grain corn. The investigation excluded seed corn, sweet corn, and popping corn.)

At the same time that CBSA was conducting its investigation, Canada's International Trade Tribunal (CITT) also began a parallel investigation to determine whether imports of U.S. corn were harming Canadian producers.

U.S. Secretary of Agriculture Mike Johanns and then-U.S. Trade Representative Rob Portman issued a joint statement (September 16, 2005) expressing their disappointment that Canada was proceeding with a formal AD/CV duty investigation, and said that the United States believes that Canada's petition calling for the investigation lacked "sufficient evidence of injury" to justify initiating such an investigation.[9] In addition, they pointed out that U.S. corn exports to Canada had actually declined during the two preceding years (2003/04 and 2004/05), while Canadian corn production had increased (see figure 1).

U.S. officials argue that a 46% decline in Canadian imports of U.S. corn from 2002/03 to 2003/04, coupled with a steadily strengthening Canadian dollar (figure 3) which makes imports cheaper *ceteris paribus*, suggested that economic forces other than U.S. dumping or subsidies may have accounted for increased Canadian imports of U.S. corn and weakened Canada's case.[10] In addition, 20 Canadian corn users from the livestock, food processors, and ethanol sectors voiced their disagreement with the Canadian Corn Producers' accusation that imports of U.S. corn were either dumped or subsidized and expressed their opposition to this case moving forward.[11]

On November 15, 2005, the CITT announced its determination that there was reasonable evidence that the dumping and subsidizing of unprocessed U.S. grain corn caused injury to Canada's domestic industry.[12] On December 15, 2005, the CBSA announced its preliminary determination of dumping and subsidizing of U.S. grain corn. As a result, provisional duties of $1.65 per bushel were imposed payable on imports of U.S. corn at any time on or after December 15, 2005, including a provisional AD duty of $0.58 per bushel and a provisional CV duty of $1.07 per bushel. (All amounts are in U.S. dollars.)

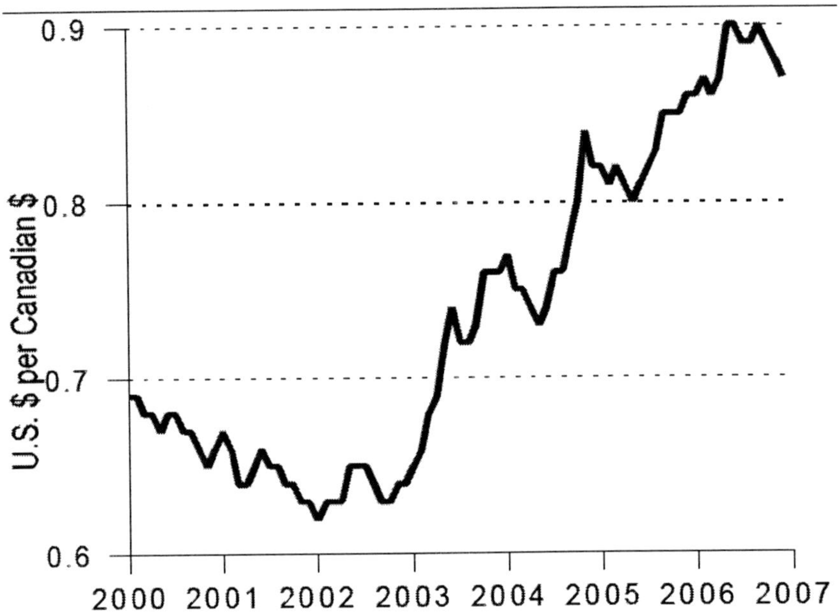

Source: Pacifica Exchange Rates Service.

Figure 3. The Canadian Dollar Strengthened Against the U.S. Dollar during 2002 to 2006.

Canadian Government Proposes AD/CV Duty Rebate Program

Following numerous complaints by Canadian corn users, the Canadian government (mid-December 2005) announced a duty-relief program and a duty-drawback program designed to help the livestock and other Canadian corn user groups obtain at least a partial rebate of the $1.65 per bushel punitive duty.[13] The duty rebate programs gave an exemption to the tariff for Canadian corn users who imported corn from the United States for use as an input, then sent the finished product back outside the country. A corn user would apply for the duty rebate as the imported corn was re-exported in the form of a value-added product. Exports were not restricted to the United States, but exports had to be made within four years of the release date of the imported corn.

Some market analysts expressed initial concerns that the duty rebate program would contribute to increased U.S. imports of Canadian agricultural products, particularly live hogs and processed pork products, since Canada's pig industry was a major user of imported U.S. corn.[14] U.S. trade officials voiced an additional concern. They suggested that the duty-drawback program could result in U.S. trade action against Canada based on how such a duty-rebate program was implemented.

CITT Removes AD/CV Duties on U.S. Corn

On March 15, 2006, the CBSA announced a final determination of dumping and subsidizing, and stated that it would continue to impose the $1.65 per bushel tariff on imports of U.S. corn until the CITT concluded its investigation of injury to Canadian producers. Shortly thereafter, on March 17, 2006, the United States requested WTO dispute settlement consultations with Canada concerning Canada's imposition of provisional AD/CV duties on unprocessed U.S. grain corn. In its WTO request, the United States' arguments included an accusation that Canada's CITT had relied on weak causality between imports and injury, while ignoring other candidates more likely causing injury, such as exchange rate movements and unusually large world corn harvests leading to weak international corn prices.

On April 18, 2006, the CITT announced its final determination, reversing its earlier position, by issuing a finding of no injury regarding the importation of U.S. grain corn.[15] Pursuant to this final finding, the preliminary AD/CV duties of $1.65 per bushel were removed and all duties already assessed were to be returned. Similarly, the United States' motivation for pursuing its WTO case against Canadian AD/CV duties was ended.

Canadian Corn Producers Review Their Options

Shortly after the CITT's final decision, the Canadian Corn Producers announced that they were reviewing their options for pursuing further legal action against imports of U.S. corn. At that time, such options included requesting a NAFTA binational panel review or possibly encouraging the Canadian government to pursue a WTO dispute settlement case. A NAFTA panel review would involve a review of whether Canadian trade authorities (in this case, the CITT) had correctly interpreted and applied existing Canadian law in reaching their negative injury determination. In contrast, a WTO case — which can only be brought by the Canadian government, not a private party such as the Canadian Corn Producers — would likely be pursued under the Agreement on Subsidies and Countervailing Measures (SCM Agreement) and would involve an investigation of whether "serious prejudice" occurred in the marketplace as a result of U.S. domestic corn program payments.

Canadian Request for WTO Consultations

On January 8, 2007, the delegation of Canada to the WTO requested consultations with the delegation of the United States under Article 4.4 of the *Understanding on Rules and Procedures Governing the Settlement of Disputes (DSU)* concerning three separate allegations involving certain aspects of U.S. commodity programs in general, and the U.S. corn program in particular.[16] This action by Canada initiated a WTO dispute settlement case (DS357) which is expected to proceed in accordance with the explicit rules and timetables of the DSU.[17]

In making its charges, Canada clearly seeks to build on Brazil's successful WTO challenge of various provisions of the U.S. cotton program (dispute settlement case DS267).[18] Other potential motivating factors include domestic political concerns emanating from a weak coalition government responding to pressure from corn producing interests following the unfavorable CITT AD/CV corn duty ruling, as well as Canada's general interest in influencing the U.S. farm bill debate in favor of lower amber-box-type support.[19] In a government news release that coincided with the Canadian government's request for WTO consultations, Canadian Trade Minister, David Emerson, said, "We hope to see the U.S. live up to its WTO obligations, particularly given that it has the opportunity to do so when it rewrites its Farm Bill this year."[20] A news report suggests that two additional factors motivating Canada's case against U.S. corn programs include the current suspension of Doha Round negotiations (where the U.S. had already offered to reform its export credit guarantee program) and the settlement of a softwood lumber dispute between Canada and the United States which freed up government trade attorneys to refocus on the WTO litigation.[21]

Since Canada's initial request for consultations, several other WTO members — Argentina, Australia, Brazil, the European Communities (EC), Guatemala, Nicaragua, Thailand, and Uruguay — have officially requested to join the consultations as interested third parties.[22] A news report suggests that Mexico is also contemplating whether or not to join as a third party.[23] News reports speculate that this growing alliance of interested third parties could add to pressure for the United States to further expand its agricultural subsidy reduction proposal in the current Doha Round of WTO trade negotiations, especially in the corn sector.

In its official request for consultations, Canada raises three explicit charges against U.S. farm programs. Each of these is discussed below.

First Allegation: U.S. Corn Subsidies Cause Serious Prejudice

Canada contends that the subsidies and domestic support provided to the U.S. corn sector have caused adverse effects to Canadian corn producers in the form of serious prejudice and the threat of serious prejudice to the interests of Canada during the 1996 to 2006 period in violation of Articles 5(c) and 6.3(c) of the WTO's Agreement on Subsidies and Countervailing Measures (SCM Agreement).[24] Article 5(c) defines adverse effects as including serious prejudice to the interests of another WTO member. Article 6.3(c) states that serious prejudice applies when the effect of a subsidy is a serious price undercutting by the subsidized product, price suppression, price depression or lost sales for a like product in the same market.

In its consultation request, Canada lists the subsidies and domestic support programs that it contends supported the U.S. corn sector during the 1996 to 2006 period. These include commodity programs from both the 1996 and 2002 Farm Acts — marketing loan payments (i.e., marketing assistance loans, market loan gains, loan deficiency payments, commodity certificates, commodity certificate exchange gains, and commodity loan interest subsidies), the production flexibility contract (PFC) payments of the 1996 Farm Act, and the fixed direct payments (DP) and counter-cyclical payments (CCP) of the 2002 Farm Act.[25] In addition, U.S. Market Loss Assistance (MLA) payments provided under six different emergency supplemental acts authorized by Congress between 1998 and 2001,[26] and benefits received under the agricultural export credit guarantee programs[27] were included in the list of support programs contributing to serious prejudice.

The Canadian government included an Annex with its official consultation request.[28] The Annex, entitled "Statement of Available Evidence," included a lengthy list of websites providing information on U.S. commodity programs, but provided no discussion of the specific program outlays other than the general discussion included in the consultation request.[29] However, in a related news release, Canada contends that in 2005/06, the United States accounted for 41% of global corn production and 68% of global corn exports, while U.S. support to corn producers has averaged nearly $9 billion in each of the previous two (Sep/Aug) marketing years —2004/05 and 2005/06 — resulting in what Canada claims is a significant distortion of its domestic corn prices.[30]

Second Allegation: U.S. Export Credit Guarantees Act as Illegal Export Subsidies

Canada argues that the U.S. export credit guarantee program operates as a WTO-illegal export subsidy. This charge stems from a previous WTO case — the U.S.-Brazil Cotton case (DS267) — where a WTO panel found (and was upheld by an Appellate Board (AB) on appeal) that U.S. export credit guarantees effectively function as export subsidies because the financial benefits returned by these programs failed to cover their long-run operating cost.[31] Furthermore, the panel found that this applies not just to cotton, but to all commodities that benefit from U.S. commodity support programs and receive export credit guarantees. As a result, export credit guarantees for any recipient commodity are subject to previously scheduled WTO spending limits.

Third Allegation: U.S. Total Domestic Support Exceeds Its WTO Limit

Canada contends that the United States has provided support to its agricultural sector in excess of its scheduled WTO commitment levels. As with the second allegation above, this allegation hinges directly on a WTO panel finding from the U.S.-Brazil Cotton case (DS267) as described below.

For the United States, its total spending limit for "amber box" programs (i.e., programs that are trade and market distorting), as listed in its WTO country schedule of commitments was $19.9 billion in 1999 and $19.1 billion in all subsequent years. Each WTO member has agreed to notify its annual domestic support outlays to the WTO for verification that it is adhering to its spending commitments. The United States has notified to the WTO its annual program spending through 2001. In these notifications, U.S. domestic support outlays remain well within U.S. WTO spending commitments. Also in its WTO notifications, the United States has notified its Production Flexibility Contract (PFC) payments as fully decoupled and green box compliant.[32] This is an important distinction because the green box contains only non-distorting program payments and is not subject to any limit.

Canada's claim that the United States has exceeded its total spending limits hinges on a previous WTO panel ruling from the U.S.-Brazil Cotton case (DS267). In that case, the WTO panel found (and was upheld by the Appellate Body) that U.S. payments made under the PFC and Direct Payment (DP) programs do not qualify for the WTO's green box category of domestic spending, because of their prohibition on planting fruits, vegetables, and wild rice on covered program acreage.[33] Instead, the panel ruled that payments under these programs should be counted as domestic subsidies directly affecting crop production (i.e., distorting) and should therefore be included with other commodity program outlays to evaluate whether the United States has met or exceeded its "peace clause" limits. Such "peace clause" limits were established under Article 13 of the Agreement on Agriculture (AA) which states that domestic support measures that comply with the AA's commitments are exempt from being challenged as illegal subsidies under dispute settlement proceedings as long as the level of support for the commodity in question remains at or below the outlays of the 1992 marketing year.[34]

Canada argues that, because PFC and DP payments do not conform with paragraph 6(b) of Annex 2 of the AA (which states that such payments should not be related to producer behavior such as compliance with a planting restriction), they should be included in U.S. amber box payments. Furthermore, Canada argues that U.S. CCP payments made under the 2002 Farm Act should similarly be counted against the U.S. amber box spending limit of $19.1 billion. In addition, Canada claims that PFC, DP, and CCP payments for all covered crops — wheat, corn, grain sorghum, barley, oats, upland cotton, rice, soybeans, and other oilseeds — should be counted against the amber box limit. Because the United States has only notified through the year 2001, no program spending under the 2002 Farm Act — including both the DP and CCP programs — has yet been notified. However, Canada charges that, when PFC, DP, and CCP payments are included in the U.S.'s amber box, then the total outlays exceeds the spending commitment in each of 1999, 2000, 2001, 2004, and 2005. In contrast, the United States, as part of its Doha policy reform proposal, recommends that CCP payments be eligible for notification as blue box payments where they would be subject to a different limit than the amber box.[35]

U.S. Response to Canadian Allegations

In response to Canada's recent request for consultations on U.S. subsidies, U.S. Secretary of Agriculture, Mike Johanns, declared that the United States would vigorously defend U.S. farm programs against any possible WTO challenge by Canada.[36] A spokesman for the U.S. Trade Representative (USTR) was critical of Canada's action, particularly in light of the significant increase in international corn prices since September 2006. The USTR spokesman said, "Given the dramatic improvement in the market over the past year, we're surprised that Canada believes that our corn programs are now causing harm in breach of WTO rules."[37] However, current market conditions are unlikely to influence any WTO investigation (should the case reach that point) since Canada is specifically challenging U.S. subsidies for the period 1996 through 2006 when corn prices were substantially lower (figure 3).

In another response to Canada's recent request for consultations, the American Farm Bureau Federation (AFBF) stated that Canada's request for a WTO consultation should have "no bearing" on the U.S. farm policy debate.[38]

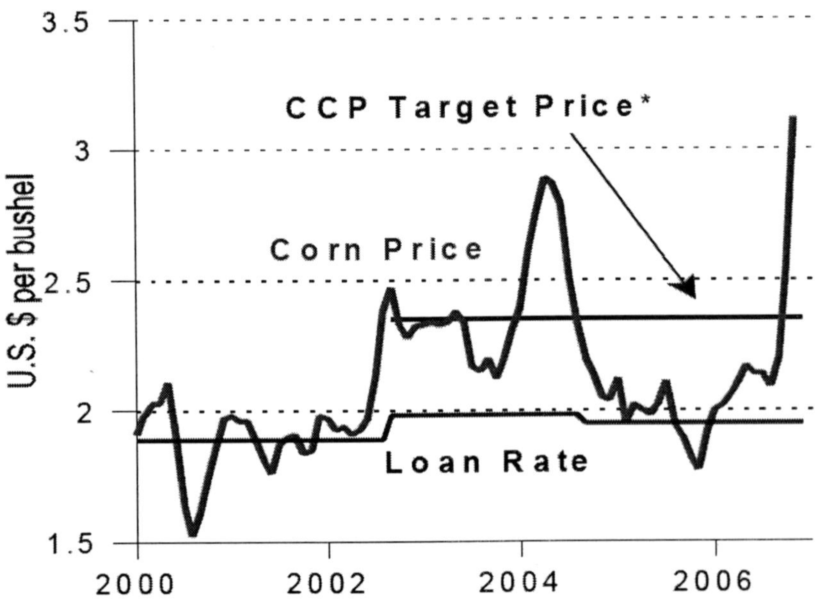

* Adjusted for direct payment per bushel.

Source: USDA, National Agricultural Statistics Service.

Figure 4. U.S. Monthly Average Farm Price for Corn Has Risen Sharply Since September 2006.

What Happens Next?

Under WTO rules, for subsidy complaints alleging adverse effects, a minimum 60-day consultation period is required before a country can ask for WTO to establish a panel.[39] If Canada and the United States are unable to reach some sort of agreement during the consultations, and Canada insists on establishing a WTO panel, this would likely not occur until the April meeting of the WTO's Dispute Settlement Body (DSB). This is because the United States could potentially block a Canadian panel request at the DSB's March meeting. While a WTO case can result in punitive sanctions being authorized, the proceedings of a formal case can take many months, and sometimes years, to reach a conclusion.[40]

For example, the U.S.-Brazil cotton case was initiated by Brazil's request for WTO consultations on September 27, 2002. A panel was established nearly six months later on March 18, 2003. The panel's final report was delivered to the WTO Dispute Settlement Body (DSB)18 months later on September 8, 2004. The case was appealed and the Appellate Body's final report was adopted by the DSB on March 21, 2005, nearly 30 months after the initial request for consultations.[41] However, the case is not yet finalized as a WTO compliance panel is currently reviewing (under request from Brazil) whether the United States has fully complied with the panel's rulings. The WTO compliance panel's chairman has said that the panel would not be able to make a determination before July 2007, thus extending the length of the U.S.-Brazil cotton case to nearly five years.

Potential Implications of WTO Case

Many market analysts and news media suggest that the U.S.-Canada corn trade dispute is a harbinger of future challenges against U.S. commodity programs. If successfully litigated, this case could affect all U.S. agricultural policy by determining that both direct and counter-cyclical payments should be counted as trade-distorting amber box support and thereby making the $19.1 billion amber-box spending limit a serious ceiling on U.S. program outlays in their current form. Furthermore, there is not a clear precedent for what constitutes successful compliance with a serious prejudice charge. Compliance through policy reform would likely require substantial reshaping of current U.S. commodity programs that use market price triggers for determining payments.

With respect to the ruling that PFC and DP payments do not fully comply with green box rules, compliance through policy reform would likely involve some type of adjustment, if not full removal, of the planting restriction on fruits, vegetables, and wild rice on acres receiving direct payments.

With respect to the ruling that export credit guarantees operate like illegal export subsidies, compliance through policy reform would likely involve incorporating user fees that reflect the market risk associated with each loan guarantee. For example, this could be achieved by removing the 1% cap on user fees charged under the export credit guarantee program. The 1% fee cap prevents charging market-based fees and contributes to the export credit guarantee program operating as a WTO-illegal export subsidy.

Role of Congress

Should any eventual changes in U.S. farm policy be needed to comply with a WTO ruling in Canada's favor, such changes would likely involve action by Congress to produce new legislation. Congress will be revisiting U.S. farm legislation this year and could potentially address some of the issues raised by Canada's WTO challenge.

During the past year, Agriculture Secretary, Mike Johanns, has been advocating that a new Farm Act should be designed to make U.S. farm policy be "beyond challenge." The Administration recently released (January 31, 2007) a proposal for U.S. farm policy reform that, if incorporated into a new Farm Act, potentially could alleviate many of Canada's concerns while minimizing the likelihood of future WTO challenges.[42] The proposal includes removal of the planting restriction on base acres receiving direct payments. It also includes adjustments to the export credit guarantee program to make them more compatible with WTO rules. Finally, the proposal includes adjustments to price-contingent commodity programs, i.e., the marketing loan program and the CCP, that would likely make them more WTO compliant.

Given the importance of corn in the U.S. agricultural economy, Congress will be closely monitoring developments in the WTO corn dispute. The House Committee on Agriculture regularly holds hearings on agricultural trade negotiations. For example, such hearings were held on April 28 and May 19, 2004.[43] Among the trade issues discussed during these hearings, both the U.S. Trade Representative and representatives of major program commodity groups provided testimony on U.S. participation in international trade negotiations.

In addition, the 110th Congress is likely to hold hearings and be in consultation with the Administration concerning the possible extension of fast track, or Trade Promotion Authority (TPA) legislation which is set to expire on July 1, 2007.[44] Such hearings and consultations would be a major vehicle for Members to express their views on the U.S.-Canada corn trade dispute, on the negotiating issues that it raises, and on the potential implications for U.S. farm policy.

REFERENCES

[1] For more information, see CRS Report RL33087, United States-Canada Trade and Economic Relationship: Prospects and Challenges, by Ian F. Fergusson.

[2] For a discussion of U.S.-Canada trade issues, see CRS Report 96-397, Canada-U.S. Relations, Carl Ek, Coordinator.

[3] For more information, see CRS Report RL32426, U.S.-Canada Wheat Trade Dispute, by Randy Schnepf.

[4] USDA, Production, Supply and Distribution (PSD) Online database, January 12, 2007, at [http://www.fas.usda.gov/psdonline/psdHome.aspx].

[5] USDA, FAS Online, U.S. Trade Internet System, January 12, 2007, at [http://www.fas.usda.gov/ustrade/USTExFatus.asp?QI=].

[6] Ontario Corn Producers' Association, News Release, August 31, 2005, at [http://www.ontariocorn.org/newsrel/newsrelease8.31.05.pdf].

[7] The "Byrd Amendment," or the Continued Dumping and Subsidy Offset Act (CDSOA), was a U.S. law providing for the distribution of import duties collected as a result of antidumping or countervailing duty orders to petitioners and other interested parties in the investigations that resulted in the orders. For more information on the Byrd Amendment, see CRS Report RL33045, The Continued Dumping and Subsidy Offset Act ("Byrd Amendment"), by Jeanne Grimmett and Vivian Jones.

[8] For more information, see CRS Report RL33752, Softwood Lumber Imports from Canada: Issues and Events, by Ross Gorte and Jeanne Grimmett.

[9] USDA News Release No. 0382.05, Sept. 16, 2005.

[10] World Perspectives, Inc., "Canada Moves to Investigate U.S. Corn," by Dave Juday, Sept. 19, 2005.

[11] Statement of the U.S. Trade Representative, Dec. 16, 2005.

[12] CITT, Dumping and Subsidizing: Determination, Preliminary Injury Inquiry No. PL-2005-001, Grain Corn, Nov. 15, 2005; [http://www.citt-tcce.gc.ca/dumping/preinq/determin/pi2f001_e.asp].

[13] Cattlenetwork.com; "Farmers to Get Rebates On U.S. Corn Tariff," Dec. 23, 2005.

[14] ProFarmer, Vol. 34, No. 4, "So... did you know they could get the $1.65 back?" Jan. 28, 2006.

[15] CITT, Dumping and Subsidizing: Finding, Inquiry No. NQ-2005-001, Unprocessed Grain Corn, Apr. 18, 2006, at [http://www.citt-tcce.gc.ca/dumping/inquirie/findings/nq2f001 _e.asp].

[16] Request for Consultations by Canada, UNITED STATES - SUBSIDIES AND OTHER DOMESTIC SUPPORT FOR CORN AND OTHER AGRICULTURAL PRODUCTS, WT/DS357/1 (Jan. 11, 2007).

[17] For more information, see CRS Report RS20088, Dispute Settlement in the World Trade Organization: An Overview, by Jeanne Grimmett.

[18] For more information, see CRS Report RL32571, Background on the U.S.-Brazil WTO Cotton Subsidy Dispute, and CRS Report RS22187, U.S. Agricultural Policy Response to WTO Cotton Decision, both by Randy Schnepf.

[19] The amber box includes those policies that result in market and trade distorting support. For a discussion of proposed reductions in WTO domestic support commitments, see CRS Report RL33144, WTO Doha Round: The Agricultural Negotiations, by Charles Hanrahan and Randy Schnepf.

[20] Government of Canada, News Release, Jan. 8, 2007, No. 2 at [http://www.international .gc.ca/tna-nac/wto-ds-en.asp].

[21] Inside U.S. Trade, "Johanns Says U.S. Will Defend Farm Programs from Canadian Challenge," Jan. 12, 2007.

[22] Official WTO documents are: (Jan. 22, 2007) Australia, WT/DS357/2; (Jan. 23, 2007) Guatemala, WT/DS357/3; and Brazil, WT/DS357/4; (Jan. 24, 2007) Argentina, WT/DS357/5; the EC, WT/DS357/6; Uruguay, WT/DS357/7; Nicaragua, WT/DS357/8; and Thailand, WT/DS357/9.

[23] Washington Trade Daily, "Brazil, Argentina and U.S. Corn Subsidies," Vol. 16, No. 16, Jan. 22, 2007.

[24] For a description and interpretation of Articles 5(c) and 6.3(c) of the SCM Agreement, see CRS Report RL33697, Potential Challenges to U.S. Farm Subsidies in the WTO, by Randy Schnepf and Jasper Womach.

[25] For more information on commodity programs see CRS Report RS21999, Farm Commodity Policy: Programs and Issues for Congress, by Jim Monke.

[26] For more information on Market Loss Assistance payments (or "market loss" payments), see CRS Report RL31095, Emergency Funding for Agriculture: A Brief History of Supplemental Appropriations, FY1989-FY200, by Ralph M. Chite.

[27] For more information on U.S. export credit guarantees, see CRS Report RL33553,

[28] Agricultural Export and Food Aid Programs, by Charles Hanrahan.

[29] Annex: Statement of Available Evidence, WT/DS357/1, pp. 5-8 (Jan. 11, 2007).

[30] Such a statement is required under Article 7.2 of the SCM Agreement.

[31] Government of Canada, News Release, Jan. 8, 2007, No. 2.

[32] Found to violate Annex I(j) of the SCM Agreement, WTO Legal Texts, p. 267, which identifies as an export subsidy, "The provision by governments (or special institutions controlled by governments) of export credit guarantee or insurance programs, of insurance or guarantee programs against increases in the cost of exported products or of exchange risk programs, at premium rates which are inadequate to cover the long-term operating costs and losses of the programs."

[33] Decoupled means it has no influence on producer's decision-making process; green box compliant means it adheres to the terms and conditions of Annex 2 of the Agreement on Agriculture.

[34] For more information on these restrictions see USDA, Farm Service Agency, Fact Sheet, Direct and Counter-Cyclical Payment Program Wild Rice, Fruit, and Vegetable Provisions, February 2003, at [http://www.fsa.usda.gov/pas/publications/ facts/html/ fav03.htm].

[35] For more detail, see CRS Report RL32571, Background on the U.S.-Brazil WTO Cotton Subsidy Dispute, by Randy Schnepf.

[36] Blue box payments are defined as "production-limiting" types of payments. For more information see CRS Report RL33144, WTO Doha Round: The Agricultural Negotiations, by Charles Hanrahan and Randy Schnepf.

[37] Inside U.S. Trade, "Johanns Says U.S. Will Defend Farm Programs from Canadian Challenge," January 12, 2007.

[38] International Herald Tribune, "Argentina, Brazil join WTO complaint against U.S. corn subsidies," Jan. 22, 2007.

[39] AFBF press release, "Statement by Bob Stallman, President, AFBF, Regarding Canadian Request for WTO Consultations on Subsidies," Jan. 8, 2007. Article 7.4, SCM Agreement.

[40] For more information, see CRS Report RS20088, Dispute Settlement in the World Trade Organization: An Overview, by Jeanne Grimmett.

[41] This timeline is discussed in more detail in CRS Report RL32571, Background on the U.S.-BrazilWTO Cotton Subsidy Dispute, by Randy Schnepf.

[42] USDA News Release No. 0020.07, "Johanns Unveils 2007 Farm Bill Proposals," Jan. 31, 2007.

[43] Hearings before the Committee on Agriculture, House of Representatives 108th Congress, Second Session, April 28 and May 19, 2004, Serial No. 108-29, at [http://agriculture .house.gov/hearings/108/10829.pdf].

[44] For more information, see CRS Report RL33743 Trade Promotion Authority (TPA): Issues, Options, and Prospects for Renewal, by J. F. Hornbeck and William H. Cooper.

In: Trade Policies and Agreements in the Era of Globalization ISBN: 978-1-60021-836-1
Editor: Paul B. Lucus, pp. 163-169

Chapter 8

TRADE PROMOTION AUTHORITY (TPA) RENEWAL: CORE LABOR STANDARDS ISSUES: A BRIEF OVERVIEW*

Mary Jane Bolle

ABSTRACT

This report is a brief overview of key issues addressed in CRS Report RL33864, *Trade Promotion Authority (TPA) Renewal: Core Labor Standards Issues*. Trade promotion authority (TPA), formerly known as "fast-track" authority, is scheduled to expire July 1, 2007. With it will expire the President's authority to negotiate trade agreements that Congress will then consider without amendment and with limited debate. For the 110th Congress, a likely issue in this debate is whether to include *enforceable core labor standards* as a principal negotiating objective in trade agreements. Accordingly, this report (1) identifies key labor provisions in the current TPA law and how they have translated into free trade agreements negotiated under it; (2) presents some legislative options, and summarizes arguments for and against listing enforceable core labor standards as a principal negotiating objective; and (3) looks at possible outcomes and implications of the legislative options.

INTRODUCTION

Trade promotion authority (TPA), formerly known as "fast-track" authority, is scheduled to expire July 1, 2007. With it will expire the authority that Congress grants the President to enter into certain trade agreements, and the authority for Congress to consider the agreements' implementing legislation under expedited procedures. Currently, the Administration is negotiating a number of trade agreements that may not be completed before TPA is set to expire. If these activities are to continue, TPA renewal may be a central issue in

* Excerpted from CRS Report RS22608, dated February 21, 2007.

the 110th Congress. Within the debate, a major issue is expected to be whether to include as a principal negotiating objective in trade agreements, "enforceable core labor standards."

The current TPA is contained in the *Bipartisan Trade Promotion Authority Act of 2002* (Title XXI of the Trade Act of 2002, P.L. 107-210). A total of nine free trade agreements (FTAs) have been negotiated under this authority. They are with Chile, Singapore, Australia, Morocco, Bahrain, Oman, the Dominican Republic and Central America, Peru and Colombia. The last two await congressional consideration. The labor issue in these trade agreements is how key provisions in each reflect two principal negotiating objectives in TPA.

The first TPA principal negotiating objective is: "to ensure that a party *does not fail to enforce its own labor laws* through a sustained or recurring course of action or inaction, in a manner affecting trade between the parties." All nine FTAs track this principal negotiating objective by providing: that countries shall "not fail to enforce their own [labor] laws ... in a manner affecting trade between the Parties" — popularly called the "enforce-your-own" provision.

The second TPA principal negotiating objective is: "to seek dispute settlement and enforcement provisions *that treat U.S. principal negotiating objectives equally* with respect to the ability to resort to dispute settlement, the availability of *equivalent* dispute settlement procedures, and the availability of *equivalent* remedies." In what labor advocates see as a "departure" from the TPA provision, procedures for labor disputes differ in several respects from those for commercial disputes and include a cap on monetary penalties (while those for commercial disputes do not.)

KEY PLAYERS AND THEIR POSITIONS

Those calling for expanded or strengthened labor provisions fault labor protections in the nine FTAs,[2] arguing that they (1) lack the enforceability of commercial provisions; (2) fail to meet some congressional negotiating objectives and barely comply with others; (3) represent a "big step back" from both the U.S.-Jordan FTA and U.S. unilateral trade preference programs such as the Generalized System of Preferences (GSP);[3] and (4) "completely exclude obligations for governments to meet such international standards as worker rights." These advocates further argue that in order to strengthen FTA provisions, the blueprint for their negotiation — the TPA language — needs to be strengthened.

Advocates of strengthened labor provisions, in promoting enforceable core labor standards, appear to have two objectives. The first objective could be characterized as humanitarian: to promote the protection of workers around the world, particularly those in developing countries where protections are weak and/or poorly enforced. The second objective could be interpreted as economic: to help "level the playing field" between U.S. and foreign workers so that U.S. workers can compete on a more equitable basis.

Opponents respond in support of the current TPA, noting that labor provisions in the nine FTAs negotiated under it: (1) are the strongest labor provisions attached to FTAs to date; (2) are the product of bilateral negotiation; and (3) both depend on and reflect mutual agreement by negotiating countries; 4) treat U.S. principal negotiating objectives "equally" in that the principal remedies for labor and commercial disputes are "equivalent;" and (5) are preferable to enforceable core labor standards because the latter could raise sovereignty issues.

Opponents have, as one key objective, promotion of U.S. investment. They often represent the viewpoints of businesses and investors, developing country governments, and the current Administration. Many business groups support the passage of TPA in order to facilitate the expansion of U.S. multinational corporations abroad — their most important avenue for continued growth. In fact, both TPA and trade agreements typically include many protections for investors. Developing countries care about protecting their ability to attract investment, and are concerned about anything that might jeopardize that ability. In the World Trade Organization (WTO), developing countries have long resisted U.S. proposals to study the relationship between worker rights and trade, concerned that such a study could lead to enforceable labor standards that could undercut their comparative advantage in low-cost labor. However, as with businesses and investors, their flexibility to compromise on the issue of enforceable core labor standards seems to be related to the strength of their desire to have an FTA with the United States.

Major Legislative Options and Arguments

Major legislative options for treatment of labor standards as principal negotiating objectives *if TPA were to be renewed*, include the following:

- Option 1: No enforceable labor standards provisions. This option would likely be viewed as a step back from the expiring TPA;
- Option 2: Renewal of the current "enforce-your-own" provisions aiming: (1) to ensure that a party *does not fail to enforce its own labor laws*; and (2) to seek dispute settlement provisions that treat U.S. principal negotiating objectives *equally*; and
- Option 3: "Enforceable core labor standards" as reflected in H.R. 3019, introduced in 2001 by Representative Charles Rangel which aimed: (1) to ensure that a party does *not fail to enforce core labor standards*; and (2) to provide that violation of these standards would be subject to enforcement under a *single set of dispute settlement procedures* that would be *applicable to all disputes* under an FTA.

The term *core labor standards* has been defined in two ways by two different sources: the International Labor Organization (ILO) which calls them "core labor standards," and U.S. trade law which refers to them as "internationally recognized worker rights." Both definitions are almost identical and share four standards or rights: (1) the right to organize, (2) the right to bargain collectively, (3) prohibition of forced labor, and (4) protections for child labor including the "worst forms of child labor"[4] They differ on the fifth standard. U.S. law identifies it as: (5) labor standards pertaining to minimum wages, maximum hours, and occupational safety and health. ILO conventions define it as: (5) freedom from employment discrimination.[5]

SHOULD ENFORCEABLE CORE LABOR STANDARDS BE INCLUDED AS A PRINCIPAL NEGOTIATING OBJECTIVE?

General Arguments

For Enforceable Core Labor Standards

Those in favor of principal negotiating objectives that call for enforceable core labor standards include the AFL-CIO, Human Rights Watch, and the International Labor Rights Fund.[6] Labor advocates traditionally argue: (1) that enforceable core labor standards help guard against a "race to the bottom," as workers all over the world compete against each other for scarce jobs; and (2) that labor standards do not interfere with natural comparative advantage in developing countries because labor standards are only one basis for comparative advantage. Others include abundance, skills, and education of available workforce; infrastructure; level of technological development of the country; and natural resource base.

Against

Opponents typically argue that (1) the enforce-your-own standards model provides a more direct, less encumbered path to economic growth; (2) most developing countries have few resources to devote to labor standards enforcement; (3) once a developing country is more economially developed and relatively near full employment, labor standards and their enforcement begin to rise on their own; and (4) imposing core labor standards on developing countries too soon could interfere with their comparative advantage in abundant and inexpensive labor, and amount to protectionism.

Arguments Related to U.S. Workers

For Enforceable Core Labor Standards

Supporters argue that a principal negotiating objective calling for enforceable core labor standards could help level the playing field for U.S. workers and make them more competitive internationally.

Against

Some opponents argue that the need or desire to earn a living is often incentive enough to encourage displaced workers to find new employment. Others argue that there are better ways to help U.S. workers than trying to level the playing field, which, at best, may only slow the offshore movement (or technological elimination of) of some U.S. jobs. A better way, some argue, would be to expand adjustment assistance benefits, educational benefits, or other training and retraining programs to cover all displaced workers — whether the job loss results from trade or technology — and help them transition into new careers.

Arguments Related to Foreign Workers

For Enforceable Core Labor Standards

Advocates of strengthened labor standards argue that enforceable core labor standards can help foreign workers share in the gains of increasing productivity and economic expansion, and thereby become consumers in their own right.

Against

Opponents argue that real gains in standard of living in developing countries come from rising productivity, not from artificially imposed labor standards including minimum wages. In addition, they argue, some workers do not want enforceable core labor standards because these could limit their ability to maximize their earnings by working overtime.

Sovereignty Issues

For Enforceable Core Labor Standards

Those in favor of enforceable core labor standards as a principal negotiating objective could argue that the ILO already requires that countries comply with ILO core labor standards as a condition of continued membership in good standing, even if those countries do not formally approve the ILO conventions. Therefore, incorporating enforceable core labor standards into trade agreements does not add much more to this requirement.[7]

Against

Opponents might respond that enforceable core labor standards interfere with national sovereignty in a way that ILO membership does not, since enforcement powers of the ILO are limited to consensus and persuasion.

If So, what Should Be the Definition of Core Labor Standards?

Arguments on the Definition of Core Labor Standards

For Enforceable ILO Core Labor Standards

If "enforceable core labor standards" is adopted as a principal negotiating objective for trade agreements, the AFL-CIO is strongly in favor of using the ILO definition over the U.S. definition (see p. 4 for definitions), because it is more current. Human Rights Watch, while not arguing for either definition specifically, stresses that the definition of core labor standards must include prohibitions against employment discrimination (which is in the ILO but not the U.S. definition.)

Against

If the ILO definition were adopted, opponents point out, foreign governments could hold existing U.S. labor laws up to scrutiny, arguing that they don't totally comply with ILO core labor standards. This is because the United States has ratified only two conventions (one on forced labor and one on the worst forms of child labor). Accordingly, the U.S. Council for International Business (USCIB) argues that many U.S. labor laws would need to be changed to come into compliance with the ILO definition of core labor standards, especially in such areas as forced labor, minimum age for employment, and employment discrimination.[8]

Possible Outcomes and Implications

Whether TPA is renewed, and whether the negotiation of enforceable core labor standards is included in any such renewal, international trade is likely to continue to expand in both volume and complexity. The economic effects on trade, investment, and labor markets of including enforceable core labor standards as a principal negotiating objective in TPA renewal could be relatively limited. They would likely depend on a number of factors including (1) the extent to which enforceable core labor standards were adopted and implemented in trade agreements; (2) the number of trade agreements affected; (3) the magnitude of U.S. trade with countries under such agreements; and (4) the extent of actual enforcement of those standards in trade agreements. In addition, the effects from any of these four factors could be dwarfed by shifts in the value of the dollar that might occur relative to other currencies.

If enforceable core labor standards were adopted as a principal negotiating objective in TPA legislation, whether or not the United States would need to make changes to its labor laws could depend on how the legislation defined the term "core labor standards."

If TPA is not renewed, or if it should be renewed without enforceable core labor standards, a number of ways might be available to promote labor standards and protect worker rights. These include enforceable standards currently incorporated into U.S. trade preference laws; continuing efforts of the ILO to promote core labor standards; the efforts of various labor advocates and international labor "watchdog" groups; economic development forces in various countries which eventually lead to rising international demand for protections of the rights of workers; codes of conduct guiding the actions of corporations in protecting the rights of international workers; and U.S. government "trade capacity building" grants which help to improve labor standards in developing countries.

References

[1] For a general discussion on TPA renewal, see CRS Report RL33743, *Trade Promotion Authority (TPA); Issues, Options, and Prospects for Renewal*, by J.F. Hornbeck and William H. Cooper.

[2] See, for example, U.S. Chile Free Trade Agreement, Report of the Labor Advisory Committee for Trade Negotiations and Trade Policy (LAC), February 28, 2003, p. 3.

[3] The Jordan FTA (in which all provisions are technically equally enforceable) requires that parties reaffirm their obligations to uphold both *core labor standards* under the International Labor Organization (ILO), and *internationally recognized worker rights* under the U.S. Trade Act of 1974. The GSP and other U.S. trade preference laws

require that eligible beneficiary countries be "taking steps to afford" their workers *internationally recognized worker rights* (defined on p. 4.)

[4] The "worst forms of child labor" include the employment of children for purposes including prostitution, pornography, drug trafficking, armed conflict, and forced labor.

[5] The U.S. definition can be found in the *Trade Act of 1974*, Sec. 507. The current TPA in the *Bipartisan Trade Promotion Authority Act of 2002*, Title XXI of the *Trade Act of 2002*, combines the ILO name and the U.S. list, defining the U.S. list as "core labor standards."

[6] Conversations with Thea Lee, Policy Director, AFL-CIO, Carol Pier, Labor Rights and Trade Senior Researcher, Human Rights Watch, and Bama Althreya, Executive Director of the International Labor Rights Fund, all January 16, 2007.

[7] *About the Declaration* (on Fundamental Principals and Rights at Work). ILO website at [http://www.ilo.org].

[8] CRS communication from Adam B. Greene, Vice President, Labor Affairs and Corporate Responsibility, USCIB, January 18, 2007, echoing the conclusion of a number of studies by the presidentially appointed Tripartite Advisory Panel on International Labor Standards (TAPILS), a research group made up of the USCIB, the AFL-CIO, and the U.S. government.

In: Trade Policies and Agreements in the Era of Globalization ISBN: 978-1-60021-836-1
Editor: Paul B. Lucus, pp. 171-176

Chapter 9

U.S.-WORLD MERCHANDISE TRADE DATA: 1948-2006*

J. Michael Donnelly

ABSTRACT

U.S. merchandise trade is trade in goods only, not services. In 2006, U.S. exports, imports, and trade deficit reached their highest historical values: U.S. exports were $1.0 trillion, a 14.5% increase; U.S. imports were $1.9 trillion, a 10.9% increase; and the U.S. merchandise trade balance reached -$818 billion, a 6.6% increase.

Merchandise trade statistics are used to measure trade in commodities and with partner countries and groups. Latest official annual trade statistics of the U.S. Department of Commerce, used in this report, show that U.S. exports remain strong and growing and that U.S. imports remain even stronger, resulting in the largest annual merchandise trade deficit in U.S. history.

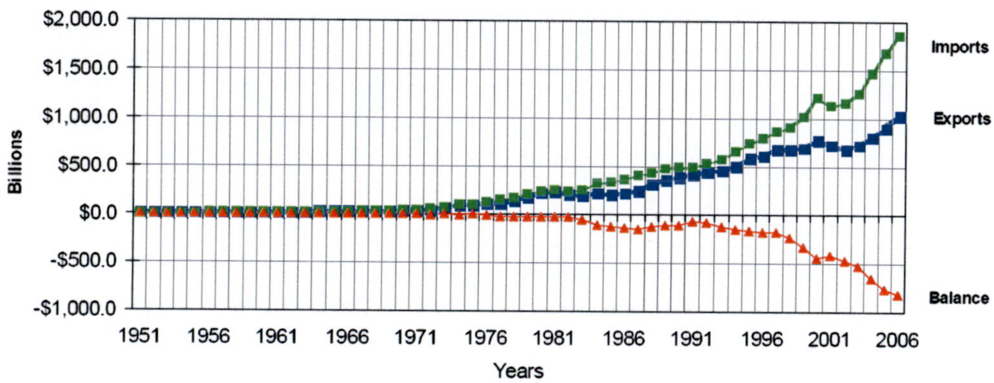

Source: U.S. Department of Commerce.

Figure 1. U.S. Merchandise Trade, 1951-2006.

* Excerpted from CRS Report RS22612, dated February 23, 2007.

MERCHANDISE TRADE VERSUS TRADE IN GOODS AND SERVICES

Merchandise trade statistics are referred to as *Census basis* statistics because they are collected, compiled, and distributed by the U.S. Census Bureau. These are the data reported here and constitute the one continuing data series using largely uniform definitions. Merchandise trade statistics are important because they alone are the basis for commodity and country trade information.

In January 1994, the U.S. Department of Commerce began reporting and publishing trade data on goods and services as the benchmark monthly trade statistic, supplementing merchandise trade data. Services trade statistics are compiled by the Bureau of Economic Analysis (BEA) on a *balance of payments (BOP) basis*. To harmonize Census merchandise data with BEA services data, statistics on goods and services are reported on a BOP basis. This involves such changes as deducting U.S. military sales from merchandise accounts, because they are considered services transactions, and adding to merchandise statistics parcels mailed to foreigners by individuals in the United States. What this means is that the goods component of trade in goods and services is different from the goods measured in merchandise trade statistics.

DEFINITIONS IN MERCHANDISE TRADE

Merchandise trade is trade in goods only, not services, and excludes capital transfers and foreign investments. Exports are defined in this report as *total exports*; they include both domestically produced goods and re-exports, which constitute imports of goods that are warehoused in the United States, then re-exported. Imports are defined here as *general imports*, which measure total arrivals of goods into the United States — imports for both immediate consumption channels and warehouses or Foreign Trade Zones. *Balance of merchandise trade* is defined here, and in standard U.S. Department of Commerce data, as total exports minus general imports. Dollar amounts are current U.S. dollars, that is, official statistics with no inflation adjustment, expressed in millions, billions, or trillions, as noted.

Valuation methods define where in a trade transaction the value of a good is measured. As goods move in international trade, they acquire more costs. Although an automobile has one cost at the end of its assembly line, it acquires a higher cost when shipping and insurance to a local dealer or port for export are added. For this report, current official U.S. government valuation practice is followed.

- Total exports are valued *free alongside*, or *FAS*. FAS figures provide valuation of exports at the port of exportation and thus exclude charges for loading onto the vessel, the transportation itself, insurance, unloading, and foreign transportation.
- General imports are valued on *Customs valuation*. Customs valuation for imports excludes costs of international transportation and insurance, as well as tariffs, and is therefore quite similar to FAS valuation. Customs valuation for imports replaced FAS valuation in U.S. government statistics in 1982.

RECENT ANNUAL TRADE TRENDS

In 2006, the latest complete year for trade data, U.S. exports increased by $131 billion, or 14%, to $1,037 billion, or $1.0 trillion. Imports increased by $182 billion, or 11%, to $1,855 billion, or $1.9 trillion. These statistics resulted in the U.S. merchandise trade deficit increasing $51 billion, or nearly 6%, to $818 billion. This 2006 merchandise trade deficit increase follows a 2005 merchandise trade deficit increase of $117 billion. Since 2002, the annual merchandise trade deficit has been growing by approximately $100 billion per year.

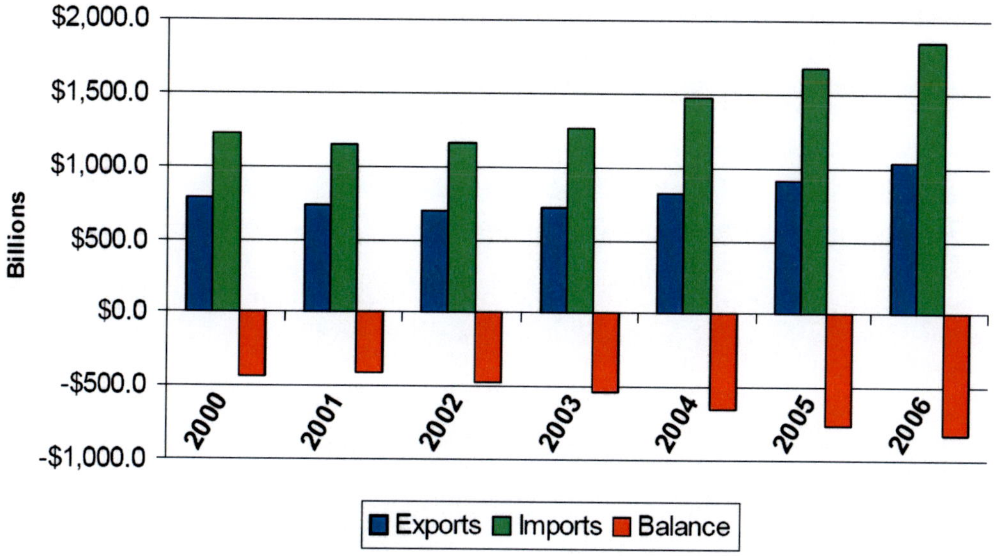

Source: U.S. Department of Commerce.

Figure 2. U.S. Merchandise Trade, 2000-2006.

As figure 2 shows, in the seven-year span from 2000 through 2006, exports increased $255.4 billion, or 33%, from $782 billion to $1,037 billion. During this time, imports grew $637 billion, or 52%, from $1,218 to $1,855 billion. This resulted in the trade deficit nearly doubling from $436 billion to $818 billion.

MERCHANDISE TRADE DATA FACTS

- Between 1948 and 2006, merchandise exports grew by over 81 times, and merchandise imports grew by 261 times.
- U.S. merchandise exports exceeded $1 trillion for the first time in 2006.
- U.S. merchandise imports exceeded $1 trillion for the first time in 1999.
- The U.S. merchandise trade balance was in surplus between 1948 and 1970.
- The first U.S. postwar trade deficit occurred in 1971.
- The trade deficit exceeded $100 billion for the first time in 1984, but did not reach $200 billion until 1998. Since 2002, the U.S. merchandise trade deficit has grown between $50 and $120 billion per year.

WHERE TO FIND TRADE STATISTICS

U.S. International Trade in Goods and Services, series *FT-900*, is the official benchmark monthly press release that reports the latest month's statistics and revises the previous month's statistics. Statistics in this report are on both a Census basis, for merchandise trade, and a balance of payments basis for goods and services trade. The December data release provides the preliminary estimate of annual trade totals and now first appears in February. Final annual revisions are normally released in the June data release of each year, which normally appears in August. The *FT-900* is available in print by subscription from the Superintendent of Documents, U.S. Government Printing Office, Washington, DC 20402, telephone (202) 512-2303. It is available in all federal depository libraries. Location of depository libraries may be searched on the Internet at [http://www.gpoaccess.gov/ libraries.html]. It is also available from both the U.S. Census Bureau, at [http://www.census. gov/indicator/www/ustrade.html], and BEA, at [http://www.bea.gov/bea/newsrel/ tradnewsrelease.htm].

The *FT-900* is prepared jointly by two agencies within the U.S. Department of Commerce, the Census Bureau Foreign Trade Division (FTD) and the Bureau of Economic Analysis (BEA). The *FT-900* may be found in many sources besides print and the Internet, mentioned above. STAT-USA Internet is a subscription service of the U.S. Department of Commerce, which provides the *FT-900* as well as exports and imports by commodity and by country. Trade data on STAT-USA Internet, [http://www.stat-usa.gov/], is in the "Globus and NTDB" section. Individual subscriptions to STAT-USA Internet are also available at [http://www.stat-usa.gov/].

U.S. trade data with the world, individual countries, and regions, as well as U.S. state export data may be found in a Department of Commerce source, TradeStats Express, which presents trade data with colorful graphics and maps; [http://tse.export.gov/].

Detailed monthly trade data with extensive commodity information is published by the U.S. Department of Commerce. Information on particular commodity trade data subscriptions may be obtained by calling (301) 457-2311 or on the FTD website at [http://www.census.gov/ foreign-trade/www/].

Economic Indicators, a monthly statistical magazine prepared for the Joint Economic Committee by the Council of Economic Advisers, contains summary trade data. The table titled "U.S. International Trade in Goods and Services," on page 35 of each issue, contains data on both a balance of payments basis and a Census basis. *Economic Indicators* is available by subscription from the U.S. Government Printing Office.

Economic Report of the President, published annually in February, contains tables that provide mainly annual merchandise trade statistics on both a Census basis and a BOP basis. It is available at [http://www.gpoaccess.gov/eop/index.html].

Table 1. Annual Change in U.S. Merchandise Trade: Exports, Imports, and Balance: 1948-2006 (Census basis as of February 2007; values in current U.S. millions of dollars)

Year	U.S. Merch. Exports FAS Value	Change From Previous Year	% Change From Previous Year	U.S. Merch. Imports Customs Value	Change From Previous Year	% Change From Previous Year	U.S. Merch. Trade Balance	Change From Previous Year
1948	12,653.1	—	—	7,123.9	—	—	5,529.2	—
1949	12,051.1	-602.0	-4.8%	6,622.3	-501.6	-7.0	5,428.8	-100.4
1950	9,992.9	-2,058.2	-17.1	8,852.2	2,229.9	33.7	1,140.7	-4,288.1
1951	13,967.4	3,974.5	39.8	10,967.3	2,115.1	23.9	3,000.1	1,859.4
1952	13,203.0	-764.4	-5.5	10,717.5	-249.8	-2.3	2,485.5	-514.6
1953	12,262.4	-940.6	-7.1	10,873.3	155.8	1.5	1,389.1	-1,096.4
1954	12,854.3	591.9	4.8	10,215.4	-657.9	-6.1	2,638.9	1,249.8
1955	14,290.9	1,436.6	11.2	11,384.4	1,169.0	11.4	2,906.5	267.6
1956	17,333.0	3,042.1	21.3	12,614.9	1,230.5	10.8	4,718.1	1,811.6
1957	19,494.9	2,161.9	12.5	12,982.3	367.4	2.9	6,512.6	1,794.5
1958	16,367.0	-3,127.9	-16.0	12,834.5	-147.8	-1.1	3,532.5	-2,980.1
1959	16,406.9	39.9	0.2	15,207.2	2,372.7	18.5	1,199.7	-2,332.8
1960	19,626.3	3,219.4	19.6	15,017.5	-189.7	-1.2	4,608.8	3,409.1
1961	20,189.5	7,335.2	57.1	14,713.9	4,498.5	44.0	5,475.6	2,836.7
1962	20,972.6	783.1	3.9	16,389.5	1,675.6	11.4	4,583.1	-892.5
1963	22,427.3	1,454.7	6.9	17,138.0	748.5	4.6	5,289.3	706.2
1964	25,690.1	3,262.8	14.5	18,684.4	1,546.4	9.0	7,005.7	1,716.4
1965	26,699.4	1,009.3	3.9	21,365.6	2,681.2	14.3	5,333.8	-1,671.9
1966	29,379.2	2,679.8	10.0	25,542.2	4,176.6	19.5	3,837.0	-1,496.8
1967	30,934.4	1,555.2	5.3	26,812.3	1,270.1	5.0	4,122.1	285.1
1968	34,062.8	3,128.4	10.1	33,226.3	6,414.0	23.9	836.5	-3,285.6
1969	37,331.7	3,268.9	9.6	36,042.8	2,816.5	8.5	1,288.9	452.4
1970	43,176.3	5,844.6	15.7	39,951.6	3,908.8	10.8	3,224.7	1,935.8
1971	44,086.6	910.3	2.1	45,562.7	5,611.1	14.0	-1,476.1	-4,700.8
1972	49,854.0	5,767.4	13.1	55,582.8	10,020.1	22.0	-5,728.8	-4,252.7
1973	71,865.2	22,011.2	44.2	69,475.7	13,892.9	25.0	2,389.5	8,118.3
1974	99,436.9	27,571.7	38.4	103,320.8	33,845.1	48.7	-3,883.9	-6,273.4
1975	108,855.6	9,418.7	9.5	99,304.7	-4,016.1	-3.9	9,550.9	13,434.8
1976	116,794.1	7,938.5	7.3	124,613.9	25,309.2	25.5	-7,819.8	-17,370.7

Table 1. (Continued).

Year	U.S. Merch. Exports FAS Value	Change From Previous Year	% Change From Previous Year	U.S. Merch. Imports Customs Value	Change From Previous Year	% Change From Previous Year	U.S. Merch. Trade Balance	Change From Previous Year
1977	123,181.5	6,387.4	5.5	151,534.3	26,920.4	21.6	-28,352.8	-20,533.0
1978	145,846.9	22,665.4	18.4	176,052.0	24,517.7	16.2	-30,205.1	-1,852.3
1979	186,362.7	40,515.8	27.8	210,285.1	34,233.1	19.4	-23,922.4	6,282.7
1980	225,566.1	39,203.4	21.0	245,261.9	34,976.8	16.6	-19,695.8	4,226.6
1981	238,715.0	13,148.9	5.8	260,981.9	15,720.0	6.4	-22,266.9	-2,571.1
1982	216,441.6	-22,273.4	-9.3	243,951.9	-17,030.0	-6.5	-27,510.3	-5,243.4
1983	205,638.6	-10,803.0	-5.0	258,047.8	14,095.9	5.8	-52,409.2	-24,898.9
1984	223,975.8	18,337.2	8.9	330,678.4	72,630.6	28.1	-106,702.6	-54,293.4
1985	218,814.9	-5,160.9	-2.3	336,526.4	5,848.0	1.8	-117,711.5	-11,008.9
1986	227,158.5	8,343.6	3.8	365,437.7	28,911.3	8.6	-138,279.2	-20,567.7
1987	254,121.9	26,963.4	11.9	406,241.0	40,803.3	11.2	-152,119.1	-13,839.9
1988	322,426.4	68,304.5	26.9	440,952.3	34,711.3	8.5	-118,525.9	33,593.2
1989	363,811.5	41,385.1	12.8	473,210.8	32,258.5	7.3	-109,399.3	9,126.6
1990	393,592.3	29,780.8	8.2	495,310.5	22,099.7	4.7	-101,718.2	7,681.1
1991	421,730.0	28,137.7	7.1	488,453.0	-6,857.5	-1.4	-66,723.0	34,995.2
1992	448,163.6	26,433.6	6.3	532,664.8	44,211.8	9.1	-84,501.2	-17,778.2
1993	465,091.0	16,927.4	3.8	580,659.0	47,994.2	9.0	-115,568.0	-31,066.8
1994	512,626.0	47,535.0	10.2	663,255.7	82,596.7	14.2	-150,629.7	-35,061.7
1995	584,742.0	72,116.0	14.1	743,542.7	80,287.0	12.1	-158,800.7	-8,171.0
1996	625,074.9	40,332.9	6.9	795,289.2	51,746.5	7.0	-170,214.3	-11,413.6
1997	689,182.4	64,107.5	10.3	869,703.9	74,414.7	9.4	-180,521.5	-10,307.2
1998	682,137.7	-7,044.7	-1.0	911,896.1	42,192.2	4.9	-229,758.4	-49,236.9
1999	695,797.2	13,695.5	2.0	1,024,618.2	112,722.1	12.4	-328,821.0	-99,062.6
2000	781,917.7	86,120.5	12.4	1,218,022.0	193,403.8	18.9	-436,104.3	-107,283.3
2001	729,100.3	-52,817.4	-6.8	1,140,999.4	-77,022.6	-6.3	-411,899.1	24,205.2
2002	693,103.2	-35,997.1	-4.9	1,161,366.0	20,366.6	1.8	-468,262.8	-56,363.7
2003	724,771.0	31,667.8	4.6	1,257,121.3	95,755.3	8.2	-532.350.3	-64,087.5
2004	818,774.9	94,003.9	13.0	1,469,704.4	212,583.1	16.9	-650,929.5	-118,579.2
2005	905,977.6	87,202.7	10.7	1,673,454.5	203,750.1	13.9	-767,476.9	-116,547.4
2006	1,037,319.9	131,342.3	14.5	1,855,423.4	181,968.9	10.9	-818,103.6	-50,626.7

Source: U.S. Census Bureau, U.S. Bureau of Economic Analysis News, *U.S. International Trade in Goods and Services*, various dates, at [http://www.bea.gov/bea/newsrel/tradnewsrelease.htm].

INDEX

A

B

C

D

E

F

G

H

I

J

N

O

P

Q

R

S

T

U

V

W

Y